PHILOSOPHY AT THE GYMNASIUM

PHILOSOPHY AT THE GYMNASIUM

ERIK KENYON

CORNELL UNIVERSITY PRESS
Ithaca and London

Copyright © 2024 by Cornell University

All rights reserved. Except for brief quotations in a review, this book, or parts thereof, must not be reproduced in any form without permission in writing from the publisher. For information, address Cornell University Press, Sage House, 512 East State Street, Ithaca, New York 14850. Visit our website at cornellpress.cornell.edu.

First published 2024 by Cornell University Press

Library of Congress Cataloging-in-Publication Data

Names: Kenyon, Erik, 1980– author.
Title: Philosophy at the gymnasium / Erik Kenyon.
Description: Ithaca : Cornell University Press, 2024. | Includes bibliographical references and index.
Identifiers: LCCN 2023051974 (print) | LCCN 2023051975 (ebook) | ISBN 9781501776748 (hardcover) | ISBN 9781501776755 (paperback) | ISBN 9781501776762 (epub) | ISBN 9781501776779 (pdf)
Subjects: LCSH: Philosophy, Ancient. | Philosophy, Ancient—Study and teaching. | Conduct of life—Study and teaching. | Mind and body—Philosophy. | Athletics—Greece—History—To 1500. | Physical education and training—Greece—History—To 1500.
Classification: LCC B171 .K37 2024 (print) | LCC B171 (ebook) | DDC 183—dc23/eng/20240308
LC record available at https://lccn.loc.gov/2023051974
LC ebook record available at https://lccn.loc.gov/2023051975

For my students

χαλεπὰ τὰ καλά

Contents

Preface: Inspiration in the Weight Room ix
Acknowledgments xix

Part I: Setting Goals with Socrates — 1

1. Bravery: *Laches* — 3
2. Discipline: *Charmides* — 11
3. Friendship: *Lysis* — 21
4. Justice: *Republic* 1 — 28
5. Wisdom: *Apology* — 38

Part II: Personal Training with Plato — 47

6. Drinking Games: *Symposium* 172a–199c — 57
7. Mysteries of Love: *Symposium* 199c–212c — 68
8. Music, Gymnastics, and Moral Development: *Republic* 2–4 — 79
9. Women at the Gym: *Republic* 5–7 — 87
10. Justice as Civic and Mental Health: *Republic* 8–10 — 101

Part III: Aristotle's Elite Performers — 111

11. A Sketch of the Good Life: *NE* 1 — 119
12. Training: *NE* 2–3 — 135
13. Greatness of Spirit: *NE* 4 — 146

14. Sportsmanship and Thinking
    on One's Feet: *NE* 5–6   155
15. Enjoying Discipline: *NE* 7   166
16. Gym Buddies: *NE* 8–9   175
17. Aspiring to Immortality: *NE* 10   188
    Epilogue: Greek Philosophy beyond
    the Gym   197

Notes 201
Bibliography 243
Index 257

Preface

Inspiration in the Weight Room

This book arose from a dare. In graduate school, I was a regular at the university's gyms (mostly to escape my dissertation on ancient philosophy). When I started teaching college full-time, the gym habit stuck. Between sets, I often got into conversations with students about school, lifting, and life. On one such occasion (I am pretty sure it was "chest day") the discussion got particularly intricate. My spotter laughed and said, "You should teach a class: Philosophy at the Gym." I suspect he was kidding, but the idea made sense. Ancient Greek moral philosophy, as I proceeded to explain, grew out of the programs of physical and civic education pursued in Athens's gyms. Images of mental health, spiritual exercise, and wrestling with ideas are woven throughout the works of Plato, Aristotle, and their successors. A few weeks before this conversation at the bench press, I had been invited to develop a general-education course to fulfill a humanities requirement. So, the next term, I taught an introduction to Greek moral philosophy via an athletic lens and called it Philosophy at the Gym.

The course filled instantly. Thanks largely to word-of-mouth publicity from a philosophy major on the men's baseball team and a member of the women's lacrosse team I knew through the Powerlifting Club, the class was made up entirely of student athletes. We opened the term with a selection of Socratic dialogues set in ancient Greek gyms. In some ways, my students could easily imagine themselves in such contexts with their training regimens, locker room banter, and worries about finding the right trainers. In other ways, these texts struck my class as bizarre. The Greek word *gymnasion*, for instance, means "naked place." The reason all those muscled men in Greek art were depicted naked is that the Greeks actually worked out naked. It is tempting to dismiss this as a cultural quirk, but the Greeks saw it as egalitarian. In the world's first democracies, any citizen could speak to the assembly. Rank was irrelevant: people just wanted to know what you had to say. Likewise, when you took off your clothes, you shed all markers of wealth and rank. Wrestlers were just two people, naked, oiled, and rolling in the sand. No branding, no high-performance athletic wear. Exposed. This clash of foreign and familiar helped students look at aspects of everyday life with fresh eyes. They saw connections between things they had thought were totally separate. They thought about their own lives with a new openness and imagination.

I offered the class the following semester, and it amassed the longest waitlist of any course in the college. Beyond the initial publicity for the class with "the professor who lifts," students were sharing their substantive experiences of the course with their friends and teammates. Sure, there were all the naked jokes and some memorable projects (it remains the only philosophy class I know of to have students show up in singlets). But students also read a hefty stack of ancient texts and archaeological studies, came to class prepared to participate and spend their time arguing enthusiastically, and wrote and revised multiple analytical essays. This was not an easy A. Despite being challenged to work hard, or perhaps because of it, students connected profoundly with this course. And they told all their friends.

Ancient Gyms

The student athletes in my course helped me realize that my "escapes" to the gym were not escapes at all. As often happens in graduate school, I had failed to connect my studies to reality. Today, philosophy is most commonly carried out in seminar rooms, libraries, and, if you're like me, cafés. None of these are athletic spaces. At the heart of most modern campuses is a library or chapel. The ancient equivalent was a gym. The standard layout had an open yard for working out surrounded by classrooms where young people would receive their civic education through heavy doses of music, literature, and public speaking.[1] We see this neatly summed up in a fifth-century *kylix* that shows two boys paired with two men who are leading them through lessons in music and writing while the head of the gym looks on with his signature staff of office (fig. 1). In short, the original gyms treated physical training as part of a more holistic project. I knew all of this well before I started teaching. What I did not appreciate was just how much my weight room conversations with students provided a path straight to the heart of Greek philosophy.

INSPIRATION IN THE WEIGHT ROOM

FIGURE 1. Attic red-figure *kylix* signed Douris Painter, circa 480 BCE. F 2285. Copyright Antikensammlung, Staatliche Museen zu Berlin—Preußischer Kulturbesitz. Photo by Johannes Laurentius.

The athletic context of the earliest philosophical schools shaped the course of philosophy itself. Plato opened his philosophical school in an existing gym, the Academy, and the main argument of his famous *Republic* relies on justice being a kind of mental health. Aristotle established his own rival school at another gym, the Lyceum, and used Olympic athletes as a model for the active life in his *Nicomachean Ethics*. Generations that followed Aristotle developed regimens of spiritual exercises, which helped shape the modern idea of religious practice. The goal of these regimens was to produce human excellence, what the Greeks called *aretē*, which we typically translate as "virtue." In short, the gym was a place for physical development *and* character development, where the young trained to be full, flourishing human beings. This was a natural context for philosophy and its driving questions: What does human excellence mean? What does flourishing consist in? And how do we get there? If we assume philosophy is all about the mind and the gym is all about the body, this merely shows how our modern culture has strayed from its ancient origins.

Modern Education: A Trifecta of Challenges

These driving questions are just as timely today as they were twenty-five centuries ago. If anything, we have lost ground in addressing them in our education system. Since the last decades of the twentieth century, the United States has confronted a trifecta of challenges that have pushed questions of character to the margins of our curricula. The result is a value vacuum, leaving students ill equipped to leverage their education to make the most of their lives as a whole.[2]

The first challenge is cultural. For most of its history, US culture was overwhelmingly Christian. Students moving through public schools would encounter Protestant values about working hard to provide for their families and serve their communities. And they studied a canon of literature carefully chosen to support these values. My own field of classics—the study of ancient Greek and Roman literature—featured prominently in this, though for reasons that classicists today have largely abandoned.[3] In the culture wars of the 1980s, people started asking why schools taught the perspectives of only "dead, white men."[4] This was a good question. Today's reading lists present a much more diverse range of perspectives. The tradeoff is that US schools taken as a whole no longer have a clear stance when it comes to questions of values. Add to this Americans' tendencies toward political polarization, which extend into religion, and we are confronted with a splintered landscape of conflicting views. Public schools deal with these conflicting values most often by simply avoiding all of them. As a result, questions about moral values and the religions with which they are associated are often not broached in schools.

The second challenge arose from the government. The No Child Left Behind Act of 2001 sought to level the playing field by bringing high-quality schooling to disadvantaged communities. This was a noble goal, but the execution was ineffective: smothering K–12 schools with excessive assessment requirements, ranking children by their ability to memorize arbitrary information, and making school funding contingent on test scores. This created a culture of testing. Students moving from the K–12 schools into college are now really good at answering questions but really bad at asking them. This should not be surprising, given the more than thirteen years they spent training that way. They are also good at checking off boxes to get to the next step. But they rarely stop to reflect on where these steps are headed.[5] Good grades in school get you into a good college; good grades in college get you a good job; a good job gets you lots of money; lots of money gets you . . .

what? Students usually say something vague about success or making a difference. Many simply assume the more money they make, the happier they will be.

The final challenge is economic. Americans have faced increasing economic challenges in the twenty-first century, including the market crash of 2008 and COVID-19 lockdown of 2020. Factor in new technologies, which make traditional jobs obsolete, and the result is an ever-widening wealth gap. For the vast majority of us, the American Dream of climbing the social ladder through hard work has been replaced by very real worries about simply paying the bills. The problem is particularly pressing for those starting out at the bottom of the economic ladder and those who, as I myself was, are the first in their family to attend college. Tuition costs, meanwhile, have soared as many colleges and universities add climbing walls, lazy rivers, flashy stadiums, and other state-of-the-art facilities to compete for enrollment. It is little wonder that students, and their parents, think about higher education in terms of return on investment (ROI).

Thanks to this trifecta of challenges, many students arrive at college stressed about money and unprepared to think about questions of values (but really good at checking boxes). In this context, major disciplines that seem to connect directly to high-paying careers (STEM and business) flourish, while those with less clear ROI (the humanities) wither. General-education courses, which offer the breadth of knowledge that has long been the strength of the US education system, are seen as obstacles to be quickly passed over on the way to what really matters: one's major. Witness the huge number of high school students earning college credit early through advanced placement courses. In short, the more than sixteen years of schooling leading to a college degree have come to be seen as merely a race to a high-paying job. What is lost is the opportunity to ask why, to think rigorously about what all the pieces of one's life will add up to. Such questions are the heart of Greek philosophy. So even if it was a fun course title that first brought all my student athletes to Philosophy at the Gym, the class became a chance to wrestle constructively with questions that were already weighing heavy on their minds. That kept them engaged through the end.

Pressing Forward: The Higher Ed Story So Far

I am not the first person to point out these challenges. Within the world of higher education, there is a whole genre of scholarship devoted to analyzing problems with school today. One of the more alarming studies addresses the question, How much learning goes on in US colleges and universities?[6] Its answer: precious little. The reason for this is simple: most students do not spend much time on schoolwork, since, on the whole, they do not have realistic, functional motivations. A good number are simply unengaged. Others dabble in various things but lack commitment. Others dream big but have no clear sense of how to pursue their goals. And then there are the "motivated but directionless," who check all the boxes but have no clear endgame.

Various individuals and organizations have noted today's value vacuum and set about filling it through a mixture of ancient religious traditions and modern psychology. In what follows, I will lay out existing attempts to push back against our trifecta of challenges. Each makes valuable, albeit limited, contributions. This book is by no means meant to offer a complete solution. Yet it fills a gap left by the rest. And, to judge by my students' responses, it does so in a way that is useful.

Attempts to undermine the culture of standardized testing are underway, though there is much work left to do. On the K–12 front, No Child Left Behind was repealed in 2015, leaving individual states to decide how to proceed. Meanwhile, groups such as the Philosophy Learning and Teaching Organization (PLATO) and the National Middle School and High School Ethics Bowls are developing age-appropriate ways to integrate philosophical thinking into the K–12 curriculum. Within higher education, the American Association of Colleges and Universities has sought to keep the traditional US liberal arts curriculum, with its hefty dose of general-education courses, relevant to students today. Given that most students today are stressed with ROI, this plays out mostly in showing how, appearances to the contrary, a traditional education is a recipe for financial success in the twenty-first-century economy. While this brings concerns for civic values into the mix and highlights the usefulness of skills in critical thinking, information literacy, and so on, it leaves students' concerns about ROI largely untouched.

The new field of positive psychology confronts assumptions about happiness and income more directly. This movement within psychology has turned away from the traditional task of fixing problems and focused instead on what it means to live well.[7] A groundbreaking 2010 study shows that one's happiness in fact goes up with one's income, but only to about $75k a year.[8] After that, it does not much matter whether you are making $80k or $800k. So, if making money is only one part of what makes a happy life, what are the other parts? Through quantitative study, psychologists have attempted to pin down the importance of factors such as flow, gratitude, and transcendence. One particularly useful concept for undergraduates is purpose. If interests are what you like doing and strengths are what you are good at, then purpose arises when you use those interests and strengths to meet a need in the world. When academic advisers ask undergraduates, "So, what do you want to do with your life?" positive psychology suggests the happiness trifecta is to figure out a need in the world that calls on you to do something you are interested in, that you are good at, and that you can get paid at least something like $75k a year to do. In practical terms, it is good for students and their families to be concerned with making money. It is even good for some to have this as their top concern. Nevertheless, this should not be their only concern. Today, courses such as Science of Happiness fill a need similar to what my student athletes felt. As a result, these courses are quickly becoming some of the most popular on college campuses.[9] Yet the gratitude journals and other resources such courses offer often bear the stamp of the lab experiments in which they were born.

Happily, most of the concepts studied by positive psychology have already been articulated in ancient religious and philosophical traditions around the world. As a result of this overlap, cutting-edge science has sparked renewed interest in centuries-old traditions. On the religious side, the Network for Vocation in Undergraduate Education (Net-VUE) has developed programs in purpose exploration.[10] These build on Christian colleges' theological concepts of vocation, calling, and service to help students connect their academic studies to life goals in ways that go beyond merely making money.[11] This fusion of approaches adds depth to the insights of positive psychology by bringing centuries of literature, art, and lived practice into the mix. NetVUE's commitment to explicitly Christian values, though, limits its ability to scale up in our post-1980s, pluralistic society.[12] In some cases, this is harmless. If Christian values work for Christian students at Christian schools, that is not bad; it is just limited. When applied to public schools, however, it can be problematic. In a recent flare-up of the culture wars, various politicians have sought to censor curricula, restrict the topics teachers may discuss, and vilify current scholarship in the social sciences. The fallout of this censorious activity is to push diverse people and voices back into the closet and onto the margins of society. Rather than get bogged down in partisan politics, I suggest we come at the problem from a different angle.

Greek thought, particularly Aristotle's, has been hugely instrumental in the development of Christianity, Judaism, and Islam alike. Within these major faiths Greek philosophy presents common, neutral territory because Greek philosophers worked from the ground up, setting any claims to divinely inspired knowledge to the side. The resulting body of thought is equally useful to students from any religion or no religion at all. Perhaps because of this, Aristotle is alive and well in the current self-help market, and ancient Stoicism is outright trending in hundreds of podcasts, vlogs, conferences, and popular works.[13] What all such approaches have in common, though, is that each draws its framework from a single ancient school. In this, they run into the same problem as NetVUE. While the revival of Aristotle or Stoicism is a step in the right direction, neither goes far enough.

If a fusion of modern psychology and ancient traditions really is the way forward, we need to find such an approach that meets the demands of our pluralistic society as it actually exists today. For example, Jonathan Haidt's *The Happiness Hypothesis: Finding Modern Truth in Ancient Wisdom* comes closest to offering a pluralistic approach to filling the value vacuum.[14] Haidt's book, which arises from his Intro to Psychology course, is not bound to any particular ancient school. In fact, Haidt does not limit himself to just Western philosophy but brings in Eastern thought as well. The end result is a splendid read with compelling connections. Yet, his survey of ancient philosophy, east and west, is limited mostly to bits of Stoicism that line up with bits of Buddhism, that line up with current thinking in cognitive behavioral therapy. While this is an impressive synthesis of ancient and modern, east and west, the end result still speaks with basically one voice.

Next Steps: Greek Philosophy for a Pluralistic Time

My strategy is to approach Haidt's project in reverse, using big ideas of happiness, purpose, and flow to anchor ancient philosophical speculation in modern evidence-based science. My goal is not to prove that the ancients were right but to use positive psychology to connect ancient thought to modern life. Through engagement with ancient literary texts, readers will be challenged to ask questions for themselves and construct pluralistic perspectives for navigating the complex world we live in. What is more, the centrality of the gym to ancient Greek culture helps Greek ethical theory fit our pluralistic context all the better. There is no one way to get in shape. But once you start making choices, say, by picking a particular sport, the range of possibilities for what works narrows. Add to this the competitive spirit that spreads easily from athletes and coaches to philosophers and teachers, and you have a recipe for a lively and flexible approach to life's big questions.

Part of going to the gym or hitting the field is trying out different strategies to prepare for unexpected situations athletic play might present. Likewise, students need different value frameworks to try on as they weigh future life choices and prepare for life's unscripted challenges. *Philosophy at the Gymnasium* seeks to fill this need by providing a series of competing frameworks. Central to this project are three interrelated ideas:

- flourishing/happiness (*eudaimonia*)
- human excellence/virtue (*aretē*)
- spiritual exercise (*askēsis*)

We tend to think of happiness as a feeling that comes and goes. The Greek notion of *eudaimonia*, which literally means "good spiritedness," is much more expansive: something like the objectively best life for a human being or human flourishing. How does one obtain *eudaimonia*? By doing the human thing well: that is to say, human excellence or virtue. Thanks to Christianity, the term *virtue* has a mostly moral sense today. That sense was present to some extent in the pre-Christian world, but the Greek idea of virtue is less being a good person and more being good at being human. The two ideas overlap, yet they also pull apart in ways we will explore. No matter how we conceptualize virtues, a final question remains: How do we acquire virtues? Here competing ancient schools agreed on a single answer: practice. Yet they disagreed about what that practice should look like.

In the chapters that follow, we will explore the meaning and interrelation of these main concepts: happiness, virtue, practice. Part 1 looks to Socrates, who through a series of dialogues set in athletic contexts calls existing understandings of these concepts into question but provides no definite answers. Part 2 turns to Plato, who views happiness as a form of mental health and advocates an elaborate program of physical and musical training as the key to a flourishing life and functioning society. Part 3 concludes with Aristotle, who takes elite performers – athletic, musical, and intellectual—as his model for happiness and works out an account of character formation that uses athletic conditioning as its model. While it might seem odd to modern sensibilities, the ancient connection between philosophy and the gym provides a useful thread for stringing all these ideas together. Approaching Socrates, Plato, and Aristotle from this perspective gives first-time readers an engaging entry point to the world of Greek moral philosophy while simultaneously providing fresh perspectives on a number of standing scholarly debates. Review of the scholarly literature will, however, be relegated to the notes. The primary task of this book is practical: to provide students figuring out what to do with their lives a set of ideas to wrestle with.[15]

Acknowledgments

Greek moral philosophy was born in the gyms of Athens. This book, likewise, is the product of multiple conversations at the Rollins College gym. Several student athletes, over multiple terms, took Philosophy at the Gym as a humanities course, puzzling through works of Plato and Aristotle while sitting on the floor of the campus yoga studio. In the weight room next door, a group of regulars provided what became a welcome spiritual exercise of elaborate between-set conversations: Brock Barfield, Yasha Carroll, Jack Dillard, Michael Dulman, Christopher Hebeler, Evans Hedges, Alon Hersch, Daniel Mock, R. T. Rogers, Jessica Smith, and Denis Terzic. Since 2020, I have pursued my work in pre-college philosophy by becoming a full-time middle school teacher. My Latin students at Friends Academy, Dartmouth, MA, have brought good humor and bold ideas as we worked out what a Greek philosophy class can look like in middle school. Meanwhile, my colleagues John Borowicz, Putnam Murdock, and Michael Williams daily illustrate the importance of athletics and the arts in moral development.

My approach to Greek philosophy is indebted to my own teachers. I was introduced to the Greek language by runner, musician, and classicist Z. Philip Ambrose. I was a student in Jacques Bailly's seminar on Plato, Christopher Shields's on Aristotle, and Tad Brennan's on the Hellenistic schools. I participated in reading groups led by Scott MacDonald, William Mann, and Gareth Matthews. I served as teacher's assistant for Gail Fine's survey of ancient philosophy and Courtney Ann Roby's of ancient medicine. And my fondness for skepticism was sharpened and refined through my dissertation work with Charles Brittain.

My editor, Bethany Wasik, provided extensive guidance as progressive drafts "bulked up" through engaging with the scholarly literature, and then "cut" by relegating most of that engagement to the notes. Along the way, Alexander Earl, Mollie Jones, Ronald Polansky, and

Michael Vazquez provided helpful feedback on individual chapters. Michael Austin and an anonymous reviewer provided useful and supportive feedback on the whole. Verity Platt, chair of classics at Cornell University, provided the appointment as visiting researcher that allowed me to complete the process of writing this book.

Two people have been part of this book from the start. Heather Reid has brought ancient athletics and philosophy back into dialogue within the scholarly community. She has also been a great support to me, from the start of the course to the completion of the book, as an editor, colleague, and friend. Jack Austin, finally, has been a tireless proofreader and a patient partner as our loft doubled as a not terribly tidy research library during quarantine.

To all these people I give heartfelt thanks. I am fortunate to belong to so many wonderful communities.

PHILOSOPHY AT THE GYMNASIUM

Part I

Setting Goals with Socrates

Socrates: Suppose there were a council to decide what your son needs to work on at the gym. Would you be persuaded by the greatest number of us or by someone who has exercised and been taught by a competent gym trainer?

Melesias: I would likely go with the person you describe.

. . . .

Socrates: So, to decide what is best, we must follow knowledge and not majority opinion.

Melesias: That's right.

—Plato, *Laches* 184e

Socrates, the father of Western moral philosophy, spent his days in the Athenian marketplace, his nights at drinking parties, and his time in-between at the city's gyms. What these venues have in common is the opportunity to talk with people. Part 1 explores Plato's Socratic dialogues set in athletic contexts. *Charmides* (chapter 2) and *Lysis* (chapter 3) are set in actual gyms. *Laches* (chapter 1) opens as characters have just watched a demonstration of fighting in armor. Book 1 of *Republic* (chapter 4) opens as characters discuss an upcoming torch race on horseback. Beyond mere entertainment, athletic competitions, as well as gym training, provided vehicles for reflecting on key aspects of life. Athens's gyms were an ancient forerunner of modern schools. When Plato sets dialogues in them, his intent seems to be to raise questions about the nature of education. Socrates, who was Plato's teacher, never wrote down his own ideas, opting instead for face-to-face conversations.[1] Plato, however, uses Socrates as a character in his own dialogues. The particular works we will look at are considered "Socratic" insofar as scholars think that they present the philosophical project, though not the actual words, of Socrates the historical individual. That project mostly involved engaging others in attempts to define key virtues: bravery (*Laches*), discipline (*Charmides*), friendship (*Lysis*), and justice (*Republic* 1). Each attempt ends in perplexity (*aporia*). The Greek term, *aporia*, literally means "no way forward." Plato's Socratic dialogues end as characters realize that important aspects of their lives are in fact more complicated than they had thought. Not all of Socrates's contemporaries appreciated this process. *Apology* presents the speech Socrates gave in reply to charges that he had corrupted the youth of Athens. While set in a courtroom rather than a gym, *Apology* ties the set of dialogues together by reflecting on the value of Socrates's conversations in athletic spaces and how they might embody a fifth virtue, wisdom (chapter 5).

In the broader arc of Greek thought, Socrates raised questions that later figures attempted to answer. As we proceed, these five central virtues—bravery, discipline, friendship, justice, and wisdom—provide a structure for our reading of Plato's and Aristotle's theories of happiness. Yet, as the game show *Jeopardy* illustrates, answers are useless if we are not clear what the questions are. Today, K–12 schools spend so much time drilling the right answers into students' heads, that there is often little chance for them to formulate questions for themselves. A bit of time with Socrates, exploring questions and lingering in perplexity, can serve as a useful antidote to our overgrown culture of standardized tests.

Chapter 1

Bravery
Laches

> Therefore, Socrates, I offer myself for you to teach and to refute as you wish.
>
> —Nicias in Plato, *Laches* 189b

Plato's dialogue *Laches* opens after a demonstration of fighting in armor.[1] We are not told the exact location, but the context is definitely athletic. At this point in the Athenian democracy, able-bodied citizens were expected to fight in the city's army when necessary. This is the era of hoplite warfare, named after all the gear (*hopla*)[2] that soldiers bore: helmet, chest guard, shin guards, shield, spear or sword. Soldiers lined up in opposing phalanxes, which collided as the two sides systematically shot, stabbed, and hacked at one another. In this system, each soldier was covered partly by his own shield and partly by that of his neighbor. Coordinated group effort was a matter of life and death. To survive, you had to be not only strong but nimble and responsive.[3]

The educational system of the day sought to prepare young men for this kind of military service by combining lessons in gymnastics and music, but neither of these terms meant quite what it does today. Music was inspired by the Muses and included singing, playing instruments, dancing, poetry, and theater. Gymnastics included all sports performed naked: track and field, wrestling, and boxing.[4] Young men were trained in both gymnastics and music at city gyms. The two came together in the long-jump (*halma*), which involved getting extra lift by throwing a

FIGURE 2. Attic red-figure *kylix* attributed to Carpenter Painter, 510–500 BCE. 85.AE.25. The J. Paul Getty Museum, Villa Collection, Malibu, California.

pair of weights (*haltēres*) behind oneself at just the right moment. The timing was so intricate that the event was often performed to music. A vase painter shows such a scene, as an *aulos* (double-flute) player stands to the right of an athlete holding a *haltēr* (fig. 2). While the fighting in armor in *Laches* seems to have been an unorthodox form of training (183c-184b), the educational context is clear.

Soccer Dads of Antiquity: *Laches* 178a-194b

Laches opens as two fathers declare that they want their sons to turn out better than they themselves did, so they seek advice from two illustrious generals, Nicias and Laches. The generals then enlist Socrates's help to determine the best plan for the boys, in particular whether they should take lessons in fighting in armor. Socrates asks what the goal would be of such lessons. The group eventually decides that the boys' character development is what matters most, in particular their ability to develop bravery. At this point, Socrates asks the seemingly innocent question, What, then, is bravery? The philosophical gloves come off as Socrates proceeds to grill the two generals about this central wartime virtue. It is tempting to skip straight to *Laches*'s attempt to define bravery, which begins halfway through the dialogue. But if we translate the work's initial question into modern-day terms, the reason for this suspenseful buildup becomes much clearer. Thinking broadly, we might ask why parents encourage sports teams and music lessons when it is unlikely that their children will later play sports or music professionally. What are students supposed to get out of these extracurriculars?

Such questions drive the first half of *Laches*. Nicias points out that fighting in armor along with horsemanship and gymnastics are all fitting for a free citizen (Greek, *eleutheros*; Latin, *liberalis*; 182a). Greece was a slave-owning society, so he means this literally. What education does a free person need in order to succeed as a citizen? Side by side with this discussion of freedom is a wide-ranging discussion of whether the art of fighting in armor is worthwhile, whether it is an "art" in the first place, and stepping even further back, what even is an art? The Greek term for "art" here is *technē* (185b), from which we get the English terms *technique* and *technical*. The Greek refers to a body of knowledge with some practical application; its Latin equivalent is *ars*. Combined, these two terms come down to us by way of their Latin forms as the *artes liberales*. In other words, the group is trying to figure out whether fighting in armor has a place in the liberal arts.[5]

How do we answer this question? We can start by returning to Socrates's question: What is any of this training for? As we arrive at the second half of the dialogue, Socrates turns to Laches and Nicias and invites them to define bravery. Given that Plato wrote in Greek, the question is not how to define the English word *bravery*. The Greek term here is *andreia*, which literally means "manliness" and can be translated as "bravery," "courage," and even "valor" (indicating a strong military connection).[6] But the characters in the dialogue want a substantial definition of the thing, not just a dictionary definition of the word. To take a modern example, anyone reading this book knows what the word *plastic* means and can use the word accurately in a sentence. But if you actually want to make some plastic, you need to find a chemist to give a substantial definition. Likewise, if you want your children to be brave, you should find an expert on bravery, someone who is actually knowledgeable about the subject.

Laches is the first to take the bait. Who better, after all, to talk about bravery than a general? A liberal-arts theme enters the dialogue here, as Laches himself talks about "the truly musical person" whose words are in harmony with his deeds (188d-e). As it proceeds, the dialogue follows a pattern that we will see frequently in Plato's Socratic dialogues. Laches's first attempt to define bravery, "keeping one's post" (190e), is dismissed as merely an example. It might be a good example, but it is too narrow to capture every instance of bravery. Since Socrates might have taken this example a bit more literally than intended, Laches takes a second pass, defining bravery as "endurance of the soul" (192c). This is problematic, though, as it covers instances of mere stubbornness and addiction. While Laches's first definition was too narrow, this second one is too broad.

To accommodate these counterexamples, Laches presents a third attempt: "wise endurance" (192d). Here, Socrates notes that there are times when less wisdom actually makes someone braver. Experts might be wiser about a field, but would not the novice who steps up in spite of his ignorance show more bravery? Imagine two scenarios where a pilot has a heart attack, and someone needs to land the plane. In one scenario, a passenger on the plane happens to be a pilot, so she steps into the cockpit and takes over. In the other scenario, no one on board knows how to fly, but a passenger steps into the cockpit and follows instructions radioed from the ground. Surely this second person is showing considerably more bravery. But still, what is bravery? In the dialogue, Laches admits defeat.

While we have not yet reached a viable definition of bravery, we have made some progress in narrowing down what a viable definition would look like. Socrates's process of cross-examination (*elenchos*) often follows a pattern where candidate definitions are shot down as being too narrow, too broad, and then self-contradictory in some mind-bending way. Given how Laches goes wrong, we can infer that Socrates is looking for something that covers all instances of bravery and nothing else, while getting at its real nature, not some superficial quality of it. That is a daunting task, but if we want to raise our children to be successful, should we not expect their teachers to say clearly what success even means? Again, the gym context is helpful. Some today think that going to the gym will make them fit, but fit can mean a lot of things. It is only by specifying concrete goals and laying out plans to pursue them that people make real progress in training. *Laches* invites such questions by thinking about fighting in armor, and it is but a small step from these to questioning the purpose and methods of education systems as a whole. A clear, coherent explanation of educational practice is exactly what Laches has failed to provide. Having reached perplexity (*aporia*), Laches hands the baton to Nicias.

Bravery vs. Virtue: *Laches* 194c-201c

Nicias has more experience with Socrates and his *elenchos*. When he is asked to take over the attempt to define bravery, he runs with an idea that he has heard from Socrates in the past, that bravery is a kind of wisdom (194d): in particular, "wisdom of the fearful and the hopeful in war and every other situation" (194e-195a). The Greek text suggests harmful things that should be avoided and daring moves that should be attempted. Thus, bravery is knowledge of how to act in the future. This seems promising: a brave person knows which risks to take, which to avoid, and she acts accordingly.

Socrates probes deeper and gets Nicias to admit that fearful things are simply future ills, and hopeful things are merely future goods. But if someone knows about goods in the future, Socrates argues, he should know about them in the present and the past as well. If the goods in question are health, harvests, and victory, then doctors, farmers, and generals can talk intelligently about such things existing at any time. It turns out, therefore, that the person who has knowledge of future goods and ills has knowledge of all goods and ills (198b-199d). This is a problem for Nicias. In setting out ground rules for their search, Laches stipulated that bravery is merely one part of virtue (190c-d), and Nicias agreed (198a). But, as we near the end of the dialogue, Socrates has shown that Nicias's definition, knowledge of the fearful and the hopeful, makes bravery the whole of virtue: a person with such knowledge would be moderate when dealing with present goods, wise when reflecting on goods from any time, and so on. Since such knowledge cannot be both a part and the whole of virtue, they conclude that they have not in fact discovered bravery.[7] At this point, everyone is perplexed, Socrates included (200e). *Laches* closes as the group resolves to go find someone else who can teach them what bravery is (201a-c).

We may rightly ask what the point of *Laches*'s rambling discussion is. Socrates's examination of Laches and Nicias failed to turn up a viable definition of bravery. In the process, though, we got a clearer sense of what a viable definition would look like. It is not just a list of brave deeds or even criteria for determining if an action is brave or not. Socrates wants to look under the hood: What is it that makes brave people act as they do? The right kind of knowledge sounds like a pretty good candidate. As Nicias said, it is an idea he has heard Socrates himself talk about. Just as the historical Socrates never wrote down his thinking, from what we can tell he also never defended his own theories, but merely questioned other people's. That said, he seems to have flirted with certain ideas. One of them, which turns up in multiple dialogues, is that all virtues are a form of knowledge.[8]

The Greek term for "virtue," *aretē*, literally means "excellence." In slightly old-fashioned English we could say it is a virtue of a wicking shirt that it keeps you cool in summer. Wicking shirts are good at being shirts. When applied to humans, virtue is being good at being human. If we were to ask someone on the streets of ancient Athens to point out human excellence, they would likely name an Olympic victor.[9] The two fathers at the start of *Laches* are looking for their sons to excel, to live full and flourishing human lives. That might include what we today would think of as being moral individuals, but it is larger than that. The question is, Can we define virtues clearly enough so that we can nurture them in our young?

The particular account of virtue that Nicias and Socrates flirt with, that it is a form of knowledge, has counterparts in current psychology. While Freud and his followers hold that many of our actions are shaped by subconscious forces, cognitive behavioral therapy (CBT) seeks to establish mental health by aligning the reality of situations with how we consciously think about them through inner self-talk.[10] We all have bad days, make mistakes, and lose games. But do we respond by throwing in the towel and deciding "I am worthless" or do we look more clearly at the scenario, saying, "I did not get enough sleep last night. I made mistakes in the final round," and move on with our lives? Practitioners of CBT do not usually talk in terms of wisdom, yet they share the basic idea with Socrates: life would be a lot better if we could think clearly and realistically about challenges we have to face. This parallel also makes both views susceptible to the same challenge: Is clear thinking all we need to get our lives right? Freud did not think so. And, as we will see, neither did Plato or Aristotle.

Failing Forward

The payoff of *Laches*'s failed inquiry lies in how characters respond to that failure. Psychologist Carol Dweck invites us to think about such things in terms of mindsets.[11] People with a fixed mindset assume that intelligence is something that you have or you do not. Such people see failure as evidence of intelligence that is already present or absent. They view the world in black and white. Because of this, they see every challenge as very high-stakes. (Think about that from a CBT perspective for a second.) People with a growth mindset, by contrast, assume that intelligence can be improved through hard work. They are thus much more likely to view challenges and failure as an opportunity to grow.

Laches puts mindsets on display in how different characters respond to perplexity. Laches, who is not familiar with Socrates's style of inquiry (188e), starts out with what seems just the right attitude: "Therefore, Socrates, I offer myself for you to teach and to refute as you wish" (189b). This could be the motto of a school. But once Socrates has finished refuting (*elenchō*) him, Laches just gets annoyed and admits to being overcome with the "love of victory" (194a-b). The Greek term, *philonikia* (a distant cousin of Nike shoes), stands in contrast to *philosophia*, the love of wisdom. Once Nicias takes over, Laches sits on the sideline interrupting periodically with petty snipes (195a-b, 196a-b, 197c, 199e-200a). Nicias's response is that Laches, since he has failed to define bravery, just wants to drag Nicias down with him (195a-b, 200a-b).

Nicias, by contrast, has dealt with Socrates before. He knows what they are getting into, and that no matter what it is they start out talking about, Socrates will make sure they themselves will eventually become the object of scrutiny (188c). He says he even takes pleasure in Socrates pointing out when he is wrong (188a-b). Unlike Laches, Nicias has the same attitude at the end as at the beginning. When Socrates rips "knowledge of the fearful and hopeful" to bits, Nicias shrugs it off, saying that they have talked enough for the day, and they can come back later and fix whatever needs fixing in their views (200b).

What should we make of the contrast between Laches and Nicias? While Plato certainly was not reading modern psychology, it is tempting to see Nicias's easygoing demeanor and apparent pleasure in getting his ideas shot down as an instance of growth mindset. Laches, by contrast, flip-flops between brazen confidence and petty sniping. A fixed mindset would explain this: by trading in black-and-white terms, Laches's stakes are ratcheted up too high. What Nicias sees as a welcome challenge, Laches sees as a threat to his intelligence.

And then there is Socrates. In this work, as in several others, he claims to be perplexed and ignorant of the answers to the questions he poses (186d-e, 200e). A surprising number of scholars do not believe him. Surely, no one would commit his life to surgically pointing out his own and others' confusion about life's most important questions! Such scholars assume that Socrates has the right answers in mind, and they set out to find them by reading between the lines. My friend and fellow cycling enthusiast Gareth Matthews has pushed back. In *Socratic Perplexity and the Nature of Philosophy*, he analyzes several varieties and benefits of perplexity found in Plato's Socratic works. *Laches* ends as the assembled group of grown men resolves to come back tomorrow to start working on finding themselves a teacher (200b-201c). Building on Gary's work, I suggest that this closing scene presents Socrates as a model of growth mindset whose enthusiasm for further inquiry is simply contagious. In the final analysis, even if Socrates might not have taught the group what bravery is, surely he has taught them to care about virtue.[12]

How are schools doing in these regards today? Does the system of standardized testing in our K–12 schools encourage students to embrace failure as an opportunity for growth or to avoid it as evidence that intelligence is lacking? It is ironic that students who come out on top of standardized tests can come out on the bottom when it comes to growth mindset. This has led to a spate of books. In *Excellent Sheep: The Miseducation of the American Elite and the Way to a Meaningful Life*, William Deresiewicz recounts how he left his position teaching English at Yale because he was so fed up with risk-averse and unimaginative students. If the ability to take intellectual risks, fail, and bounce back is necessary for authentic and useful learning, why is our school system rewarding students for doing just the opposite?

One remedy for this might sit in *Laches*'s opening question about fighting in armor. Playing a sport gives ample opportunity to fail, dust yourself off, and go back into the game. In my experience, student athletes often excel at receiving criticism of their academic work, admitting that they have room for improvement, and digging into revisions. Despite what popular wisdom would tell us, this seems to be an instance when the smart kids have something to learn from the athletes.[13]

Chapter 2

Discipline
Charmides

> "If he is willing to strip naked, his face will seem ugly: his body is completely beautiful," Chaerephon said.
>
> Everyone else agreed with Chaerephon, but I said, "By Herakles, you are describing an irresistible man if, that is, he should have one other small thing."
>
> "What's that?" asked Chaerephon.
>
> "If he also has a well-formed soul," I replied.... "So why don't we strip that part of him naked before we have a look at this body?"
>
> —Plato, *Charmides* 154d

A typical Greek gym consisted of two areas that were often run together: the *palaistra* (wrestling school) and the *gymnasion* (place for naked sports). If we take the *palaistra* from Olympia as an example, we find a large courtyard open to the sky surrounded by covered walkways on all four sides (fig. 3).

A number of rooms surround this central courtyard. The largest are the bays (*exedrai*), each of which had one side open to the central courtyard. In some, the other three sides were lined with benches (rooms VI, VIII, and XVIII); in others, not (V, VII, and XVII). The largest of these (XII) was the *ephēbeion* in which the city's youth (*ephēboi*) received their lessons in music, literature, and civic responsibilities. It was this connection to civic education that made the Athenian gym known as the *Akadēmeia* a natural location for Plato to set up his philosophical school. As for the smaller rooms, it was the Greeks' practice to exercise naked and oiled: each *palaistra-gymnasion* thus needed a locker room for people's street clothes (XIV), a room for storing oil, a room for applying dust (which, like chalk today, was used to help with grip), and rooms for showers and baths (X).[1] As you can imagine, wrestling under the

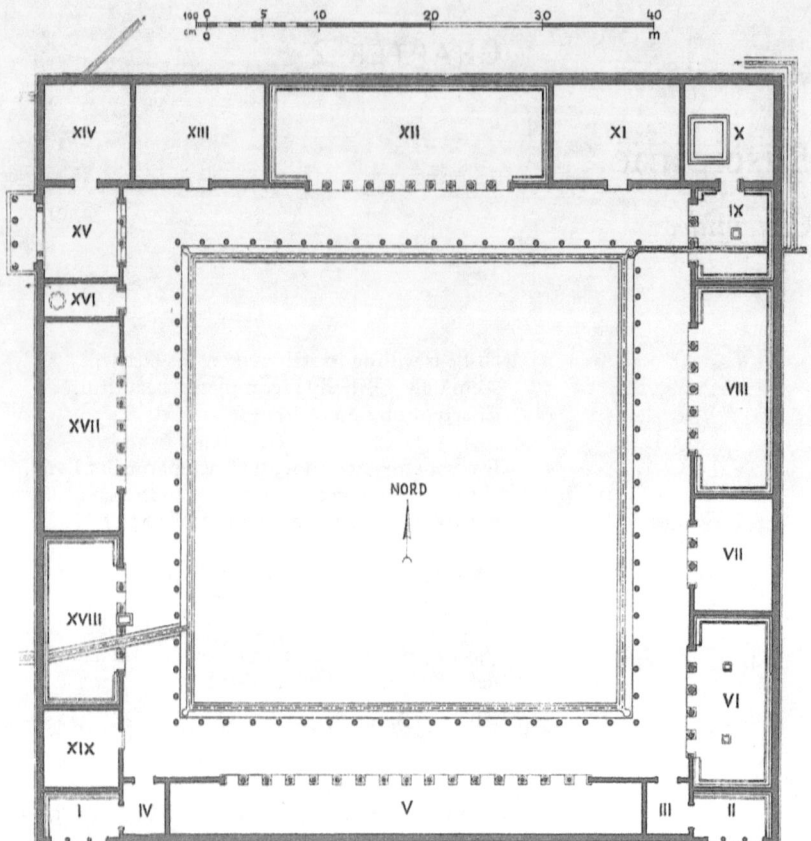

FIGURE 3. Plan of the *palaistra* at Olympia from Hans Scheif, *Die neue Ausgrabungen in Olympia und ihre bisherigen Ergebnisse für die antike Bauforschung.* Ber. IV, Taf. 3. Europäische Studienmappen, Berlin 1943.

Mediterranean sun was a sweaty affair. The resulting mix of oil, dust, sand, sweat, and maybe blood was known as *gloios* and was thick enough that cleaning up after a workout involved scraping it off with a special stick called a *strigil*. (There are records of athletes selling their *gloios* for high prices; we can only speculate why anyone bought it.) Additional rooms provided spaces for punching bags, ball games, and massages.

Unlike most athletes today, the ancients had a pretty minimal kit, which had mostly to do with grooming. In vase paintings, you can spot the athletes by their oil flask, sponge for the bath, and sometimes a *strigil*. More active scenes might have a discus, javelin, and weights for the long jump (*halētres*). The last piece of equipment was known as a dog leash (*kynodesmē*): a bit of leather used to tie back the penis, thus keeping it out of the way while working out.[2]

The Naked Truth: Athletics, Democracy, Philosophy

You may well wonder why the Greeks thought that naked sports were a good idea in the first place. We are not sure. Literary sources claim that early Greek runners competed wearing loincloths. One day a runner's fell off, and he just kept going. The practice went viral.[3] On a practical level, anyone who has spent time in the Mediterranean in the summer will sympathize with the desire to wear as little as possible and, particularly after physical activity, to scrape the gunk off one's skin with a stick. Whatever the origin of nude athletics, over time it became part of the Greek identity distinguishing the Greeks from those they saw as their less civilized neighbors, most notably the Persians.

On an ideological level, naked sports went hand-in-hand with democracy and philosophy. What could these possibly have to do with one another? When you have taken all your clothes off, there are no markers of rank or social status left. All you bring to a contest is your strength and skill. What is more, there are judges standing by to whip even the cities' leading men for committing fouls. In the absence of a professional army, it was a civic duty to stay fit so as to be ready when the need arose to fight for one's city. You could therefore also get whipped simply for being out of shape. In the same vein, Greek democracy was fully participatory. While a city's citizens (its free, landowning men) comprised only a small slice of the overall population, anyone who made it into that elite circle could stand in the assembly and make his case on the political issues of the day.[4] Philosophy pushed this egalitarian ideal even further. Socrates does not care about the status of his discussion partners. Plato depicts him in conversations with the young and old, generals, slaves, and everyone in between. If anything, Socrates delights in taking down politicians whom the city sees as wise, and in pointing out the wisdom of craftspeople whom the high and mighty routinely overlook.

Far from a mere cultural quirk, nudity is a central thread running through Greek sports, democracy, and philosophy. Even today, we talk about the naked truth as facts stripped of all pretense and niceties. It is in this spirit that Plato's *Charmides* opens.

CHAPTER 2

Getting Naked with Socrates: *Charmides* 153a-162b

Plato's *Charmides* is set in an Athenian gym and gives us a glimpse of the antics that took place there.[5] Having just returned from a military campaign, Socrates heads straight for the *palaistra*. Once he has greeted his friends and answered their questions about the battle, his first question is about the state of philosophy, young men, and whether any were outstanding for wisdom, bodily beauty, or both. Enter Charmides, Plato's uncle, whose name shares a root with the English word *charming*. And charming he is. Not only the older men, but even the youngest boys are awestruck by his beauty. Unlike some gyms today, men working out at the *palaistra* had few inhibitions about checking each other out. In fact, the Greeks had their own version of competitive physique or male beauty contests.[6] Socrates's friend Chaerephon puts it bluntly: "Just wait till he strips, and you get to see him naked." Socrates agrees that that will be lovely. But first Socrates wants Charmides to "expose" his soul. Conventions of nude exercise thus provide a springboard for looking at the naked truth of Charmides's character (154d).

At this point, Charmides's guardian, Critias, whips up a pretext: Charmides has had trouble with headaches, so Critias calls him over and introduces Socrates as a doctor who can help. Charmides takes a spot on the bench between them. Socrates catches a glimpse down Charmides's robe and for once is at a loss for words.[7] Pulling himself together, Socrates explains that he has an herb to help with headaches that can be used in conjunction with singing a charm. From here he lays out a holistic approach to medicine, saying that just as one cannot treat part of the body without treating all of the body, one cannot treat the body without also treating the soul. Therefore, before Socrates can give Charmides this charm, he must test the state of Charmides's soul, in particular whether he possesses the virtue *sōphrosunē* (155d-157d).

Sōphrosunē is hard to translate into contemporary English, for the simple reason that contemporary culture rarely worries about it. "Temperance" is the normal translation. In somewhat old-fashioned English, this brings connotations of reaching a careful balance, for instance, when tuning an instrument or alloying metals. The temperance movement, however, advocated completely abstaining from alcohol, coloring the English term in ways that the Greeks would not have meant. The term *prudence* suffers from the same problem, as it makes us think of prudes. From the opening pages of *Charmides*, it is clear that Socrates is no prude. *Moderation* gets closer: the person who goes out and gets a good buzz but does not black out. But the Greek virtue *sōphrosunē* extends beyond just social drinking. We can talk about being discreet and not making a mess of a sticky situation, having your ducks in a row, or maybe even being street smart. Moore and Raymond make a case for translating *sōphrosunē* as "discipline."[8] This is somewhat problematic insofar as discipline refers both to a process of punishment (disciplining) and to the intended result of that process: what we might call being self-disciplined. On the other hand, its Latin root, *disco*, has to do with learning as is captured in English phrases such as interdisciplinary studies. This nicely captures the street smarts sense present in the Greek (*sōphrosunē* is related to *sōphrōn*, "being sound of mind"). In the end, "discipline" is perhaps the least problematic option, provided we keep clear that we refer to the end state, not the process of getting there. It also nicely captures the athletic resonances at play in many ancient discussions of the virtue.

However we translate the term, the fact remains that US culture is not very disciplined. If one cookie is good, then two will be great! Children are conditioned from an early age to compete for "likes." As soon as the iPhone 18 is in your pocket, Apple is marketing the 19. Driving all of this is our free-market economy, which depends on a population that constantly spends more: buying goods and replacing them as soon as possible. One of the reasons we spend money on vacations and activities is to post pictures of ourselves having fun. If everyone in the United States suddenly started living moderately and prudently, our economy would collapse. Look at the economic havoc that arose from the COVID-19 lockdown! Yet, if we reflect on our time staying home and spending less, we might ask ourselves: Is there an alternative to the consumerist hamster wheel we are trapped on, constantly seeking more? Would we be happier simply living with enough? If so, how do we start?

These are the sorts of questions Socrates has in store for Charmides. Socrates begins by prompting Charmides to agree that if someone has discipline in his soul, then he will be able to talk about it (159a).[9] So if Charmides can simply answer a few questions about what discipline is, then he will have shown himself to possess it. As usual, it is not the meaning of the Greek word, *sōphrosunē*, but the reality to which the word refers that Socrates wants.

The arena is set for the first round of questioning (159a-162b). Charmides seems to have discretion in mind, as the first definition he offers is "to do things calmly." The Greek (*hēsychaō*) means both "act quietly" and "act slowly." Socrates latches onto the second meaning and points out that there are times when we need to do things quickly. Charmides tries again: it is to do things modestly. But, as Socrates points out, there are also times when bold actions are required, such as asking for help when one would rather not have to. At this point Charmides remembers a view of discipline he has heard from someone: "minding one's own business." But, Socrates responds, if raising crops is a farmer's business and making a plow is a blacksmith's business, then a farmer and a blacksmith who minded their own business would be unable to trade crops for plows. If we expand the point, then it seems that minding one's own business rules out transactions entirely, which would bring society to its knees. At this point, Charmides bats his lashes at Critias, who is clearly the "someone" who came up with this last definition, and passes him the baton.

Discipline and Leadership: *Charmides* 162c-176d

Charmides's second round begins as Critias comes to the aid of his definition. His first attempt is to split the hair between doing, making, and working (163a-c). This is a bit hard to follow in translation, but the point seems to be distinguishing between one's life's work in a lofty sense and more menial, day-to-day tasks. Socrates will not have it. Critias tries again, claiming that discipline is "doing good things" (163c). But would it count, Socrates asks, if someone accomplished good things without realizing it? Can a doctor, for instance, sometimes treat people in useful ways and sometimes treat people in un-useful ways, not realizing whether he is being helpful or not? The idea here seems to be that there are times when it is appropriate to cure people and times when it is appropriate not to try—for instance, when treatment will only prolong suffering and delay inevitable death. Critias is not comfortable with the idea of a doctor who can act with discipline by accident, so he offers a revised definition: discipline is knowledge of oneself (164d). The definition picks up the famous phrase written at the entrance to Apollo's temple at Delphi, "Know thyself" (164d-165b).[10]

While that sounds all well and good, Socrates asks what it actually means. Knowledge, after all, needs to have some object. Critias takes one last pass and states that discipline is "the knowledge of itself and other kinds of knowledge" (166c). It is at this point that translating *sōphrosunē* as "discipline" comes in handy. At Socrates's prompting,

Critias spells out his meaning: a disciplined person will know what he knows and what he does not know (167a).[11]

Let us pause for a second. Imagine a person who knows what she knows and what she does not know. How would such a person act? To be honest, she might act like Socrates. At *Apology* 20d-21d, as we will see, Socrates claims a kind of "human wisdom," which amounts merely to "I do not think I know what I do not know." In practice, such a person would be confident when she knows what she is doing, and cautious when she does not. Would not such a person show discretion and street smarts? As with any promising idea, Socrates proceeds to shoot this one down too. His argument comes in three waves.

Socrates's first and least impressive wave of argument is that discipline is odd (167c-168e). After all, if we think about other things that take objects—vision, hearing, desire, wish, love, fear—we do not find things that take themselves and other things as their objects. It is perhaps true that we cannot see vision or hear hearing. But it seems simply false that we cannot fear fearing. As Franklin Delano Roosevelt put it, "The only thing we have to fear is fear itself!" Likewise, many of us have looked forward to a day when we could look forward to leg day at the gym. In any event, Socrates grants, by way of hypothesis, that such self-reflective acts are possible, and he moves on to his more substantial arguments.

Socrates's second and more serious critique of discipline is that it is useless (169d-172d). His argument turns on what we now refer to as first- and second-order knowledge. First-order knowledge takes something out in the world as its object. The doctor, as Socrates puts it, knows health. Second-order knowledge takes another body of knowledge as its object. Socrates's example is medicine. Knowledge of medicine as a body of knowledge seems to amount to knowing the medical field's foundational principles, general criteria for knowledge, structuring norms, and so on. In our terms, this is philosophy of science. The trouble is that first-order and second-order knowledge can pull apart. You could have a doctor who knows health but not medicine, and a disciplined person who knows medicine but not health. (This may seem counterintuitive, yet I have met plenty of scientists who know their subject matter intimately but get annoyed when asked about how they know whether they can trust observations, or whether the causal explanations they posit capture the world as it actually is.) If we grant this distinction, Socrates argues, then doctors will be able to judge other doctors, while disciplined people cannot. A doctor who also happens to be disciplined would be best of all. But what about all those other bodies of knowledge outside of medicine: navigation, farming, and so on? For society to function, experts in several different fields are needed. At some point, the person calling the shots will not be able to know all the first-order content of these various fields. The more complex the group, the more often people in charge will have to delegate responsibilities. With modern corporations and nations, the range of specialized first-order knowledge is dizzying. There is too much knowledge in the world today for any one person to master. But if that is right, and leaders must still delegate tasks, how can any individual possibly know everything necessary? Critias held out discipline as the key to this, but, given the current line of argument, his understanding of discipline is simply not up to the task.

At this point, Socrates lends Critias a hand: perhaps the point of Critias's definition is that a person with discipline will do everything with knowledge (172a-175a). Here Socrates entertains the possibility that a person with discipline can spot someone pretending to be a pilot, a doctor, and so on. (We might again find a model for this in Socrates himself. Even if he lacks first-order knowledge of navigation or medicine, he is able, by questioning alleged experts, to expose those who *lack* the knowledge they claim.) Socrates and Critias agree that a person with this capacity to sniff out frauds would live a happy life. But what kind of knowledge would make that person happy? Critias is forced to say, "Knowledge of good and evil." With that, however, they all have simply looped back to an idea they already rejected (163e).

The upshot is that this discussion is a total mess. If Charmides, Critias, and Socrates all show themselves incapable of saying what discipline is, it must be that none of them actually possesses it (159a). Charmides concludes—perhaps playfully, perhaps ominously—that he will force Socrates to "charm" him every day (175b-176d).

Education for the Twenty-First Century

What should we make of *Charmides* today? To those working on modern college campuses, Greek gyms can come across as one big Title IX violation. Still, Socrates's attempts to "expose" Charmides's and then Critias's souls raise central questions about the relationship of school and society. Those questions are just as pressing today as they were in Athens's fledgling democracy. I will close by drawing out the current implications of two of them.

First, in challenging Critias's idea of discipline as knowledge of knowledge, Socrates raises serious concerns about the possibility of leaders delegating responsibilities. Such worries motivate the standard US undergraduate curriculum, which combines deep knowledge of a major discipline with the broad knowledge of a general-education curriculum. In the US system, if you want to be a doctor, you should focus on science but know enough about computers to talk with IT personnel and enough about human beings to talk with your patients. That is why we make science students take literature courses, and humanities students take math. The end result is not so much a hierarchy with one person at the top, as a cluster with enough overlap between individuals to hold things together. As the world becomes more interconnected, the tasks we all face become more complex, and the need to talk across disciplinary boundaries becomes all the more pressing. It is ironic that as colleges across the world are coming to see the value of the US approach to education for the twenty-first-century economy, the United States itself is busily abandoning it for more narrowly focused job training.[12]

Second, among the reasons the United States is walking away from its signature mode of education is that students themselves often have trouble articulating this system's value. In my past teaching experience, I took part in designing general-education curricula for a college's traditional, residential students and its program for nontraditional, adult learners. Faculty worked across disciplinary lines to produce beautifully structured curricula that integrate transferable skills, broad knowledge bases, disciplinary focus, and project-based, real-world learning. Yet, when asked to talk about ways this education might apply to potential jobs, students often fumbled. What was missing was the ability to articulate all of this learning. As a result, the faculty built a Capstone Seminar into the one general-education curriculum and an Intro to the Pragmatic Liberal Arts into the other, forcing students to talk about the structure of their education.[13] Scientists and educators today refer to this as metacognition. In Socrates's terms, these students needed a bit more knowledge of knowledge. Apart from merely getting ahead in interviews, the ability to articulate how one fits into a larger scheme and how skills developed in one context can translate into another has been shown to improve the learning process itself.[14] For these reasons, the American Association of Colleges and Universities has led the charge to restructure curricula around learning outcomes such as critical thinking, information literacy, written expression, and ethical reasoning. If school is practice for life, then focusing on these outcomes helps us connect the dots.[15] Students who do this throughout their studies will find more meaning in their schoolwork and draw more use from it after they graduate. While Critias's knowledge of knowledge may not have held up as a formal definition of discipline, his discussion with Socrates raises issues that we would do well to think through today.

Chapter 3

Friendship

Lysis

> "Come over here, Socrates," said Hippothales as he showed me an enclosed space facing the wall and an open door. "We spend our time here. There are other men too. Many of them are really attractive."
>
> "What is this place," I replied, "and what do you do here?"
>
> "It is a new wrestling school, just built. We spend most of our time here talking about things. We'd love for you to join us."
>
> —Plato, *Lysis* 203b-204a

One reason that gym-goers in *Charmides* are so unabashed in complimenting each other's nude, oiled physique is that homoerotic relationships were a widely accepted part of Athenian society.[1] Such relationships were not seen as competing with heterosexual marriage. Socrates himself had a wife, Xanthippe, yet flirted tirelessly with other men and had at least one long-term lover, Alcibiades. None of this counted as cheating. We have far less information about women's experiences in antiquity, yet we know from the poet Sappho of Lesbos that similar relationships existed between women. Homoerotic relationships also had an educational dimension. Because of this, such relationships often, but not always, involved some kind of age gap. In my experience, these age gaps can trip up some modern readers. Before we pass judgment on ancient practices, let us note three respects in which modern society has parted ways with earlier cultures and generations.

First, life expectancy in Socrates's Athens was significantly shorter than it is today. As it works out, a young man would first take an older lover at about the same age that a young woman would take an older husband: around fourteen years old.[2] By some reckonings, this was essentially middle age.[3]

Second, ancient Greece had more of an apprenticeship culture than we do today. If you wanted to be a blacksmith, you did not go to school to major in metallurgy. You apprenticed with a blacksmith. The *gymnasion*'s combination of music and gymnastics provided a basic education for future citizens, but more advanced education followed the apprenticeship model. An older lover would take his younger partner to drinking parties, help him network, and provide him with an apprenticeship in citizenship. This helps explain the same-gendered nature of such relationships. Factor in the extreme social separation between the sexes—husbands and wives moved in mostly separate social and professional circles—and we can see why men would look for companionship among people they actually spent time around.

The third, and perhaps greatest, disconnect between us and the ancient Greeks is highlighted by modern feminism. Among other things, feminism championed the idea that marriage should be between equals. The rationale for this viewpoint is obvious: wives, for no good reason, took second place to husbands through most of human history. In the twentieth century, new ideals of equality between spouses made their way into the popular consciousness. This general idea bled into the queer community. Gay male relationships in the nineteenth and early twentieth centuries were mostly between people who are unequal in age, social status, or both: take Oscar Wilde and his younger lover Lord Alfred "Bosie" Douglas, for instance. While members of gay or lesbian couples today may present themselves as more masculine or more feminine, such identities do not typically dictate which person's opinions and career take precedence. Today's gay community is much more likely than the last century's to shape itself around the feminist ideal of equal partnership. This new standard of equality is, no doubt, a good thing for gay and straight couples alike. But we should recognize that it makes our society the exception when compared to long stretches of human history.

Whatever we may think of mixing romance and education, many ancient Athenians embraced it. It was also a fairly formal affair, with roles assigned to the parties involved. The older man was known as the "lover" (*erastēs*), from the active form of the Greek verb for "erotic love." The younger was known as a "beloved" (*eromenos*), from the passive form of the same verb. To make sure everything was on the up and up, a particular slave, known as a *paidagōgos*, was assigned to bring young men to and from school. The title *paidagōgos* (child leader) is the root of the term *pedagogy*, which now covers education as a whole.

These relationships also followed conventions for the exchange of gifts and favors. Common gifts from the lover to his beloved included roosters, hoops (used in a game), oil flasks (used at the gym), and drinking cups (used at drinking parties). Flasks and cups often depict the beloved with the label *kalos*, which means "fine" or "beautiful," with both physical and moral connotations. In return, the beloved would provide favors, which amounted mostly to kissing and cuddling. Sexual penetration was generally frowned upon, though a kind of intercourse "between the thighs" was common. The gym, as a place where fit, naked men of various ages gathered to oil up and wrestle, became a natural setting for this form of courtship.

All of this provides the backdrop for Plato's dialogue, *Lysis*.[4]

Flirting at the Gym

Lysis opens as Socrates is walking from the Academy to the Lyceum, two gyms that were the future sites of Plato's and Aristotle's philosophical schools. Along the way, he runs into some friends who call him into a new *palaistra*. Socrates's first question is who there is good-looking (*kalos*; 204b). At this point, the assembled company starts teasing Hippothales, a would-be lover, who is clearly smitten with the beautiful young man Lysis. In something approximating locker-room banter, Hippothales's friend Ctesippus mocks Hippothales's attempts to court Lysis by writing poetry about the wealth, athletic victories, and mythic descent from Zeus of the young man's ancestors (205b-d). In context, such behavior is not strange so much as unimaginative: such themes are the bread and butter of victory odes, which poets like Pindar wrote to celebrate victories at Olympia and other ancient games.[5]

Socrates points out that Hippothales is shooting himself in the foot. By treating his would-be beloved in terms suited to an Olympic victor, Hippothales will give the young man a swelled head, making him harder to catch. Hippothales is like "a hunter who scares off his prey" (206a). Rather than tell Hippothales the right way to flirt with men at the gym, Socrates decides to show us his moves. A lesson in flirtation ensues. Hippothales watches from the sidelines, while Socrates engages Lysis and his friend Menexenus in a conversation about friendship. With this setup in place, their discussion proceeds in four rounds through which Socrates leads Lysis and Menexenus into perplexity.

In the first round (207d-210d), Socrates argues briefly that Lysis's parents must not love him because they do not let him do various things, like drive the mule team. What is worse, they even put a slave, the *paidagōgos*, in charge of Lysis who is freeborn. Lysis takes the bait, replying that this is because he has not yet come of age. Socrates replies that it is not merely age but knowledge that makes people worthy to be entrusted with responsibilities. Since Lysis is still a student, it must be that his parents, and everyone else, will love him only when he has learned more and "become wise." Lysis apparently appreciates this perplexing conclusion: youthful whispers ensue as Lysis asks Socrates to question Menexenus too. The moral of the story so far? It is best to talk with a potential conquest by "cutting him down to size" (210e).⁶

In the next two rounds, Socrates tries to determine what kind of person is a friend, by going through all possible options and ruling them all out. The Greek term *philos* has a broader range than the English word *friend* and encompasses not just people but anything that is dear to us. This explains some of the oddness of their discussion. Starting with Menexenus (212a-213d), Socrates makes use of the lover/beloved distinction and points out problems with all possible combinations. The basic idea is that if only one person loves the other, then it is possible to love our enemies and hate our friends. But if friendship requires that the object of one person's love loves him back, then it is impossible to love horses, wine, or wisdom, which would rule out philosophy as the love of wisdom. Menexenus is stumped.

Socrates turns again to Lysis as he begins the third round (213d-218c). This time he brings in moral terms: bad people cannot be friends to bad people, he argues, since they will act unjustly toward each other. Good people are self-sufficient, so they would not need other good people as friends. Can good people, then, be friends to bad people? That would mean, Socrates argues, that unlike people would be friends, and unlike people are opposite, so that does not work. The just, after all, cannot be friends to the unjust! In this, Socrates leans into the moral implications of the Greek *kakos* (bad). In the context of friendship, we might translate this as "toxic." We have all seen scenarios of toxic friends. But what is the opposite of a toxic person? A healthy person? A solid person? Whatever we call him, can such a person really be a friend to a toxic individual? As a final option, Socrates considers someone who is neither good nor bad but neutral, and asks whether this person could be a friend to a good person. This option seems to gain traction. Socrates suggests a parallel: a body is neither good nor bad but neutral, and because of disease, it is a friend to medicine. But the victory is short-lived.

In the fourth round (218d-221c), Socrates draws a distinction: a person is a friend (a) to someone, (b) on account of something, (c) for the sake of something. In the medicine scenario, a patient is a friend to a doctor, on account of disease, for the sake of health. In this case, it seems that health is our real friend. And we can expand this beyond just medicine: whenever we are a friend to someone, it is for the sake of the good, so it seems that the good is our real friend. But we are not friends to the good for the sake of something else, so their conclusion about friendship in round three fails to hold up. Furthermore, this suggests that we would stop being friends to the good if somehow the bad were to disappear. And that just seems backward.

The conversation ends as Socrates concludes that either desire has nothing to do with friendship, and this has all been chatter (221d), or that a friend is what "belongs to us" (221d-222b). With the second response, we seem finally to arrive at a conclusion. Hippothales takes it this way, and beams as Socrates concludes that a young man must therefore passionately love his lover. But this victory is also short-lived. As Socrates attempts to spell out what belongs to means, the group loops back to positions they have already rejected. At this point the *paidagōgos* shows up to take the young men home, and the work concludes in perplexity all around.

Flirting with Philosophy

What should we make of the *Lysis*? Put another way, what is *Lysis* about—the nature of friendship or the correct way to flirt? Seeing it as merely a lesson in flirtation would go some way to explain why so many of Socrates's arguments seem obviously flawed. Still, it is possible to draw a serious point from an undertaking that is basically silly. The comedies of Socrates's contemporary Aristophanes often presented serious political commentary through humor that would make a sailor blush even today: the ten minutes of jokes about excrement at the beginning of *Peace*, for instance, or the giant flaming phallus of *Thesmophoriazeusai*. The Greeks even had a term for the serious in the silly (*spoudaiogeloios*). Perhaps the point of *Lysis* is to figure out how Socrates's arguments are flawed. This is not to say that there is a secret message in *Lysis* for those who read between the lines, but rather that legitimate perplexity about the nature of friendship can itself act as a springboard for moving beyond superficial assumptions.[7]

One place to start looking for a more serious takeaway is the opening round's assumption that we only love people who are useful. This is mirrored in the third round's assumption that good people will not love each other because they do not need anything from each other. Is love based on need? If not, then what is it based on? Another promising connection comes in the brief mention of philosophy (218a-b). Here, the philosopher—the lover of wisdom—sits between the actually wise person and the person so ignorant that he does not even know to seek wisdom. Is this a more positive take on Socrates's initial argument that Lysis will be loved when he has become wise?

If we can set aside sexual connotations, which are basically absent from *Lysis* to begin with, there is something special about teacher-student relationships. Such things are not merely about two people enjoying each other's company. Such relationships point beyond themselves, as they help the student grow. They are, in *Lysis*'s terms, "for the sake of the good." Participants in such relationships play different roles, but they are not "opposed." Schools today sometimes treat teachers as knowledgeable, students as ignorant, and education as a form of knowledge transfer. People who think this way tend to see good students as sponges that soak up information. Understood this way, I could see student and teacher as opposed: forced into a transactional relationship not unlike "the rich and poor, . . . the sick and the doctor" (215d).

We find a clearer parallel today among coaches. It is not that a coach has the ability to run fast, which she somehow transfers to her players. If anything, coaches are often past their physical prime. The point, rather, is that coaches guide student athletes as they improve through their own hard work. Furthermore, a coach who praises athletes to the point that they get "swelled heads" rather than helping them focus on what they need to improve is a terrible coach. The setting of *Lysis*, a *palaistra*, invites us to draw such parallels. Just as wrestlers compete with each other to make each other stronger, Socrates wrestles intellectually with Lysis and Menexenus to help them improve their powers of reasoning. As we have seen in their discussion, to begin the search for wisdom, one first has to admit one's own ignorance.

There is no perfect, modern parallel to the ancient gym. The modern world has largely separated coaching from teaching, athletics from academics. Romantic relationships between teachers and students clash with ideals of equality between romantic partners. Whether or not there is a right answer in *Lysis* for those who read between the lines, the dialogue works through a constellation of ideas that were interconnected for the Greeks and we might think about as forms of tough love. The text invites us to think more rigorously about important aspects of our lives: friendship, teaching, growth. It also gives us a chance to bring into dialogue parts of our world that we normally see as separate. What can teachers learn from coaches? Should we look for romantic relationships to make us better people? Should we, as students, seek out people who tell us we are wonderful or those who help us see what we need to work on?

Chapter 4

Justice
Republic 1

> Thrasymachus agreed to all these things, not as easily as I am now telling it. Oh no, he was dragged along and only just barely. And he was sweating profusely (it was summer). Then I saw something I had never seen before: Thrasymachus blushing.
>
> —Socrates in Plato, *Republic* 350c-d

Sports have been wound up in politics since the beginning. Egyptian Pharaohs were considered such exemplary athletes that asking them actually to compete was seen as an insult. Greek warlords of Homer's *Iliad* and *Odyssey*, composed around 800 BCE, routinely defend their social status through wrestling, chariot racing, and discus.[1] For over a thousand years, the Greeks honored an Olympic truce, as warring cities set their disagreements aside to allow safe travel to and from the games. And an Olympic win was seen not just as a personal victory but as an accomplishment of the winner's home city. The modern world is not so different. Given the United States' particular history, however, the interplay of sports and politics often revolves around issues of race. This played out during the buildup to World War II, as the United States sent Jesse Owens, an African American track-and-field athlete, to the 1936 Olympic Games presided over by Hitler in Berlin. Owens proceeded to win four gold medals, allowing the United States to thumb its nose at Germany's emerging ideals of racial purity. The United States itself was hardly perfect, though, and even as an Olympic hero, Owens returned home to face racial segregation (the 2016 film *Race* pointedly depicts Owens being forced to use the service entrance to a banquet held in his honor). All of this provides context for a more recent collision of politics and sports.

"No Justice, No Peace"

The football player Colin Kaepernick introduced the gesture of taking a knee during the singing of the national anthem in 2016 to draw attention to racial injustice and police brutality. The gesture went viral in 2020 following the death of George Floyd, an African American man who suffocated because of excessive police force. Since then, the gesture has become strongly associated with the Black Lives Matter (BLM) movement. Taking a knee raises a number of philosophical questions: Do athletes perform on behalf of their communities, or do they merely provide entertainment? Is it bad sportsmanship to use athletic events to make political statements? Given the severe backlash against Kaepernick and those who followed him, we may even ask whether it is un-American or unpatriotic to speak out against one's own country.

Greek philosophy has little to say about the politics of race for the simple reason that modern concepts of race did not exist in antiquity. The ancients noticed differences in skin color, yet they attributed no more moral significance to this than we do to the color of people's eyes or hair. Augustine of Hippo, the focus of my graduate studies, was a late ancient philosopher from North Africa whose skin color we do not know because none of his contemporaries thought it was worth mentioning. Granted, the Greeks and Romans also practiced slavery. Yet, unlike the United States and other modern countries, they did not attempt to justify slavery on the basis of skin tone.[2] People became enslaved mostly by losing in battle or falling into extreme poverty.

Greek philosophy has more to say about the justice invoked by the racial justice movement. We might imagine Socrates attending a BLM rally, hearing the chants of "No Justice, No Peace," engaging a protester in conversation, and winding around to the question, What is justice? Presumably he would shoot down the most immediate answer—punishing George Floyd's killers—as merely an example and not the whole of justice. In response, our imagined protestor might suggest treating all people the same way, regardless of race. This, however, might go too wide. There are some who argue that since the US economy was built on the basis of slave labor, the United States as a whole owes a debt to descendants of enslaved people. The only way to pay such reparations is by treating races differently. At this point, our protester might suggest that justice has something to do with the structure of our society and its institutions. If so, the real question is, What? Happily, we do not need to imagine what Socrates would say about justice, since the attempt to define justice is the central project of *Republic*. Portions of this discussion can help us look at our current political landscape with fresh eyes. Getting to these insights, however, takes a bit of setup.

Opening Conversation: *Republic* 327a-331d

Republic is split into ten books.[3] *Republic* 1 resembles a self-contained Socratic dialogue, which starts with a day in the life of Socrates, brings up a controversial question, seeks to define a particular virtue, shoots down candidate definitions, and ends with everyone perplexed (*aporia*). It even opens with an athletic event: in this case, an upcoming torch race on horseback as part of a festival honoring the goddess Bendis. Unlike other dialogues, however, *Republic* reaches *aporia* and then keeps going for another nine books. Gym training is woven throughout later books, as is the idea that the virtues are a kind of mental health. These ideas are largely absent in book 1. Instead, we find war and politics, which (along with athletic events) embody the ancient Greek spirit of competition (*agōn*). These competitive topics of discussion, in turn, are mirrored by the verbal sparring between Socrates and a teacher of public speaking, or sophist, Thrasymachus. Scholars disagree as to whether *Republic* 1 was written as a stand-alone work that Plato later came back to, or as an intentional part of the whole from the start.[4] Either way, it provides a sort of trailer for questions and theories to come.[5] We will look at it here in the context of Socratic philosophy and return to books 2 to 10 in part 2 on Plato.

If *Republic* 1 is a trailer, then the opening dialogue between Socrates and Cephalus (327a-331d) is a trailer within a trailer. The festival has taken Socrates away from downtown Athens to visit the city's port, Piraeus. While there, Socrates encounters his elderly friend Cephalus, who claims to enjoy conversations in his old age, now that he has lost the desire for sex, parties, and drinking. Socrates, polite as always, points out that it might be Cephalus's great wealth that explains his happiness. Cephalus agrees but not for the reason most people think. The real use of wealth is that it frees one from having to cheat, steal, or engage in other activities that could bring punishment in the afterlife. The tone of this conversation would fit a not terribly exciting dinner party, but the philosophical point is that happiness is not a matter of one's external circumstances but rather of what one does with them. There is much more to be said about this idea, but this is only a trailer.

Socrates uses the talk of criminal activity to raise a question about justice. At this point, Cephalus hands the conversation over to his son and heir Polemarchus and heads off to a sacrifice.

Traditional Definitions of Justice: *Republic* 331c-336a

As Polemarchus takes over the conversation, Socrates brings up the more basic question: What is justice (*dikaiosunē*)? He even offers the first definition: "paying what is owed" (331c). Polemarchus offers the second: "benefiting friends and harming enemies" (332d). The first seems simple enough: if you borrow money, pay it back. The second fits well within military contexts. From what veterans have told me, soldiers in combat scenarios focus on taking care of their friends. In many cases this is accomplished by taking down enemies to stop them from harming those friends. Harming enemies may sound harsh for civilian life, but if we are honest, we tend to think this way when things get competitive: we want our political candidates to win, and their opponents to lose. The same goes for sports teams, college applications, and job interviews. If everyone is doing it, does that make it right?

Socrates quickly shoots down the first definition, paying what is owed. If a friend loans you a weapon and then has a mental health crisis, the just thing to do is not to give it back to him. Why? Because this would harm your friend. This leads naturally into the second definition, benefiting friends and harming enemies. Socrates has four responses. The first (332d-333e) treats justice as a craft (*technē*) and asks what it is useful for. After Socrates runs through various scenarios where other crafts are obviously more relevant (sailing, raising horses, etc.), Polemarchus agrees that justice is useful for storing resources but not for using them. Socrates replies that justice then seems pretty useless. The second response (333e-334b) relies on the fact that the person who knows how to be of benefit in a certain area is able to harm in the same area: doctors make the best poisons. Socrates concludes that justice is an art of stealing. Polemarchus is flustered but does not give up. Socrates's third reply (334b-335a) is to ask whether friends in this definition are the people who actually are good and useful to oneself, or are simply believed to be so. Polemarchus opts for the second option, which leads to more contradictions. He quickly backpedals, specifying that friends are those who are thought to be, and actually are, good and useful.

CHAPTER 4

Socrates's final reply to Polemarchus is the most philosophically hefty: Is it ever just to harm anyone (335b-336a)? Polemarchus replies with what will strike many as the obvious answer, that it is just to harm bad people. Socrates responds: If justice is a virtue and if virtue is human excellence but harming people makes them worse, then we make people less virtuous through virtue. Since that makes no sense, Polemarchus admits defeat and drops the idea that justice is benefiting friends and harming enemies. This all goes by so quickly that it is easy to dismiss it as simple wordplay. But if we look at this exchange from the perspective of the BLM movement, the implications are huge.

The US criminal justice system is largely based on retributive justice. This is the idea that people who do bad things deserve to be punished. The trouble is that this approach can turn people who have committed small crimes (or no crimes at all) into hardened criminals. Add to this that African Americans make up 13 percent of the overall population but 39 percent of the prison population, and you have an efficient system for grinding down people who already start out at a disadvantage.[6] Is this just? One attractive alternative is a system based on rehabilitative justice, which views sentencing as a form of treatment rather than punishment. Norway has such a system. Norway imprisons only 70 of every 100,000 people and reincarcerates 20 percent of them within three years. The United States imprisons 693 of every 100,000 people with a reincarceration rate of 68 percent.[7] It is, of course, possible for a system to aim for both forms of justice. In the United States, however, the aims of retribution ("he is a bad person who deserves to be punished") tend to undermine rehabilitation efforts ("he is a sick person who needs to be treated"). It is also impossible to justify the death penalty on the grounds of protecting the overall population, since legal fees for executing a prisoner outstrip the cost of a life sentence.[8]

Returning to our imagined conversation between Socrates and a BLM protester, we may now add a final critique: the problem is not only that the US justice system disproportionately harms African Americans; it is that it harms anyone at all. The point of a justice system, on Socrates's line of reasoning, is to make people just. A system that singles out sections of the public and makes them more unjust is flawed at a fundamental level. What is the alternative? *Republic* 1 is a Socratic dialogue, and a trailer at that, so the only answers we get are what justice is not. Be that as it may, some of Socrates's arguments pack a punch all these centuries later.

Philosophy vs. Sophistry: *Republic* 336b-354c

The intersection of sports and politics also plays out in antiquity through the competitive culture of public speaking. As we saw in chapter 2, nude athletics, democracy, and philosophy embodied egalitarian and competitive ideals that were central to Greece's self-image. In the Athenian democracy, any citizen could bring political proposals to the assembly and bring charges against neighbors in court. And, as we will see in chapter 5, the ability to convince a crowd could be quite literally a matter of life and death. In this context, teachers of public speaking were highly valued, and the competition of such teachers for students was fierce. In the public eye, these sophists (teachers of wisdom) were sometimes hard to distinguish from philosophers (lovers of wisdom). Perhaps for this reason, Plato goes to great lengths in several works to contrast them. Thrasymachus, the star of *Republic* 1's second half, is one of Plato's most memorable attempts. His name, which means "bold in battle," reflects his character. Fed up with Socrates's discussion with Polemarchus, Thrasymachus bursts in, telling Socrates to get real. For readers who have had the sense that Socratic questioning is pointless intellectual bullying, Thrasymachus's interruption comes as a breath of fresh air, as he calls out Socrates for his entire philosophical project of cross-examining others' views. Socrates replies by claiming not to know what justice is, and Thrasymachus complains all the louder (336b-338b). With this, an intellectual sparring match begins, with sophistry and philosophy going head-to-head.

Thrasymachus's name is also reflected in the ideas he brings to the discussion. He sees the world in terms of winners and losers. What matters to him is winning, and he is willing to do whatever it takes to come out on top. His disregard for sportsmanship or any other norms of conduct is reflected in his own definition of justice, "the advantage of the stronger who rule" (338c-d). This is the kind of view that cynical people usually call realistic. Today, we might say that justice is whatever the people with money and power decide it is. While we rarely talk this way, the reality of American democracy is that big money backs both major political parties, and for decades, if not centuries, has been making sure that policies are made in big money's own best interests. Having laid out how things really are, Thrasymachus waits for everyone to be impressed. Socrates has other ideas.

Socrates opens by asking whether it is just to obey rulers and whether rulers can be mistaken about what benefits them. Thrasymachus agrees to both. Socrates points out that by Thrasymachus's own definition justice could call on us to harm rulers, which would be unjust (338e-340c). The crowd of onlookers at Cephalus's house loves this. Thrasymachus replies that his definition refers to a ruler "in the precise sense"—an ideal ruler that real-world individuals can fall short of. Rulers in this sense will always do what is in their own self-interest. In this, Thrasymachus treats ruling as a kind of craft (*technē*). Socrates runs with the idea, pointing out that all other crafts seek to benefit not their practitioner but their charges: doctors benefit patients not doctors; horse breeders benefit horses not themselves, and so on. By analogy, a ruler in the precise sense benefits his charge, not himself (341c-342e).

At this point, Thrasymachus calls Socrates a "snot-nosed brat" (343a) and launches into a rant about how shepherds benefit themselves, not their sheep, how justice is for chumps, and injustice on a grand enough scale, such as taking over one's government, is perfect happiness (343b-344c). Having poured all this out "like a bath attendant" (344d), Thrasymachus attempts to leave the room. But his friends pin him down so that Socrates can respond. Socrates's first line of argument is that caring for things can be a pain (345b-347d). Sheep are stupid and smelly. That is why we compensate shepherds for caring for them. The craft of shepherding, though, is concerned only with the welfare of sheep. Likewise, ruling a state is a lot of trouble, and that is why we compensate people for doing it. Flipping typical views on their head, Socrates claims that the compensation a real ruler wants is not money or honor but not being ruled by a worse person.

Socrates then turns to Thrasymachus's idea that justice is for chumps. As Thrasymachus puts it, wisdom is getting ahead unjustly; only a fool plays by the rules; happiness is attained by outdoing everyone else however you can. In other words, Thrasymachus views life as a game with clear winners and losers. Socrates responds to this in three waves. The ideas go by quickly and without anything close to adequate support. Again, this is just the trailer. In the process, though, we get a hint of big ideas to come.

The first wave of argument focuses on Thrasymachus's idea of outdoing (*pleonekteō*; 347e-352d). If we treat injustice as a kind of wisdom, then it is something one can be an expert in. In other cases of expertise, an expert wants to outdo nonexperts but not other experts. A nonexpert, by contrast, wants to outdo everyone. Socrates offers the example of tuning an instrument. An actual musician will not be interested in outdoing other actual musicians when it comes to tuning a string. If an instrument is in tune, it is in tune. End of story. Someone who does not know anything about music, however, could think, "I am going to tune this better than other people who get it in tune!" Socrates, who is championing philosophy in this match, looks to the musician's musician and the athlete's athlete. This is a jab at Thrasymachus whose ultimate concern as a sophist is not swaying experts but swaying crowds. Still, we might object that the example of tuning assumes that there is a right way to tune something, a perfect middle ground between sharp and flat. Why should we think justice is like tuning in this respect? What, in this context, dictates the right amount? Thrasymachus, however, does not raise these questions. Instead, he agrees to each step in Socrates's response, although "reluctantly and with a great quantity of sweat" (350c-d).

In the second wave, Socrates turns to Thrasymachus's idea that injustice is profitable (352d-354a). Socrates argues that a group of unjust people cannot achieve a single purpose, presumably because they will always be lying and cheating each other. By analogy, he argues, an unjust individual cannot achieve anything because he will be an enemy to other people, to the gods, and to even himself. At the moment it is unclear how one can be an enemy to himself. Should we assume some sort of inner conflict? (The idea returns at length in books 2–10.)

Socrates's final response is to present an argument from function (353d-354a). A thing's function (*ergon*) is what can be done only or best with that thing: hedge clippers, for instance, are for clipping hedges. A thing's virtue, meanwhile, is to perform that function well: cutting hedges with ease and accuracy. The soul's function is living, which often includes ruling (*archō*) and caring for (*epimeleomai*) things (353d-e), and virtues such as justice are what allow us to live well. A thing that performs its function well is in its best state. In the case of humans, the best state is happiness. Therefore, justice is not in fact for chumps but the key to happiness. There is a lot going on in this passage. This argument will come back in *Republic* 2-10 and provides the central argument for Aristotle's ethical theory as well. In the present context, though, Socrates undermines his own conclusion. Having laid out this theory, he points out that he has argued that justice is profitable without first saying what justice is. All of this is built on sand. No one has yet gotten a handle on justice, and the discussion ends in perplexity.

Thrasymachus's Contribution

Republic 1 hints at profound ideas through discussions that are frustratingly brief. In terms of the work's drama, Thrasymachus steals the show. His outbursts and cynicism come as reality checks in the midst of what can sound like pointless banter. Socrates's responses hint at ideas that will be fleshed out later. For the moment, though, let us focus on Thrasymachus's contribution, which gives us three main takeaways.

From a psychological perspective, Thrasymachus has some good points. When it comes to "outdoing" others, studies of contentment have shown that in judging one's own wealth, people do not use objective standards, such as how much they need; rather, they compare themselves to the people around them. This is what psychologists call the adaptive-level phenomenon.[9] In this sense, happiness (at least in terms of self-contentment) really can be thought of as "outdoing" others. Does this form of contentment add up to the best life for a human being? As Cephalus has pointed out, happiness is not a matter of your external circumstances so much as what you do with them. This is the chief insight behind cognitive behavioral therapy, of which Socrates seems to be an early pioneer.[10]

From a methodological perspective, Thrasymachus also has a point when he calls out Socrates for his practice of merely refuting others' ideas. Sure, we can throw words around and think through ideas that people carry around with them, but what guarantee do we have that this will actually accomplish anything? In *Republic* 1, Socrates leaned heavily into the meaning of the Greek word *aretē* to draw conclusions that he then admitted were not based on anything solid. While this approach to wrestling with ideas may have various benefits for those involved, is actually arriving at correct answers one of them?[11] Plato himself seems to have realized this problem. In his non-Socratic works, he sets aside Socrates's characteristic approach to refuting others and takes a new approach, one based in a substantive theory of human nature. This is exactly what is missing from Socrates's function argument, which makes claims about human nature without first defining what a human being is.

From the perspective of competition, Thrasymachus's sophistic approach to debate serves as a foil to Socrates's philosophical one. Up to this point, Socrates's discussion partners have been willing participants even after their views were shot down. Charmides and Critias (jokingly) say they will force Socrates to continue the discussion of discipline another day. Lysis and Menexenus actually enjoy having their ideas about friendship ripped to bits. Laches gets flustered after he fails to define bravery, but it is Nicias that he sees as his rival, not Socrates. Thrasymachus is different. As a sophist, his livelihood depends on training young men to speak persuasively in law courts and political assemblies on topics such as justice. People paid dearly for such training (337d). By attacking Thrasymachus's ideas, Socrates represents a direct threat to Thrasymachus's livelihood. By pitting these characters against each other, Plato contrasts Thrasymachus's "logic of domination" with Socratic "cooperative inquiry."[12] The one seeks to win at any cost; the other invokes norms of conduct and sportsmanship (even if it is still unclear what those norms are grounded in). These two approaches to discussion are mirrored in the ideas these same two characters set out as Thrasymachus defines justice in terms of outdoing others, and Socrates responds by talking about harmony and care. As one scholar puts it, "Book 1 is a struggle between a sweaty sophist who wants to throw his weight around and a friendly philosopher who wants to spend his spare time today in Piraeus checking out a new festival for a girl-power goddess."[13] In short, Thrasymachus is a sore loser.[14] Socrates, by contrast, enjoys a good contest and is open to improving his own knowledge and skills by sparring with a worthy opponent.

Chapter 5

Wisdom
Apology

> What is fitting for a public benefactor who is a poor man forced to use his free time to admonish you all? Nothing is more fitting, men of Athens, than that such a person be provided free meals at City Hall. This is more fitting for him than for one of you who wins with a pair or a team of horses at Olympia. For the Olympic victor makes you seem happy. I make you be happy.
>
> —Socrates in Plato, *Apology* 36d

Not everyone appreciated Socrates's tough-love approach to making his companions better people. Over decades of questioning fellow Athenians at the city's gyms and embarrassing leading men in front of crowds of amused onlookers, Socrates made a number of enemies. He also attracted a number of protégés, some of whom ended up on the wrong side of Athens's war with Sparta. All this eventually caught up with him when a group of disgruntled Athenians hauled Socrates into court and argued for the death penalty. Plato's *Apology* (from the Greek word for "defense speech," *apologia*) portrays Socrates's response. Legal trials were referred to as competitions (*agōnes*). If *Republic* 1 shows philosophy on the offensive in the debate with sophistry, sophistry fights back in *Apology*, putting Socratic philosophy and Socrates's life on the line. We will thus draw our exploration of Socratic philosophy to a close with *Apology*, which embodies the spirit of competition that Socrates put to philosophical use during his many conversations at the gym.

Innocent or Guilty: *Apology* 17a-35d

Athens's democracy did not distinguish between civil and criminal courts. When someone committed a crime, it fell to individual citizens, not the state, to pursue punishment. When Socrates was finally brought to court, it was by two individuals, Anytus and Meletus, who likely had powerful allies behind them. This system also lacked a set code for what punishment fit what crime. Instead, trials went in two rounds. In the first, a jury of 501 citizens voted on the defendant's innocence or guilt. If he was found guilty, a second round would ensue as the defense and prosecution suggested alternative penalties for the jury to decide between.

In this system, each side went after what they could reasonably get away with. Typically, this would encourage moderation on both sides, since juries typically shied away from radical proposals. But little about Socrates's trial was typical. We do not have verbatim transcripts from the trial, but Plato's *Apology* gives a literary version of Socrates's self-defense.[1] Given how fond Athenians were of taking each other to court, sophists and other authors produced a large number of speeches and theoretical works on rhetoric. To judge by these, any normal person would begin a defense speech by trying to capture the goodwill of the jury. Socrates begins by refusing to submit to the conventions of the court (17a-d) and proceeds to lecture jurors on how they should do their job: listening for truth, not how it is expressed (17d-18a). With this, we are off!

Socrates is also atypical in that he breaks the case against himself into old and new charges. The so-called old charges are not part of the formal case at all. Rather, they are rumors that people have been repeating for years that Socrates "studies all things in the sky and beneath the earth, and makes the weaker argument the stronger" (18b). This alludes to Aristophanes's comedy *Clouds*, which depicts Socrates as a sophistic quack who trades in mad-scientist theories and will teach how to win any argument to anyone willing to pay. In articulating and then denying these rumors, Socrates is attempting to uproot bias among the jurors. Apart from pointing out that no one present has actually heard him talk about such things, the best evidence he brings in his defense is his poverty (31c). Still, one wonders where such rumors started. This is where things get really unusual.

Socrates recounts a time his friend Chaerephon—the one who was excited to see Charmides naked—visited the oracle at Delphi (20e-21a). This religious center, sacred to Apollo, had an extensive *palaistra-gymnasion* and hosted the Pythian Games, named for the mythological Python slain by Apollo. Like the Olympic Games, this was a crown competition in which victors would be awarded a crown woven from a simple branch. This was such a coveted honor that cities such as Athens would pay their victors by giving them free meals for life. Unlike the Olympics, the Pythian Games included a *musikos agōn* in which musicians would compete alongside other athletes in a massive amphitheater next to the racetrack.[2] Visits to the oracle happened in a nearby temple. When people came seeking Apollo's advice, a priestess breathed fumes from a thermal vent believed to house the Python's rotting corpse. This would put her into an altered state of consciousness, and she would proceed to ramble incoherently. Priests standing by translated these ramblings into short poems for those who came seeking advice. While the oracle was well respected, it was also notoriously ambiguous. In Socrates's case, Chaerephon asked who was wiser than Socrates. The oracle responded, "No one." Having been handed down this message from a god, Socrates set out to refute (*elenchō*) it.

To this end, Socrates started questioning politicians who were famous for their wisdom. What he found was that neither he nor they knew anything worthwhile. Still, he concludes, "I am likely to be wiser than they to this small extent: I do not think I know those things that I do not know" (21e). After the politicians, he turned to poets and playwrights, only to discover that they were terrible at interpreting their own works (22b). The one place he found a bit of wisdom was in lower-class craftsmen who actually did know something about their respective crafts. Even here, though, he found that the limited knowledge they had made them overestimate their knowledge of things they did not in fact know about (22c-e).

Socrates concludes that the god meant that human wisdom is pretty worthless, and the best a mortal can do is to be like Socrates and acknowledge this fact (23a-b). "Human wisdom," therefore, consists in not thinking you know what you do not. This is contrasted with "divine wisdom" which is actually worth something and would, presumably, provide actual answers to Socrates's questions about virtue and the good life (20d-21d, 23a-b, 29b).

Socrates's project of refuting his fellow citizens in an attempt to refute an oracle might seem like a quirky activity born of Socrates's overfondness for questioning. Socrates presents it as a "service to the god" (23b, 28e) and himself as "god's gift to the city" (30a, 30e, 31b). Running with this idea, Socrates suggests that the city should worry about its own welfare: given its size, it is like a "sluggish horse" that needs to stirred up by a heaven-sent "gadfly" (30e). While Socrates may appear to be merely annoying, he is in fact serving god and country, and his incessant questioning is meant to get his fellow citizens to "care for virtue" (31b). In sum, Socrates is god's gift to the city, and the city would shoot itself in the foot by killing him. There is a lot going on here. But let us focus on one particular oddity: How did Socrates get from the oracle's simple message, "No one is wiser than Socrates," to a divine mission of rousing his fellow citizens to care for virtues by questioning them about moral terms? The two things seem simply unrelated. Modern psychology, I suggest, can help us connect the dots.

Psychologists distinguish between interest (things we like doing) and purpose (the needs of the world that individuals can meaningfully attend to).[3] One way of making sense of Socrates's story is to see him as having a deep-seated interest in asking questions and examining people. This seems to have arisen before the oracle's message to him. Yet that message, if we take his account at face value, set him off on a project that he found engrossing. Over time he discovered that what he was doing was actually useful for others. While individuals might not enjoy having their flaws pointed out, such confrontations can serve as a reality check. For the powerful and famous who believed their own press, encounters with Socrates provided opportunities to reflect on what actually matters in life. As we have seen time and again, Socratic examination gets his companions, or at least most of them, to "care for virtue." With this, Socrates's interests found a purpose. Since the oracle, which was famous for being cryptic, sent him down this path, why not see the whole thing as a divinely appointed mission?[4]

The other upshot of Socrates's mission is that it won him fans. If there is anything that today's politics shows us, it is that seeing politicians humiliated is really entertaining. As we have seen in *Lysis* and *Charmides*, the young men of Athens's gyms all know who Socrates is. Some of them even started imitating his methods for questioning others (*Apology* 23c). It is for this reason, Socrates argues, that the city's leading figures cooked up the prosecution's "new charges"—namely, "Socrates is guilty of corrupting the youth and of not believing in the gods in whom the city believes, but in other new spiritual things" (24b). Socrates's response to the charge of impiety is a bit limp (26b-28a). As one scholar argues, Socrates's ideas about the gods as perfectly moral beings is more in line with Judeo-Christian monotheism than Greek polytheism: his fellow citizens were right to feel threatened![5] That said, Socrates's aligning himself with the god Apollo in particular might be significant. Rather than quote Homer about the gods or claim direct inspiration, as he does elsewhere, Socrates presents a message handed down from a religious site famous for hosting one of Greece's most important games. As a patron deity of athletics, music, and medicine, Apollo represents ideals pursued throughout the gyms of Greece. In turn, Socrates presents himself as a doctor for the soul (*Charmides*) with a concern for bringing harmony to one's character (*Laches*) through a spirit of collaborative competition spread throughout the dialogues. Read against these works, *Apology*'s invocation of Delphi may make a better case for Socrates's traditional, Greek piety than Socrates's direct response to the impiety charge does.

What of Socrates's corruption of the youth? If he has done so unintentionally, Socrates argues, then he should be corrected not punished (26a). But if he has done so intentionally, then he has made them wicked, and given that wicked people harm the people around them, it would make no sense for Socrates to have put himself in harm's way intentionally (25c-e). As he did in *Lysis*, Socrates invites us to think about toxic friends. Would anyone willingly create toxic relationships? We might talk playfully about corrupting people. Still, typical antics at the club will not turn people toxic. If anything, they can give rise to war stories that help build bonds of friendship. For corruption, we might think of convincing friends to try steroids or heroin. Which of these is closer to the fate of Socrates's companions: harmless antics that might be beneficial in the long run or toxicity that destroys individuals and those around them?

Judging by Plato's account in *Apology*, Socrates was a mischievous but positive influence. None of his younger friends spoke out against him. More importantly, none of their fathers or older brothers did either (33d-34b). On the contrary, Socrates's younger friends as well as their fathers are grateful for how he helped shape these young men's lives. This fits again with modern psychology, which has shown that one of the keys to developing a sense of purpose in one's own life is to have purposeful role models.[6] It does not even matter whether the particular purpose of one's models lines up with one's own. What young people need is to see what it looks like to structure a life around meaningful service to the wider world. In this respect, Socrates was a rock star. He ends the first round of his defense by showing how his eccentric behavior stems from his commitment to his divine mission (31c-35d), and he insults the conventions of the courtroom by telling the jury that they would harm themselves if they got rid of him.

Setting a Penalty: *Apology* 35e-42a

Given Socrates's efforts to insult his jury, it is perhaps surprising that they voted him guilty by a margin of only thirty votes (36a-b). It is now time to decide the penalty, and Meletus suggests death (36b). Any normal defendant would suggest exile or a hefty fine. The system is set up for moderation, after all, and such fines provide the jury a way to retain a clean conscience. But this is not a normal trial. True to form, Socrates suggests that what he really deserves for his service to the state is to be fed for life at state expense as the winner of an Olympic chariot race would be. After all, "the Olympic victor makes you think you are happy. I make you be happy" (36d-e). Socrates's singling out chariot races may be significant. Winning an event at Olympia or Delphi was seen as an outward manifestation of one's inner excellence (*aretē*). Chariot races were a possible exception insofar as it was the owner of the team, not the driver or horses, who was crowned victor. This opened up the possibility for someone with enough money to buy his way to an Olympic victory. Socrates seems to have this in mind, as he immediately goes on to say, "Besides, he does not need food but I do."[7] After insulting the jury a bit more, he suggests a fine that is so low that his friends rally and increase it thirtyfold (38b). The jury is not amused and votes for his death.

With this, the world's first democracy sentenced the father of Western moral philosophy to death by poison. Before we are too quick to condemn them, note that it was standard practice in Athens for people on death row to bribe their way out of jail and flee to a neighboring city. The jury likely had this in mind. Plato's dialogue *Crito* even shows Socrates's friends showing up at his jail cell, bribe in hand. Socrates responds with a philosophical reflection on whether it would be right to break the laws he has lived his life by. In the end, he decides to go through with the death sentence that his jurors likely thought would never actually happen.

It seems safe to say that Socrates went out of his way to annoy the jury. But to what end? Is he merely spiting them? Has his pride gotten the better of him? Or is he teaching Athens and posterity a lesson? How individual readers answer this question will likely line up with how they respond to dialogues that end in perplexity. After three or more failed attempts at defining a term, do you conclude that there is no answer? Do you throw up your hands and say that bravery and the rest are whatever you want them to be? Or do you buckle down and decide that we need to put serious work into figuring out what we are actually doing with our lives?

The end of *Apology* gives some of the most direct advice we find in Plato's Socratic works: "The unexamined life is not worth living for a human being" (38a). "It is not difficult to avoid death, gentlemen. It is much more difficult to avoid wickedness, for wickedness runs faster than death" (39b). "A good person cannot be harmed in either life or death" (41d). It is not clear that any of this amounts to divine wisdom. None of these quotes answers Socrates's questions about defining virtues. If anything, he is using terms like "good" and "wicked" without defining them! Is this part of human wisdom, then? As with "If I do not know something, I do not think that I know something," Socrates's final words of wisdom are heavier on process than on content. In the end, Socrates's human wisdom amounts to a provisional way of getting through life when divine wisdom still escapes us.[8]

The Life of Inquiry

It is not such a stretch to see the United States as a big sluggish horse in need of the occasional gadfly. But who in our culture performs this service? As people isolate themselves in echo chambers and tune out ideas they disagree with, who is providing reality checks and making people care about virtue? Furthermore, we live in a time of cultural pluralism the likes of which Socrates and his neighbors never imagined. While the examined life might make a nice motto for an inspirational bracelet or a T-shirt, can we really proceed by way of provisional, processed-based values when we find ourselves seriously in doubt about which moral standard to follow?

Our survey of Socratic philosophy drove home the importance of the virtues, particularly for guiding education, as well as the difficulty in actually defining them: bravery (*Laches*), temperance (*Charmides*), friendship (*Lysis*), justice (*Republic* 1), and wisdom (*Apology*). While Socrates set out this philosophical agenda, he never provided answers to his own questions. Nevertheless, Socrates models a certain way of life. In tracing how he goes about his divine mission, we looked at these Socratic dialogues through the lens of current psychology. Given the requirements of modern empirical science, positive psychology tends to study a set of big ideas in isolation from each other: flourishing, friendship, mindset, interest, purpose, and so on. Our survey of Socratic dialogues provides a framework for connecting the dots and seeing these big ideas as part of an organic whole. Socrates thus provides us with a model for a way of life that integrates insights of current science into a coherent whole.

Socrates's life of inquiry, as we may call it, starts with personal interest in pursuing the truth through rigorous questioning. In today's age of standardized testing, this is highly countercultural. As we have seen, though, Socrates seems to be having a good time: he surrounds himself with bright and beautiful younger men, skipping the small talk and going straight to what makes them tick. Students engaged in discussion-based courses may get a taste of this joy of shared inquiry. Those who are not lucky enough to have had this sort of education can perhaps think back to B.S. sessions with their friends, or late-night conversations that "got real." In the closing lines of *Apology*, Socrates imagines an afterlife in which he could question famous figures from history. How great would it be to spend eternity engaged in inquiry (40d-41c)!

Socrates is not merely playing games, however; he is providing a service to his community. In terms of cognitive behavioral therapy, Socratic cross-examination gets people to rethink their self-talk (*Laches*). If all goes well, such people will be more careful when using value-laden terms to evaluate situations. Or, to put it in terms from *Charmides*, "stripping away" pretentions gets people to "care about virtue" rather than wealth, power, popularity, or whatever else culture says will make people happy. This, all by itself, can help get people out of quite a few bad situations. In this, Socrates embodied the tough love typically found in coaches (*Lysis*), and he clearly found a purpose, a life project, that he was willing quite literally to die for. If his tactics in *Apology* seem miscalculated, then we should ask what he hoped to accomplish. If it was to escape death, he did a terrible job. If it was to provide a model for posterity, then he put on a performance for the centuries!

Socrates also provided a model of growth mindset (*Laches*). Most people dislike being told that they are wrong. Yet, to take him at his word, Socrates delights in having his faults and false opinions pointed out to him. This enthusiasm is contagious as Lysis, Menexenus, Nicias, and even a couple of "loser fathers" get on board with the idea that with hard work we can make progress. Still, is this enough? Can people today actually build a life around a dogged and unending pursuit of knowledge? Most, though not all, philosophers who followed Socrates in antiquity thought not.

As we move forward in our survey of Greek ethics, we will explore how different figures, and, increasingly, different schools, gave their own answers to Socrates's questions about human flourishing and the virtues. Insofar as subsequent thinkers offered competing theories, we will move from having no answers to having too many! We will thus enter into a new kind of perplexity. At the same time, we will keep tracing big ideas from modern psychology, watching each school combine them into different organic wholes. This fusion of ancient ethics and modern science provides readers with a multitude of competing frameworks to try out as they wrestle with life's challenges today.

PART II

Personal Training with Plato

> Every soul is immortal.
> —inscription, Berkeley Plato

The ancient long jump (*halma*) involved a complicated set of movements in which athletes would use a set of hand weights (*haltēres*) to give themselves added momentum. Timing was so important that the event was normally performed to music played on a flute (*aulos*).[1] Today, swimmers and other athletes talk about finding a rhythm. How literally should we take this? "Finding" suggests that the right answer is already there waiting to be discovered.[2] In the case of swimming, water and individuals' anatomy interact in certain optimal patterns that maximize speed and endurance. When we find one of these patterns, everything falls into place.[3] We often use visual language to describe such moments: when working through a math problem, a lightbulb flashes and we see the answer. According to Plato, our ability to find patterns such as these tells us something profound about human nature: that we are rational beings capable of grasping truth with our minds.

Today, such abstract ideas may seem divorced from gymnasiums, where people care for their physical bodies. The ancient gym, however, was a place where the physical and the intellectual met. In addition to athletic events familiar today, a musical competition (*musikos agōn*) was included in many ancient athletic competitions, most notably the

Pythian Games held at Delphi. Greek mathematicians beginning with Pythagoras understood music to be composed of numbers in time, as tones are strung together through rhythms and harmonies, all expressing whole-number proportions.[4] The rhythmic nature of music spilled over into other athletic events. The Pythian Games opened with the musical competition, and the winning flute player would go on to accompany the pentathletes' carefully timed long jumps.[5] In short, Greek athletic culture embodied ideals of rhythm and proportionality, which were intimately tied to music and analyzed mathematically by philosophers. It is against the backdrop of this particular athletic culture that we will approach the thought of Plato.

The Berkeley Plato

The Academy was a functioning gym when Plato set up a philosophical school there, yet few scholars have taken this setting into account when interpreting Plato's philosophical project. What, after all, could training for the body have to do with ideas of the mind?[6] An archaeological discovery in the basement of a women's gym in Berkeley, California, addresses this question. In 1902, a benefactor purchased a collection of antiquities for the University of California, Berkeley, including a portrait herm. This sculpture form most often depicted the god Hermes by way of a flat narrow stone surface for an inscription with a head and shoulders mounted on top, to which a phallus was attached more or less where one would expect relative to the statue's head. Herms were everywhere in ancient Greece, and often used as signposts. (Hermes was the patron god of travelers.) At gyms they were also used to display portraits honoring the local *gymnasiarchos*: the person in charge of managing the finances, staff hiring, and general operation of a gym. This particular herm bears the inscription "Plato, son of Ariston, the Athenian," along with two quotations from Plato's works (fig. 4). For its first century at Berkeley, it was dismissed as a modern forgery, in part because of the asymmetry of its ears, and placed in a gym basement.

In 2002 archaeologist and Berkeley professor Stephen Miller revisited the herm as part of the research for his groundbreaking book, *Ancient Greek Athletics*. Through chemical analysis of the herm's marble, iconographical analysis of the bust's ribbons and headband, and stylistic analysis of the inscription's font style, Miller argues that this was not a modern forgery but, rather, a Roman copy (perhaps from the

PERSONAL TRAINING WITH PLATO 49

FIGURE 4. The Berkeley Plato. Marble portrait herm, circa first century CE copy of Greek original. Copyright Phoebe A. Hearst Museum of Anthropology and the Regents of the University of California, inv. no. 8-4213.

early second century CE) of a Greek portrait herm of a *gymnasiarchos*. Whereas previous art historians saw its mismatched ears as a sign of a sloppy forgery, Miller argues that the one larger ear is, in fact, the mark of an active boxer who has developed cauliflower ear from repeated punches. In short, an ancient statue of Plato has been hiding in plain sight, one that depicts him as an athlete and the head of a gym.[7] If Miller is right, Plato was not an observer on the sidelines in the company of athletic trainers and music teachers; he was actively hiring, managing, and training with them. The Berkeley Plato's two inscriptions point to central philosophical ideas we will turn to in part 2.

The first inscription reads, "Every soul is immortal." This is a key idea in several of Plato's so-called middle dialogues. The chronology of Plato's works is controversial, yet it is possible to separate them into three rough categories.[8] In the early or Socratic dialogues, the Socrates character uses a method of cross-examination (*elenchos*) to question others about moral terms. The efforts all end in perplexity (*aporia*), as we saw in part 1. Scholars take these dialogues to reflect the project if not the actual words of the historical Socrates. In the middle works, the Socrates character uses a method of hypothesis to defend theories about the soul's immortality and the human mind's ability to engage with immaterial realities such as numbers. Scholars see this middle Socrates as a mouthpiece for Plato's own ideas. In the late dialogues, Plato, still speaking mostly via the Socrates character, criticizes ideas set out in the middle dialogues. The soul's immortality is central to the middle dialogues' thinking about psychology, ethics, and knowledge. It is through this immortality that the human soul shares in the divine.

The second inscription reads, "Blame the one who makes the choice. God is blameless." This comes from the end of *Republic*.[9] The context is a myth about the afterlife and reincarnation. The choices human individuals make during life shape their character. When it comes time to be born again, character guides each individual's choice of lives. While a god may oversee the process, it is up to human individuals to choose. Those who are taken in by superficial considerations of wealth, power, pleasure, and so on lead lives of misery as a result. Those who choose more wisely go on to live lives akin to the gods'. Taken together, these quotes point to the idea driving Plato's ethics, that human happiness involves becoming "like a god."[10]

What are the gods like? For the ancients, the question has an obvious answer: images of the gods were everywhere. The gods look like beautiful, healthy, youthful athletes. In this, they are perhaps not so different from the students at Plato's philosophical gym. As with music, the long jump, and swimming, Plato and his contemporaries saw such beauty as a matter of proportion. Whereas athletic events let numbers play out in time, ancient sculpture, like practices in modern bodybuilding that it inspired, let numbers play out in space, through the proportions between parts of the body, as set out in the sculptor Polykleitos's guide, the *Canon of Polykleitos*.[11]

How does one become like a god? Through a proper regimen of gym exercise and diet, individuals may sculpt their bodies to approach divine proportions. In Plato's time, such considerations fell under the single umbrella of therapy (*therapeia*). According to one scholar of ancient medicine, the line between drug prescriptions and food recipes was blurry.[12] To us, blurring the distinction between cooking and medicine degrades the medical art, yet it has the advantage of integrating concerns for health into everyday life in ways that resemble modern efforts in preventative medicine. How do individuals sculpt their souls to approach divine proportions?[13] For this, Plato looked to physical training for guidance. He lays out the most elaborate parallel at *Gorgias* 462a-466a: the art of gym exercise (*gymnastikē*) creates health in the body, and when we become physically ill, the art of medicine (*iatrikē*) restores bodily health. Likewise, the art of politics (*politikē*) creates health in the soul, and when we become spiritually ill, the art of justice (*dikaiosunē*) restores spiritual health.[14]

Talk of spiritual or mental health has an intuitive appeal that has lasted through the centuries. To put these analogies into practice, however, requires us to cash out the metaphor. First, what does it mean for the soul to take on divine proportions? Since Plato takes the soul to be immaterial, it cannot embody numbers in the literal way that the body can. Second, Plato's ideas about bodily health and spiritual health do not run simply on parallel tracks: they interact with each other in complex ways. Sorting these issues out is a central task of Plato's psychology and moral philosophy, which we will address throughout part 2. In doing so, we must be careful not to allow modern assumptions about the nature of health, medicine, and training to distort our understanding of Plato's argument. Before turning to his works, therefore, let us take a brief excursion into the field of medicine as Plato knew it.

The Hippocratic Corpus

The Hippocratic Oath remains the single most famous medical text to this day.[15] Its traditional author, Hippocrates, was a fifth-century BCE physician. The collection of sixty or so medical treatises attributed to him is known as the Hippocratic corpus, though scholars believe that many if not all of these works were written by people other than Hippocrates.[16] The works themselves reflect the agonistic spirit of Greek culture, as physicians compete against each other in a lively "medical marketplace."[17] Many texts within the corpus set out theories by explicitly rejecting alternative perspectives, some of which can be found elsewhere in the corpus. What is worse, given the habit of doctors throughout history to find their own views in the thought of their predecessors, we are often unsure of which century a given work was written in.[18] Despite these inconsistencies, we can still trace some general themes.

In approaching ancient medical texts, we must distinguish between what we might call an ontological view of disease and a view of disease as imbalance. In the first case, disease is, or is caused by, a foreign *thing* that does not belong in a person's body: a cancer, virus, bacteria, parasite, and so on. Treatment, in this scheme, involves getting rid of what does not belong: killing it with drugs or removing it from the body. In the second case, disease is at root an imbalance among things that do belong in the body: glucose, electrolytes, water. Treatment, in this scheme, is a matter of somehow adjusting levels until things are back to where they should be.

In very broad terms, Western medicine today defaults to the ontological view, while Eastern medicine defaults to the imbalance view. Ancient Greek medicine has more in common with Eastern medicine than with its Western counterpart today. There are exceptions. The Greeks had an ontological conception of disease: some illnesses were explained by the presence of a spirit (*daimōn*), which could be removed through religious rituals.[19] However, the Greeks tended to contrast such ideas with scientific or "rational medicine," which focused on keeping the body in balance.[20] To lay out this mode of thought, let us look at three works in the Hippocratic corpus that likely date back to Plato's time.[21]

The first treatise, "Nature of Man," opens by arguing against the view that the body is made either of a single element—earth, air, fire, or water—or of a single bodily compound—blood, bile, and so on ("Nature of Man," 1–2). To account for observed phenomena, the author argues, the body must be composed of multiple substances (3), which he identifies as blood, phlegm, black bile, and yellow bile. Health consists in having these "humors" in balance, and illness arises when any of them shifts into excess or deficiency (4). How does this happen? Humors can be mapped out on the axes of hot/cold, dry/wet. If we find ourselves with an excess of phlegm in the winter, it is because phlegm is cold and winter is a cold season (7). Summer is warmer, so our blood increases. Why do people get depressed in the fall? That is when black bile is on the rise. (The English word *melancholy* is taken directly from the Greek for "black bile.") In addition to seasonal disorders, lifestyles and airborne epidemics also cause illness (9). In these cases, patients should either change their lifestyle or breathe less air. The general strategy behind these suggestions is treatment by opposites.[22] If someone is too sedentary, make them exercise. If someone eats too little, feed them more. When illnesses are located in a particular spot in the body, you can adjust the humoral balance by strategic bleeding, and the author helpfully lays out which veins to cut for which treatments (11). Urine provides a window into the body's inner balance (12-14), and is used to explain why athletes' flesh goes soft when they give up their athletic lifestyle (12). As Brooke Holmes puts it, "The Hippocratic body is fundamentally dynamic, animated by forces in an agonistic relationship with one another and always engaged with a teeming mass of external forces (winds, foods, etc.) that it struggles to resist or conquer."[23]

The second treatise, "Regimen for Health," builds on this general theory to describe plans for preventative medicine, with a recommendation to counteract or compensate for whatever season one is in as a way to retain balance: drinking more liquids during dry seasons and so on (1).[24] The author takes into account individual body types (2-4): people with dry skin should generally drink more liquids; people needing to lower their weight should exercise on an empty stomach and eat while out of breath (4). In addition to cutting veins, adjusting diets, and exercise regimens, there are drugs for restoring balance: emetics to make you vomit and enemas to give you diarrhea (5). The author also has advice on child development, noting, "Babies should be given their wine diluted and not at all cold" (6). The work closes with instructions for what exercises best fit each season of the year and how to respond to problems such as exercise-induced diarrhea (7). While the details of Hippocratic medicine may strike us as silly, we can at least appreciate the systematic way in which ancient doctors wove together theory, observation, and practice.[25] What is more, the emphasis on preventative medicine sets concerns for diet and exercise at the heart of medical science: in addition to all its other roles, the ancient gym served as a medical site.

The third treatise, "Airs, Waters, Places," sets such thinking within the framework of environmental and social determinants of health. Such thinking sits at the cutting edge of current medicine and social justice work today.[26] Heightened rates of diabetes in certain minority populations, for instance, have been shown to result from restricted access to quality diet and higher consumption of fast food.[27] High rates of COVID-19 infections among African Americans resulted not from genetics but from a combination of chronic stress, socioeconomic disparities, and a greater number of people living in multigenerational households.[28] Hippocrates embraces similar thinking, looking not to innate differences between populations but to ways in which environmental factors and cultural customs (*nomoi*) shape the illnesses, body types, and even moral character of people living in different places. When it comes to prevailing winds (3–6), cities facing north or south will suffer from extremes of temperature. Eastern winds produce moderate climates, making for the greatest health. Western winds, by contrast, introduce too much variability and cause health complications. In terms of water sources (7–9), ground springs facing east provide the purest and most temperate water. Rock springs, stagnant water, and rivers fed from multiple tributaries all introduce complications. Astrological events, such as the rising of the Dog Star or the two solstices, also signal complications, not for any religious reason, but because they mark seasonal transitions in hot and cold, wet and dry (10–11).

Having laid out these general principles, Hippocrates applies them to different regions of the known world (12–24). Scythia in the north is too cold, thus encouraging weight gain. Egypt in the south is too hot, encouraging sinewy bodies (18–19). Greece occupies a balanced Goldilocks zone, encouraging a robust physique. Yet even moderation can be taken too far. Asia, or the Near East, enjoys the most temperate climate, making for abundant crops and men "well made, large and with good physique" (12). Yet the too slight variation in Asia's climate accounts for these same men's "mental flabbiness and cowardice" (16). Custom (*nomos*) compounds the problem, as Asia's monarchs discourage general populations from developing bravery. Greece, meanwhile, enjoys the overall temperate climate of Asia, while the seasonal variation of Europe produces people with a "fierce, hot-headed and courageous" temperament. Custom further strengthens this, as democracy and other forms of self-rule encourage risk taking, which leads to the "brave, warlike nature of Europeans" (23). It is easy to dismiss Hippocrates's Eurocentrism as simply a form of cultural bias. Yet, like social justice movements today, Hippocrates does not attribute racial difference to the nature of people but to a combination of environment and custom. His goal in all of this is to help overcome challenges to specific demographics through artful city planning (10) and context-specific regimens for health.

Hippocrates's theory had staying power.[29] Well into the nineteenth century, barbers bled people for medical purposes (as advertised by the red stripe of a barber's pole). Even today, folk wisdom about wet feet causing the flu can be traced back to Hippocratic humoral theory. Modern Western medicine made great strides in the twentieth century by setting Hippocratic thinking aside and focusing on ontological conceptions of illness. The price of that shift was overspecialization, which led doctors who fixed one problem at times to cause another.[30] As we move further into the twenty-first century, medical professionals are starting to argue for more holistic approaches.[31] Even though we typically think of that as an Eastern focus, ideas about balance and holistic treatment sit at the start of the West's own rational, medical tradition.[32]

With this, we have set the stage for approaching Plato. While an athlete and *gymnasiarchos* himself, Plato did not write on physical health at length. Ideas from medicine and training, however, inform his thinking on a wide range of issues. By reading *Symposium*'s discussion of erotic love (*erōs*) against a Hippocratic background, we can see how one of the work's characters, the doctor Eryximachus, provides crucial insights for understanding the work as a whole (chapter 6). This goes against the grain of most scholarship, which sees Eryximachus as merely a comic interlude. And by reading the dialogue against the embodied rhythms of the ancient long jump, we may see how the discussion of lofty ideas in *Symposium*'s second half is a natural outgrowth of the earthy ideas that lead up to it (chapter 7). In this, *Symposium* provides a warm-up, as it were, for *Republic*'s more elaborate attempt to spell out the virtues and their cultivation in terms of mental health and spiritual exercise. *Republic* 2–4 returns to the gym as a site of moral education, this time defending a theory of a three-part soul, which, like a Hippocratic body, must be brought into balance with itself through a regimen of musical and athletic training (chapter 8). *Republic* 5–7 opens by asking whether women, whom Socrates sees as just as fit as men to rule, should receive the same course of nude education at the city's gyms. Like *Symposium*, this line of inquiry closes by employing ideals of embodied proportionality to set traditional gym training within a lofty and elaborate course of study through which individuals may come to understand the abstract principles that structure physical and political activities (chapter 9). *Republic* 8–10, finally, looks to Hippocratic thinking on social determinants of health, arguing that virtue, as a form of mental health, requires a dynamic balance between the individual and his or her broader environment. The work closes, once again, looking to the human soul's connection to immortal realities, as summed up in the Berkeley Plato's second inscription (chapter 10).

Chapter 6

Drinking Games
Symposium 172a-199c

> Medicine, therefore, is guided in all matters by the god Eros, as is gym training and farming.
>
> —Eryximachus in Plato, *Symposium* 186e-187a

Rihanna's 2023 halftime show set a new record by attracting 121 million viewers.[1] Her performance, which doubled as a pregnancy announcement, was relatively low-key compared to shows in previous years. Halftime shows attract a huge following, including people who have little interest in football. (Rihanna brought in 6 million more viewers than the game itself.) While there is no official competition in these annual mini-concerts, comparisons abound as each show attempts somehow to outdo the rest. The scale, spectacle, and athletic context of the halftime show, as well as its combination of musical one-upmanship and often quite athletic choreography, present a point of contact between athletics and art in contemporary popular culture. In this, we get a glimpse of what was a normal occurrence in ancient Greece. Religious festivals often included plays, parades, sacrifices, public feasts, and athletic competitions. Festivals at Athens were lavish enough that ancient politicians complained that the city spent more on its festivals than on its military.[2] Tragedies and comedies were judged no less than athletic competitions were, and included elaborate singing and dancing, meant to impress. Comedies were particularly blunt about this. At points, characters break the fourth wall, address the jury directly, and present the playwright's argument for why his play is best. In short, religious festivals were the halftime shows of antiquity.

CHAPTER 6

One such festival, the Lenaia, in honor of Dionysus, provides the backdrop for Plato's dialogue *Symposium*. The poet Agathon has just won first place in the tragedy competition of 416 BCE. *Symposium* depicts a drinking party attended by Socrates and his friends to celebrate this win. The athletic context is not as obvious as Socratic dialogues set in gyms, yet the work fits into our overall project via three interrelated strands.

First is the setting, which shows the gym's spirit of competition (*agōn*) spilling into other aspects of Greek culture. Ancient athletics, philosophy, politics, and theater all participate in a culture of *agōn*. This plays out in *Symposium* through the friendly competition of drinking games that provide the dialogue's literary structure.[3]

Second is the social function of the ancient symposium. Like the ancient gym, the symposium has no one modern equivalent. The closest we can get is a high tea mixed with a fraternity party mixed with a college seminar. Like a tea party, the symposium was a formal event with various dishes used for various purposes. People reclined on couches, and drank according to elaborate conventions. But they were not drinking tea. We have thousands of drinking cups, storage vats, and bowls in which wine was mixed with water to produce a drink with an alcohol content close to that of modern beer. As the event progressed, participants would get more and more intoxicated. Games included something called a wine toss. Flute girls were present to serve as prostitutes, though they played actual flutes too. Like the gym, the symposium was also a key site for homoerotic mentoring relationships. A lover helped his beloved learn to be a man and everything that entailed. Symposia were an opportunity for young men to network with peers, while gaining experience in various intellectual, artistic, and sexual pursuits.[4]

The third and final strand is *Symposium*'s main theme: erotic love (*erōs*). Plenty of that went on in the gyms of Athens, as we saw in part 1. In *Lysis*, Socrates goes so far as to give a lesson in flirtation through an ultimately unsuccessful attempt at defining friendship. There are various Greek words for love. *Philia*, the main subject of *Lysis*, is comprehensive and can include everything from family and romantic partners to wine and wisdom. *Erōs* covers sexual desire and other strong attachments. It is also the name of the god Eros (Latin, Cupid), who, depending on which mythology you consult, is either the pudgy infant son of Aphrodite or a primal force of nature.[5] One of the most promising ideas in *Lysis* is that friendship points beyond itself as friends strive to be better people. The same general idea returns in *Symposium* where it is connected with a spirit of friendly competition through which individuals may improve. *Symposium* sets this idea within a matrix of religious practices. While Dionysus is mentioned only in passing, he casts a long shadow over the event through both the drinking and the Lenaian festival. Tangled up in all of this are ideas drawn from mystery cults, a religious form that involved complex rituals of purification, initiation, and revelation. Different mystery cults were connected to different divinities, most notably Dionysus and Demeter.[6] In Plato's hands, the mystery cult provides a framework for reconceptualizing *erōs* as a way of transcending mortal life and striving after the divine.

In the end, these three strands come together. Where the gymnasium offers a venue for friendly rivalry and mutual improvement, *Symposium* presents erotic relationships as a vehicle for improving one's character and striving after the divine. To us, workout routines, character formation, and religious experience may have little to do with one another. To Plato, they are merely different facets of a single striving for transcendence. This is the constellation of ideas to be explored through Plato's *Symposium*.

Agathon's After-Party: *Symposium* 172a-178a

Symposium is set the night after Agathon's initial victory party. Agathon and his friends overdid it the first time, and they have now gathered for something tamer, the ancient equivalent of postgame beer and wings with friends. After an opening scene involving invitations lost in the mail and Socrates actually taking a bath, Socrates and the work's narrator, Aristodemus, show up at Agathon's house (172a-178a). Eryximachus, a physician and one of the guests, sends away the flute girl, opting instead for some male-only time (176e). Taking the lead as master of ceremonies, he suggests that they each give a speech in praise of *erōs*. As often happens in Greek religion, it is hard to draw a clear line between the god and the psychological phenomenon. Agathon and his guests praise the god by weaving between mythology and their various experiences of desire. Since Plato's Greek does not follow English conventions of capitalization, I will speak simply of *erōs* and leave readers to ponder whether passages refer to the god, the emotion, or both.

The praise of *erōs* is particularly well suited to the guest list: Pausanias and Agathon are a couple, as are Socrates and Alcibiades, who crashes the party toward the end. Through their different speeches, we glimpse homoerotic relationships from the perspectives of both the lover and the beloved.[7] As with *Lysis* and *Charmides*, the particulars of these relationships may strike current readers as somewhat foreign. Today people talk about heteronormativity: the assumption that heterosexual perspectives are the correct default for thinking about the world. Plato's *Symposium* presents what we might call homonormativity, making love between a man and a woman seem decidedly second-best. In my experience, gay students tend to read this as a kind of homecoming. Straight students tend to find it uncomfortable, hilarious, or some combination. Whatever the reader's orientation, the big ideas presented in the work have stood the test of time, as they get at basic questions about what it means to be human and the role that erotic love plays in our lives.

In Praise of Love: *Symposium* 178a-199c

The bulk of *Symposium* is taken up with a series of six speeches in praise of *erōs* and a seventh in praise of Socrates. The key to interpreting the work's main argument is to see how these speeches fit together in a coherent progression. Before turning to these holistic questions, let us briefly set out the main lines of the first five speeches.

Phaedrus

The first speaker is Phaedrus (178a-180c). He appears in another Platonic dialogue, bearing his name, which shows him and Socrates on a stroll outside the city discussing the nature of *erōs*. In *Symposium*, Phaedrus makes *erōs* as noble as possible, citing Hesiod and Parmenides to describe *erōs* as an ancient god and cosmic force (178b-c). From there, he quickly turns to *erōs*'s educational role. A young man looks up to his lover and cares what his lover thinks. This leads the young man to feel shame (*aischynē*) and pride (*philotimē*; 178d) in the right things. Phaedrus even suggests that an army made up entirely of male-male couples would be the best possible.[8]

Looking to mythology to drive home the honor/shame aspect of *erōs*, Phaedrus starts by citing Alcestis, a woman who was willing to die for her husband, Admetis.[9] Next is the musician Orpheus, who went to the underworld to retrieve his dead wife, albeit unsuccessfully. Phaedrus's grand finale is Achilles, star of Homer's *Iliad*, who went into battle to avenge the death of his lover, Patroclus.[10] What interests Phaedrus is that Achilles does this in the face of a prophecy. As the son of an immortal sea nymph and a mortal man, Achilles faces the choice between a short, glorious life or a long life of obscurity. In choosing to go back to battle, Phaedrus argues, Achilles decides to die for Patroclus. This is remarkable, first, since Patroclus is already dead and, second, because Achilles was the beloved not the lover. On this detail, Phaedrus corrects the tragic poet Aeschylus, who thought that Achilles was the lover (180a). If we are honest, homoerotic relationships do not figure in Homer's heroic worldview. The most obvious reason we cannot find clear details in *Iliad* as to who was lover and who was beloved is that they were actually just friends. Athenians of Plato's time, by contrast, saw this as an obviously romantic relationship.

Pausanias

Pausanias offers the second speech (180c-185c). In the spirit of friendly competition, the first thing he does is correct Phaedrus for not distinguishing between the two forms of *erōs*. This reflects the twofold nature of *erōs*'s companion, Aphrodite. The older, heavenly Aphrodite is the "motherless daughter of Ouranos" (180d). While that sounds lofty, Pausanias is playing with some fairly graphic imagery. According to Hesiod, Ouranos (literally, Sky or Heaven) imprisoned his children, the Titans, in the underworld. His son Kronos, Zeus's father, therefore, used a sickle to castrate his father, and threw his genitals into the sea. All that "heavenly" semen did not go to waste, and Aphrodite was born out of the resulting foam (her name sounds vaguely like "from the foam" in Greek). Such thinking inspired Botticelli's famous painting *Birth of Venus*. While we might sense some tipsy logic coming into play here, the point is serious: heavenly Aphrodite is the best sort. By contrast, there is the younger deity, common Aphrodite, who is the daughter of Zeus and Dione. When discussing *erōs*, we must likewise be careful to distinguish between the heavenly and common versions (180d-e).

Pausanias deals with common *erōs* first (180e-181c). He argues that actions are not in themselves good or bad but become so depending on how they are performed. In the case of common *erōs*, the problem is that people are too undiscerning. Someone under the sway of common *erōs* is just after sex, and does not care whether he gets it from a woman or a young man. And he does not particularly care how young that man is (181d). This is because he is more in love with the body than the soul. Heavenly *erōs*, by contrast, is a companion to the motherless Aphrodite. Thanks to this all-male pedigree, this love is purely between men (181c-e). This is a love more for the soul than the body. For this reason, heavenly lovers are not attracted to young boys, but to those whose minds have sufficiently developed.

Pausanias finishes by explaining different customs (*nomoi*; 128a) surrounding homoerotic relationships. In a very Greek moment, he speaks out against the Persian empire, which has outlawed them entirely. Like the love of wisdom (*philosophia*) and love of the gym (*philogymnastia*), *erōs* between male citizens strengthens social bonds and overthrows tyranny (182b-c). Pausanias proceeds to explain that the Athenian practice of having young men chaperoned by a *paidagōgos* might seem to condemn homoerotic relationships, but is in fact a way of separating common and heavenly lovers (182d-184e). By encouraging potential lovers to do anything for the object of their affections and encouraging potential beloveds to play hard to get, Athenian custom sets up a contest (*agōn*) to test what sort of relationship it would be (184a).[11] Pausanias ends with the educational role of homoerotic relationships, arguing that, no matter the outcome, it is always honorable to give oneself to a lover for the sake of pursuing virtue (184c-185c).

Eryximachus

The comic poet Aristophanes should come next, but he has the hiccups. The group's doctor, Eryximachus, steps up, offers various hiccup remedies (185d-e), and proceeds to give his own speech in praise of *erōs* (185e-189a).[12] While he may come across as a bit of a nerd (214b), his contribution is profound.

Mirroring Pausanias's critique of Phaedrus, Eryximachus critiques Pausanias for insufficiently developing the distinction between heavenly and common love. All the sciences, it turns out, study the effect of *erōs* on different aspects of life. Eryximachus begins with medicine (186b-e), which is the "science of the effects of love on the filling and emptying of the body" (186c-d). He has in mind Hippocratic practice, which sought to balance the body's humors through diet, exercise, and drugs.[13] The goal, according to Eryximachus, is to restore love between opposed bodily elements: hot and cold, bitter and sweet, wet and dry. The doctor's role is to distinguish between good/heavenly/healthy *erōs* that brings balance and bad/common/diseased *erōs* that destroys balance.

Eryximachus applies the same thinking to athletic training (*gymnastikē*), farming, astronomy, music, and religion (187a-188d). Just as doctors and trainers adapt regimens for the changing seasons of the year, farmers must keep crops in balance as seasons change because of the influence of heavenly bodies studied in astronomy. Music ends up being a process of reconciling long and short syllables, high and low pitches, and the effect they have on listeners. Religion through sacrifice and divination helps restore balance between gods and humans. Erotic relationships between human individuals are thus just one part of a much bigger picture. When *erōs* is "pursued with discipline and justice toward the good" (188d), the results are happiness, civic harmony, and prosperity.[14]

Aristophanes

In his opening critique, Aristophanes claims that people have greatly undervalued the god *erōs*, and that Pausanias and Eryximachus have gone about praising *erōs* in the wrong way. Pausanias focused on the nature of the god, while Eryximachus focused on ideas from the sciences. Aristophanes examines human nature. He is the only one present who does not immediately look down on love between men and women. In fact, his speech (189d-194e) explains the origin of different sexual orientations. In a comic spin on Hesiod, Aristophanes presents a myth in which the original humans each had four arms and four legs arranged in some kind of wheel that made them very fast. Zeus worried that they would seize Olympus from the gods, so he cut them in half, creating the bipedal humans we know today. The process, among other things, explains the origin of the six-pack stomach (190e-191a).[15] These new humans, however, wasted away in longing for their "other halves." Zeus eventually took pity, and came up with a solution, relocating human genitals to allow individuals to come together in sexual union. In this way, *erōs* "seeks to heal the wound of human nature" (191d).[16]

What does this have to do with sexual orientation? It turns out that the original humans had three genders: male, female, and androgynous. The last of these, when split, turned into pairs of heterosexual men and women. There are many adulterers in this group (191d-e). The original men, by contrast, gave way to pairs of homosexual men. These are "the best of boys" when they are young, because they are most masculine: they delight in manly things and in embracing men (191e-192b). Homosexual women do not get much mention (191e). Bisexual people get no mention at all.

Aristophanes ends by extending his myth. When someone finds his or her other half, the two want to live their lives together, though they cannot say what it is they want from the other (192c). Aristophanes suggests that what they would really like is to be "welded together" by

Hephaestus (192d). In this way, the two could melt together, becoming one person. In sum, *erōs* "is the name for our pursuit of wholeness" (192d-193a).

Agathon

It is now down to Agathon and Socrates. None of Agathon's tragedies survives complete today. *Symposium* describes him as a talented, aristocratic young man and the most handsome in the room. Little wonder that Socrates ends up on his couch.[17] When it comes time for Agathon to speak, Socrates butts in, attempting to engage him in a cross-examination. Phaedrus sees that this will derail the task at hand and promptly shuts it down (194).

Agathon brings the pattern of opening critiques to a new level, claiming that all the speakers so far have congratulated human beings on receiving gifts from *erōs*, rather than saying what exactly *erōs* is. Having started with this philosophical insight, the rest of Agathon's speech in praise of *erōs* proceeds like a child's Valentine's Day card, extolling *erōs*'s surpassing beauty. (As Socrates will soon point out, Agathon describes the experience of the beloved in a homosexual couple: to be the sweetheart, fawned over and given presents.) Agathon corrects Pausanias: *erōs* is not ancient; he is the youngest of the gods, because he flees old age, and spends his time around beautiful, young people (195a-c). Nothing harsh or bad, such as castrating one's father, ever happens when *erōs* is present. He is delicate, and touches only pretty, delicate things. He is like a flower (195d-196b). Taking a more philosophical stance, Agathon argues that love is the root of the virtues of justice, moderation, bravery, and wisdom (196b-197c). Tipsy logic continues as *erōs* is said to have "the biggest share of moderation." In mythology, Ares, the god of war, fell in love with Aphrodite, thus proving that *erōs* is brave. Agathon's point about justice seems to be that if everyone just spent their time giving each other presents, everyone would get along. As for wisdom, Agathon falls back on the convention that *erōs* inspires people to become poets (Agathon's and Aristophanes's own profession), animal breeders, craftsmen, prophets, and diplomats.[18]

Taking Stock: The First Five Speeches

We have reached the halfway point in the dialogue, and we have seen speakers proceed with friendly competition: correcting others, expanding ideas, and dipping into tipsy logic, saying things that sound ridiculous but are still, perhaps, profoundly true. Until fairly recently, scholars tended to dismiss these opening speeches, Eryximachus's and Agathon's in particular, as not contributing anything useful to *Symposium*'s philosophical inquiry into *erōs*. More recent work has turned to the question of how these speeches fit together.[19] I suggest that by setting these ideas against the background of the gym and taking seriously the banter through which each speaker critiques those who went before, we can find a structure running through these five speeches that continues into the work's second half. The result is a reading of the work that highlights the centrality of Eryximachus's and Agathon's contributions to the whole.[20]

In one sense, characters' opening critiques claim that previous speakers did not get the question right. Thus, each speech goes beyond the last by exposing the question behind the question. Phaedrus starts by claiming that erotic relationships will keep lovers from doing anything shameful. But this begs the question, What makes an action shameful? Pausanias answers: loving bodies more than souls. But this raises a further question: Why is it shameful to love bodies more than souls? Given that Eryximachus lays out a cosmos in purely physical terms, his speech may seem a poor place to look for body/soul comparisons. Recall, however, that he criticizes Pausanias for not taking the heavenly/common distinction far enough. Eryximachus proceeds to find instances of healthy and diseased love in everything from gym work to farming to astronomy. All of these are ruled over by medicine, which Eryximachus defines as the science (*technē*) of balancing *erōs*'s effects of filling and emptying to create heavenly love. While Eryximachus does not make it explicit, science belongs to souls not to bodies.[21] We should therefore ascribe more worth to souls that act by using science than to bodies that are acted upon by those souls. But this raises the further question, Why does balance/proportion make something healthy and heavenly? Aristophanes responds by focusing on human nature, and spells out *erōs* as the search for wholeness, which brings long-lost other halves back together. This insight relies on the idea shared by ancient medicine and aesthetics that balance and harmony are a means to wholeness. The Greek for "whole" (*holos*) means both "whole" and "sound," as in the Latin motto for ASICS shoes: *anima sana in corpore sano* (a sound mind in a sound body).[22] In anything with parts, whether a human body, a musical instrument, or a piece of architecture, wholeness is brought about through balance of those parts.[23] This raises yet another question: Why is wholeness worth seeking?

Taking a different approach, Agathon criticizes his companions for describing what love does for humans, not what love is. By laying out an account of *erōs* in terms of beauty, Agathon provides a context for the ideas raised by the previous four speakers. If the result of the previous speakers' critiques was to move to ever more basic questions, Agathon now suggests a basic answer that can be used to connect all of this. Why is wholeness worth seeking (as Aristophanes argued)? Because it is beautiful. Beautiful wholeness is brought about by the harmonious, balanced gatherings of gods and humans (as Eryximachus argued). Under the sway of such harmony, nothing is done by force. This lack of force accords with "the laws (*nomoi*) which are king of the city" (196c; compare Pausanias). In such a state, all virtues flow naturally, giving people the correct attitudes toward honor and shame (as Phaedrus argued). Read this way, neither Eryximachus nor Agathon provides a merely comic interlude. Eryximachus brings key concepts from medicine to the table, while Agathon ties a neat philosophical bow on everything that went before. Likewise, the tipsy banter with which speakers roast each other is not mere window dressing: it lays bare the basic structure of the dialogue's first half.

If my reading is correct, then *Symposium*'s first half pursues a strategy that Plato refers to in other dialogues as a method of hypothesis.[24] The method starts by offering a hypothesis awaiting confirmation. The next step is to offer a more basic hypothesis, which would explain the truth of the first: one that answers the question behind the question. Investigators continue this process until they cannot go any further. Ideally, this will culminate in a nonhypothetical first principle (*archē*), though it is possible to stop short of that. The method concludes through a two-step confirmation as original hypotheses are shown to follow from the later ones, and as the nonhypothetical first principle is rigorously tested. If the process is completed, Plato counts the result as knowledge. If the process is cut short before confirming a nonhypothetical principle, then any conclusions produced up to that point are deemed provisional.

By following this method, inquirers dig into ever more basic questions. Basic here means both more simple and more fundamental. This progression is important for two seemingly opposite reasons. First, people rarely start out asking basic questions. The method of hypothesis thus helps readers get to the level at which philosophical theorizing typically operates. Second, by following the method, people can connect philosophical questions with things they actually care about. If this process is skipped, philosophical questions can sound strange or pointless. These movements (finding the basic questions behind everyday concerns and connecting basic questions to everyday concerns) are effectively two sides of a single coin. Among other things, they serve as a teaching strategy, providing a method for getting people to think about ideas, both familiar and novel, from a series of different perspectives.

Plato's process for confirming a first principle is notoriously hard to pin down. At the very least, it involves checking an idea for internal consistency through a process reminiscent of Socratic *elenchos*. At other times, it asks how well a hypothesis rings true to lived experience or makes good sense of human psychology.[25] The four speeches leading up to Agathon's speech capture various experiences and ways of conceptualizing *erōs*: honor and shame (Phaedrus), heavenly vs. common (Pausanias), cosmic processes (Eryximachus), and longing for wholeness (Aristophanes). In setting out a hypothesis connecting *erōs* and beauty, Agathon in effect says: Each of you has a piece of the picture. Here is the whole. Everything your theory can do, mine can do better.[26] Socrates congratulates Agathon on his method of praising love, but he points out contradictions within Agathon's hypothesis, and offers a rival theory that resolves them. Put another way, Socrates criticizes Agathon for not yet arriving at a basic question: there are yet more questions behind the hypothetical answer Agathon gives. To evaluate the force of this critique and the strength of the alternative hypothesis Socrates presents, we must take one more digression into *Symposium*'s cultural context in the next chapter.

Chapter 7

Mysteries of Love
Symposium 199c-212c

> To go about this undertaking correctly, he must as a young man devote himself to beautiful bodies. First, he must love one body and through this love give birth to beautiful ideas. Later, he must realize that the beauty of the one body is brother to the beauty of any other body. And if he is set on pursuing bodily beauty, he must realize how insane it would be not to think that the beauty of all bodies is one. When he realizes this, he must establish himself as a lover of all beautiful bodies, and he must look down on the wild gaping after one body and think it a small thing.
>
> —Socrates/Diotima in Plato, *Symposium* 210a-b

In Plato's Athens, there were at least two spheres of what we could call religious life: state cult and mystery cult.[1] State cult involved massive temples, public processions, athletic and theatrical contests, and public sacrifices offered on behalf of the city as a whole. Greek temples had functional altars upon which animals as large as bulls were sacrificed. That was a messy undertaking, so altars tended to be in front of rather than inside temples.

Mystery cult was pursued by individuals. The Eleusinian mysteries were the most famous in antiquity, yet the details of their ritual remain elusive. To join the cult, individuals would go through a process of purification and an initiation ceremony that culminated in the cult's mysteries being revealed through a series of complex and secret rituals. Such cults provide the model for the basic form of the Greek life of American collegiate fraternities and sororities, as well as Christian rituals of baptism and communion.

At Eleusis, the process of purification proceeded in stages. At certain points, priestesses would come into Athens with baskets containing genital-shaped baked goods. Initiates would bathe in the ocean with a piglet, which they would then sacrifice and throw into a pit. As they processed from the city to Eleusis, a suburb of Athens, a man dressed as a flute girl would jump out from under a bridge and tell obscene jokes. Unlike most ancient temples, the main building at Eleusis was designed to host its rituals on the inside. This gave people running the ritual greater control over initiates' experience. From what we can gather, the ceremony involved contrasts between deep darkness and bright lights, protracted silence and loud noises. At some point a (hopefully) symbolic baby was thrown into a fire, and the final moment involved watching a stalk of wheat being broken.

The Homeric *Hymn to Demeter* provides what may be the key to making sense of this seemingly random set of events. The pigs thrown into the pit reenact Demeter's daughter Persephone being kidnapped by Hades and taken to the underworld. The dirty jokes reenact a servant who subsequently tries to cheer Demeter up. The baby in the fire has to do with a mortal child Demeter seeks to make immortal by baking him. The final bit with wheat connects to Demeter's role in agriculture. The meaning of the genital doughnuts is unclear.[2]

What we can be sure of, and what matters for present purposes, is the basic process: initiates were ritually purified in preparation for induction into a mystery. Membership had its privileges. Ancient Greek views of the afterlife varied, yet the general consensus was that all humans ended up in Hades. That said, some parts of Hades are more enjoyable than others, and entry into the Eleusinian mysteries secured a spot in the Elysian fields. Initiation also brought a new perspective. This seems to have mostly related to how people understand the cult's rituals, which were spectacular enough that people would return multiple times after being initiated.

Socrates/Diotima's Speech: *Symposium* 199b-212c

Mystery cult's basic pattern of purification, initiation, and acquisition of a new perspective provides a framework for Socrates's speech in praise of *erōs*. Or, more exactly, for the speech he recounts in praise of *erōs*. Rather than give his own ideas, Socrates recites a speech given by Diotima, a wise woman who taught him the art of erotic love (*ta erōtika*; 201d). She may have been a historical figure or a fiction invented by Socrates on the spot. Either way, Diotima is presented as something like a priestess in the mysteries of love.

Socrates introduces this speech by taking a second pass at examining Agathon (199c-201c) and turning the young poet's cuddly view of love on its head. Just as Diotima once found the young Socrates (204c) doing, Agathon is thinking about love from the perspective of the beloved. Socrates forces Agathon to think through what it is like to be a lover. The upshot of their conversation is that we love either what we do not have, or what we now have but worry about losing in the future (200d). What is it we need but have such a tenuous connection to? Beauty and goodness. Being a lover ends up being an ordeal as we labor over beauty, which we tenuously grasp. In terms of the method of hypothesis, Agathon's speech concealed one more question: How is *erōs* related to beauty? The answer Socrates gets Agathon to give is "Through lacking it."

Having questioned Agathon, Socrates turns the tables once again, and recounts how Diotima questioned the young Socrates (201d-203e). The upshot here is that *erōs* is an in-between sort of thing. Just as correct opinion is situated between ignorance and understanding without being either of them, *erōs* is neither ugly nor beautiful, neither miserable nor happy, neither mortal nor immortal: *erōs* is a spirit (*diamonion*; 202e) straddling the mortal and immortal worlds. Having left everyone a bit perplexed, Socrates launches into Diotima's speech.

Diotima presents *erōs* through a myth of her own (203b-207a). On the day Aphrodite was born, Plenty and Poverty were guests at the party.[3] Plenty gets drunk and passes out, at which point Poverty makes love to him. Their child is *erōs*. As with Achilles, *erōs*'s mixed parentage explains his in-between nature. Like his father, Plenty, he is a lover of goodness, beauty, and wisdom. Like his mother, Poverty, he does not have any of these things and thus spends his time pursuing them. His ultimate goal is to possess the good forever. How can mere mortals accomplish this? The answer Diotima gives is reproduction.

Even animals feel the effects of *erōs*, and by mating in the presence of beauty attain a kind of immortality. There is more than one way to be pregnant, though (207a-209e). Most people are "pregnant in body" (Diotima seems to have men in mind here) and thus make love to women, who help them attain immortality through childbirth. Other people are "pregnant in soul" (she is still talking about men) and thus turn to younger men to "beget" virtues and ideas. Diotima cites artists, poets, and legislators as examples of people who have attained immortality through their creative work. What does this have to do with making love to younger men? Even according to ancient ideas of procreation, ideas and virtue are not something that can be exchanged via bodily fluids. So, while physical intercourse leads to babies, some kind of spiritual intercourse leads to creative endeavors. What does spiritual intercourse actually amount to? Here the modern meaning of symposium comes through the strongest: by coming together in joint inquiry and creative endeavors, mentors and their students can create beautiful works together. One of the most beautiful is the character of the student himself. Among other things, Greek homoerotic relationships are a mode of education. According to Diotima, such bonds are firmer and more valuable than mere animal reproduction because their children are "more beautiful and more immortal" (209c).

Diotima ties all this together by explaining *erōs* in terms of mystery cult (209e-212b). She presents what later philosophers would call a spiritual exercise: a systematic way of thinking designed to reorient one's thinking. The first step in Diotima's spiritual regimen is to recall a time you felt erotic desire for someone's body. What do we really want in such situations? Diotima's answer: to possess that beauty forever through physical intimacy. Likewise for bodies in general. Next, recall a time when you felt strong attraction to someone's character or customs (*nomoi*). Diotima suggests it is the person's virtue, or at least their potential for virtue, that we love. Likewise for character in general: beautiful character arouses in us a desire for a spiritual connection, in which we enjoy and nurture that person's character and perhaps even take it on ourselves. Next, recall a time when you felt a strong attraction to someone's intellect. Having your mind stretched can be enjoyable. Diotima suggests that beautiful ideas arouse a desire to engage in learning and creative projects. What do these three sorts of *erōs* have in common? According to Diotima, what we are really after in all of this is beauty itself. We find particular beautiful things in the world all around us (bodies, customs, ideas), but by going through the mysteries of love, stripping away the particulars and purifying our gaze, we ascend to a vision of a single beauty behind all of them. This is the final revelation of Diotima's erotic mysteries.

Diotima's account of *erōs* attempts to explain a huge range of human activity. To evaluate it as a philosophical theory, we must first ask: How huge? Does it make sense to say that all our desires ultimately strive for immortality through the possession of beauty? When I brush my teeth in the morning, am I really thinking deep down, "I want immortality through the possession of beauty," or do only certain desires aim at this lofty goal? The root of the interpretive problem sits in the passage where Socrates's conversation with Diotima moves quickly from the desire to possess beautiful things to the desire to possess good things to the desire to possess good things forever (204d-205a). How exactly do we connect the dots between goodness, beauty, and forever? Most scholars either equate beauty and goodness, or see beauty as an aspect of goodness. Insofar as dental health is a good, and healthy teeth are attractive, this lands us back at the toothbrush problem. Gabriel Richardson Lear takes an alternative approach, arguing that when we encounter beautiful things, "their goodness strikes us as being impervious to the passage of time.... For Plato, to experience something as beautiful is to sense in the present moment an infinite perfection."[4] On this reading, only those desires count as erotic that jar us out of complacency with everyday goods like dental health and move us to strive for immortality as best we can. But what exactly does this entail?

Striving for immortality can mean a couple of things for a human being. One is to stretch one's legacy as far as possible, whether through having children, building a reputation, or creating a piece of art that outlives its creator.[5] These strategies rely on quantity of time and run into the problem that we cannot control what happens to our descendants, reputations, or creations after we die. There is also the more basic question about what possible effect our future legacies can have on our happiness in the here and now. One response is that it is not a matter of actually being remembered, but of living our lives in a way that makes them worthy of being remembered.[6] This brings us to the second way to understand a human being's striving for immortality, which is to live our lives in a way that is as close as possible to the way the immortal gods do. Here it is not quantity of years but the quality of our lives that matters. In *Symposium*'s terms, this means bringing our time-bound lives into sync with timeless paradigms of number, proportionality, and beauty. As Eryximachus showed us, this imposition of timeless ratios onto time can happen in a huge range of cases, from the gym and farming to music and astronomy. Perhaps the feeling of time slowing down that elite athletes use today to describe flow was on Diotima's mind when she talked about the collision of the mortal and immortal, time and eternity.[7] If this is right, we should strive to look like the gods by imposing immortal ratios on our mortal bodies (as Eryximachus counseled), to move like the gods through our rhythmically balanced actions, to desire like the gods by having our desires for things reflect their worth (compare Pausanias's idea of valuing souls over bodies).[8] Most importantly we should strive to understand the world as the gods do.[9] In short, *erōs* is the drive for transcendence.

While this might sound like a noble set of aspirations, does it actually explain *erōs* in a relationship between two human beings? Individual people feature in Diotima's mysteries of love, yet they occupy the bottom stages of the ascent to beauty. Even if we move beyond loving people's bodies to loving people's characters and then their ideas, we eventually leave individuals behind as we set out onto the "great sea of beauty" (210d) and behold beauty itself, "absolute, pure, unmixed, not polluted by human flesh or colors or any such nonsense of mortality" (211e). Diotima seems to make *erōs* an impersonal affair, as she treats people as steps on some kind of ladder in the ascent to beauty. Gregory Vlastos defends this position in his 1973 essay, "The Individual as an Object of Love in Plato," which sparked a lively debate.[10] One way to answer Vlastos's worries about Diotima's seemingly impersonal view of personal relationships is to set her speech in its broader contexts.

Mystery cults provide the first context. Many scholars have read Diotima's ascent to beauty as presenting a three-stage process of purification via love of bodies, with "lesser mysteries" focused on honor, and "greater mysteries" in which some secret knowledge is revealed.[11] On this reading, we must be purified of our love of bodies and then set those bodies aside (perhaps like the piglets of the Eleusinian ritual). In philosophical terms, this reading drives a wedge between beautiful bodies and beauty itself.[12] More recent studies suggest the point of actual mystery cult was not to reveal a secret doctrine but to offer an unusually intense experience of divinity, such as the face-to-face encounter with Dionysus at the end of Euripides's play *Bacchae*.[13] While such experiences do not bring any particular knowledge, they alter the way we perceive things. This explains why individuals would return to the mysteries multiple times. Repeat visits, after all, would make little sense if the point was merely to reveal a secret idea. If we apply this thinking to *Symposium*, the final revelation of beauty itself is not so much a new piece of knowledge as an intense experience. As with any intense experience (athletic, musical, theatrical, religious), we can say various things about the experience of beauty itself, but all such descriptions fall short. When it comes to human individuals, this reading suggests continuity between the various stages on the ascent. While Diotima talks about the ascent in terms of "steps" along the way, we should be careful not to get caught up on the idea of a ladder that we ascend and then discard. While talk of "Diotima's ladder" is widespread, it does not appear in *Symposium* itself.[14] Perhaps mountain climbing would be a better metaphor: the higher we go, the more we appreciate the view.

To say we "look down on" the initial stages of the ascent is not to say that we want to replace them.[15] Rather, we come to appreciate how each element fits within an ever more holistic picture.

The second context is the larger educational enterprise to which the symposium and the gymnasium belong. While romantic relationships provide the occasion for Diotima's ascent, they need not be its focus: if Diotima does not spell out interpersonal relationships for people who have seen beauty itself, it may simply be because she is talking about something else.[16] If the ascent is in fact the search for happiness, then to think that our happiness relies on another person is "deeply misguided," even if that is the point of Aristophanes's speech.[17] The main thrust of Diotima's speech is that the ascent to beauty is at every point creative. Whether it be the generation of fine speeches, laws, or virtues, Diotima describes the philosophical encounter with beauty in terms of pregnancy and creation. The ancient symposium and gym were spaces for intimate, caring relationships, which served as apprenticeships for aspiring citizens. The connections between this and Diotima's ascent are clear. If people today tend not to think of intimate relationships as vehicles for improving self and partner, that may simply be a sign of our culture's impoverished status compared to Diotima's ideal.[18]

In sum, how we evaluate Diotima's account of *erōs* rests in no small part on what we take that account of *erōs* to be. At the root of the scholarly debates are different assumptions about Plato's understanding of goodness. Coleen Zoller contrasts "austere dualism," according to which all goods are goods of the mind, and "normative dualism," according to which bodily goods are accepted as real goods, albeit at a lower level than goods of the mind. Scholars typically assume that Plato has the former in mind. Zoller argues that the latter makes better sense of Plato's writings, and puts his thought more squarely in line with current social justice movements.[19] There is a related question about how we understand the vision of beauty as a highest good. Vlastos's critique rests on the assumption that beauty is a highest good in the sense that it is valuable in itself and for no other reason. As a result, anything that leads us to the vision of beauty is a mere means, a step along the way. One response is that this is "a common (and correct) way of understanding Aristotle," but not of Plato, who contrasts it with the idea that "the best goods are those we seek both for themselves and for their consequences."[20] This supports a reading according to which "we are to live our lives in response to something superior to ourselves," such as beauty itself, which deserves our "admiration, wonder, and devotion," and provides a model for how we should live.[21] To decide which way to go on these various interpretive questions, we can look at how a particular expert in the mysteries of love approaches relationships: Socrates. For this, we have one final speech.

Party Crasher: *Symposium* 212c-223d

Having brought us to this height of mystic revelation, and tied a neat philosophical bow on everything that came before, Socrates is interrupted by a ruckus outside. It turns out to be his own beloved, Alcibiades, who has been doing his own drinking. A lot of it. As a result, he does not even see Socrates at first and ends up startled to find himself sitting on a couch next to him. The two men interact like an old married couple, both of whom flirt with Agathon. Since it would not be civilized to drink in silence (214b), Alcibiades decides to give a speech in praise of Socrates, whom he roasts mercilessly.

At this point, the project of praising *erōs* seems to be derailed. Yet we must remember that this speech lets us glimpse how one member of a homoerotic relationship thinks about the other. In this particular case, Alcibiades is the younger, attractive, rich, and politically powerful beloved. Socrates is the older, ugly lover who usually dresses like a bum and has spent his life avoiding politics. Alcibiades compares him to a satyr. Everything else about their relationship is turned on its head. It is Alcibiades who pursues Socrates, wrestling with him at the gym, inviting him to dinner, and even plotting a sleepover. Alcibiades's goal in all of this is to seduce Socrates into making Alcibiades a better man. Socrates is swayed by none of it, and Alcibiades's ego is shattered as his advances are shot down.

What should we make of Socrates shunning Alcibiades's beauty? On the one hand, Socrates refuses to engage in literal sexual intercourse. On the other hand, Socrates does not shut down their relationship. The two of them spend time together and do a lot of talking. Furthermore, Socrates plays the gadfly, getting Alcibiades to worry about improving his character. If anything, Socrates's refusal to go along with Alcibiades's plan advances this project. Alcibiades seems to think of virtue as something you can get via exchange; hence his plan to give his body to Socrates in exchange for virtue.[22] Socrates knows better: virtue is something you need to develop for yourself, though mentors can help by providing models, asking questions, and getting you to put the work in. From this perspective, Socrates is giving Alcibiades what he is asking for, but it is a decidedly tough-love approach. (As a historical note, the actual Alcibiades had a notorious political career in which he repeatedly switched sides in Athens's war with Sparta, profaned the Eleusinian mysteries by performing them in public, and, in a night of drunken mischief, desecrated several herms by breaking off their phalluses.)[23]

Particulars of their relationship aside, this portrait of Socrates as a philosophical lover provides another way to confirm Diotima's account of *erōs*. Just as Diotima did not hear the other speeches at Agathon's party, Alcibiades did not hear Socrates's retelling of Diotima's speech. The cross-references are there nevertheless. To see the method of hypothesis at play, we must simply connect the dots.

If we work backward, Diotima's speech provides answers to the questions sitting behind the previous five speeches. By making *erōs* an in-between thing, she answers Socrates's question to Agathon regarding how *erōs* relates to beauty: *erōs* seeks to possess the good forever through various kinds of reproduction. This is a mortal way to engage with immortal reality. It provides the kind of stability that Aristophanes described in terms of wholeness. In practical terms, this is often done by imposing immortal proportions onto mortal bodies and their actions.[24] *Erōs*'s constant striving casts Eryximachus's focus on medicine in a new light. If we survey the mathematical arts of the day, arithmetic and geometry study static objects (numbers and shapes), while music and astronomy study objects that exist in time (sounds and the motions of the heavens). But this second pair was most often reduced to processes that were static across time (such as the relationship between pitches).[25] A physician's work, by contrast, is never done. Like the other mathematical arts, medicine engages in immortal proportions, yet it does so in the most mortal of ways, tending to changes within the body and its environmental context through an "agonistic relationship" that forever strives for balance yet never secures it for long.[26] A philosophical lover-mentor will likewise always be consulting immortal ideas to care for his beloved.[27] In such a scheme, he must love ideas more than his beloved's body or soul, but in the sense that immortal ideas provide the standard for shaping body and soul, not vice versa. This is not to shun the individual but to love him correctly. Insofar as the soul can actively engage with and impose these ideas on bodies, Diotima goes beyond Pausanias by giving a reason for valuing souls over bodies. These immortal ideas supply the ultimate standard for judging Phaedrus's concerns for honor and shame. More importantly, Diotima's idea that mortals can engage with immortal happiness by bringing their bodies, actions, character, and understanding into sync with immortal ideas provides a profound alternative to Phaedrus's more traditional idea of living on through posthumous reputation.

If we work forward, Diotima's theory is shown in practice via Alcibiades's portrait of Socrates, especially the way Socrates engages with younger men. Socrates performs honorably in battle, yet without worrying about getting credit for it, thus embodying a more substantial approach to Phaedrus's ideas about honor and shame. While he clearly enjoys the company of attractive younger men, he shoots down Alcibiades's sexual advances for the sake of Alcibiades's education, thus showing that he meets Pausanias's criterion of loving souls more than bodies. While Socrates does not heed Eryximachus's concern for moderate drinking, he is able to drink everyone else under the table without showing any signs of inebriation.[28] He is gregarious but also perfectly fine spending time lost in his own thoughts (compare Aristophanes's concern for wholeness). And while he may not be as physically attractive as Agathon, all the men fall for him, as he devotes his life to engaging others in creative philosophical inquiry. In short, Socrates is at every position of Diotima's ascent at once.[29]

If *Symposium* has struck some scholars as short on arguments, it is because of the piecemeal way the text has been read.[30] Building on this insight, I suggest that *Symposium*'s argument is spread across all seven speeches, each of which fits into an organic progression shaped by the method of hypothesis. In the end, I take this argument to be provisional. Diotima's ascent is about beauty itself. There is one more basic question to be asked: What is beauty itself? To this, Diotima does not give an answer but merely points the way. Still, not all provisional answers are equally valuable. If my reading is correct, we should judge *Symposium*'s overall account of love by how well the initial speeches uncover ever more basic questions and ring true to our lived experiences of *erōs*; by the extent to which Diotima's account of *erōs* provides a useful framework for understanding those experiences; and by the extent to which Alcibiades's presentation of Socrates provides an attractive model for us to emulate.

Symposium and Spiritual Exercise

Outside of religion, transcendence is not a common goal in life in the United States today. Thanks to various economic forces, worries about the here and now tend to eclipse any desire to step outside of time. The proliferation of social media has brought worries about reputation to levels unmatched since the age of chivalry. The main exception to this might be sports. One day while teaching *Symposium*, I rambled on about ecstatic experiences of great music only to see blank stares all around the classroom. Eventually one student raised her hand and asked, "Is it like when you get into a flow state swimming?" To which, I answered, "Yes!"

One thing our gyms have in common with their ancient counterparts is training. For us, as for the Greeks, the pursuit of athletic excellence is never-ending. *Symposium* invites us to see this familiar aspect of our lives in a new light, as an instance of the mortal pursuit of immortal beauty. And it challenges us to extend this pursuit to other parts of our lives, in particular to think about intimate relationships as a vehicle for the joint pursuit of excellence in all aspects of our lives. *Symposium*'s exploration of *erōs*, beauty, transcendence, and training provides a practice run for the much more elaborate project set out in *Republic*'s account of gym training's role in pursuing mental and political health, to which we now turn.

Chapter 8

Music, Gymnastics, and Moral Development
Republic 2–4

> It seems that some god gave these two arts, music and gym training, to human beings for the sake of the spirited and philosophical parts of the soul, and only incidentally for the body and soul, so that the parts of the soul may be brought into harmony with each other, being tightened and loosened to the right degree.
>
> —Socrates in Plato, *Republic* 411e-412a

Republic 1 sought to answer whether justice is more profitable than injustice. But without a viable definition of justice, the effort descends into perplexity, as we saw in chapter 4. While book 1 resembles other Socratic dialogues, *Republic* 2 opens as Socrates states, "I thought I was done with the discussion. But it all turned out to be only a prelude" (357a). Glaucon moves the discussion forward by challenging Socrates to say what justice is, and to show that it is valuable in itself, not just for its consequences. Socrates responds over the course of the next nine books.

Socrates's overarching strategy is to find justice first in a city, and then use that as a model for finding justice in the soul. He proceeds to lay out an ideal city and in *Republic* 3 sets out a curriculum combining music and gym training for educating its ruling class. In *Republic* 4 he steps back to argue that the city is divided into three parts, and that justice is a kind of civic health as each class tends to its own work, therefore contributing to the good of the whole. Using this as a model, he argues that the soul is composed of three parts, and that its own virtues amount to a kind of harmony and mental health.

If we do not agree that bodily health is valuable for its own sake, the entire project unravels. This particular concept of health is drawn from Hippocratic theories of holistic balance. Hippocratic practice, in turn, is deeply involved with regimens of diet and exercise. *Republic* draws these ideas together and makes early education in music and gym training the foundation upon which balanced souls and harmonious governments are built. In short, the gym, as the site of both musical and physical training, is the key to personal happiness and civic concord.

Glaucon's Challenge: *Republic* 2 (357–367)

Republic 2 starts with one of the most economical pages of philosophy ever written. Glaucon divides all goods into three classes (357; see table 1).

Some of these seem uncontroversial. Harmless pleasures, such as a couple of cookies that do not impact your health, are good for their own sake and not really much else.[1] Medicine, by contrast, is good for its consequences but not the sort of thing you would seek out for its own sake. Money, likewise, is good not in itself but for what it can buy.

According to Glaucon, health, sight, and knowledge are good both in themselves and for their consequences. The consequences of being healthy are that people find you attractive, you are capable of engaging in various activities, you are able to live free from pain, and so on. The consequences of having sight range from avoiding collisions to enjoying beautiful objects. Knowledge is likewise useful for accomplishing tasks. This much seems uncontroversial. But are health, sight, and knowledge also valuable in themselves? Knowledge for its own sake seems simple enough: sports fans will spend considerable energy exploring players' statistics for no practical purpose. They simply enjoy knowing about sports. What about health?

If you could have all the consequences of health but not actually be healthy, would you choose to be that way? Given advances in medicine, this is becoming more and more possible. Rather than spend time at the gym, you can get silicone muscle implants, which increase the apparent strength of muscles while compromising their actual function. Rather than controlling your diet, you can undergo liposuction.

Table 1

CLASSES OF GOODS	EXAMPLES
1. Good only in itself	Harmless pleasures
2. Good in itself and for its consequences	Health, sight, knowledge
3. Good only for its consequences	Medicine, exercise, moneymaking

Rather than getting a natural dopamine release from exercise, you can stimulate brain chemistry through drugs. Rather than getting a general sense of energy and well-being from cardiovascular health, you can take stimulants to get through the day. Rather than getting a good night's sleep from having taxed your body through exercise, you can counteract your stimulants with alcohol and sleeping pills. This might be hard on your liver, but there are treatments for that as well. In short, if you could look, feel, and act just as a healthy person can but without being healthy, would you do it?[2]

The point of all of this is to lay out the driving question: What kind of good is justice (358b)? Glaucon personally thinks that justice is a middle sort of good (good both in itself and for its consequences), yet he is afraid that most people think that justice, like medicine, is good only for its consequences. He therefore challenges Socrates to explain (a) what justice and injustice are, (b) what power each has in the soul, and (c) why justice is a good in itself and not only for its consequences (366d-367e). To drive home what he is after, and what Socrates is up against, Glaucon sets out how "most people" would respond to this challenge (358d-362c).

Justice, according to this account, is simply an agreement people make not to harm each other. No one seeks justice willingly. To prove it, Glaucon offers a thought experiment: a shepherd, ancestor to Gyges, king of Lydia, finds a magic ring that makes him invisible (359e-360e).[3] Making use of this, he sleeps with the king's wife, kills the king, and takes over the kingdom. If you had an invisibility ring, would you still play by the rules? If you could act unjustly without suffering the consequences, would you do it? Glaucon drives the point home: If you had the choice between being just but seeming unjust (and thus suffering the consequences of being seen as unjust) and being unjust but seeming just (and thus reaping the rewards of being seen as just), which would you choose? Glaucon's brother, Adeimantus, takes it a step further, pointing out that acting unjustly helps one make money, which can be used to bribe people and gods alike (362d-367e). If that sounds right to you, then clearly you do not value justice for itself, only for its consequences.[4] With this, the challenge is set.

"We Built This City": *Republic* 2 (368–374)

Up to this point, we have been talking about the justice and injustice in individual people. Socrates sets out his strategy, which is to step back and look for justice and injustice on a larger scale: a city. Once that has been described, he will return to the original task of seeking something analogous in an individual's character/soul (368a-369b). This is a heuristic strategy: it is not that justice in the soul will be a certain way because justice in the city is a certain way. Rather, finding justice in the city will give us a set of questions to ask and ideas to work with as we examine the soul. This task takes up the next two and a half books.

The first stage is to imagine a healthy city (369b-372d), small in scale, catering to simple desires, lacking delicacies, and self-sufficient as a community. Such a place is apparently too bland for Athenian sensibilities. Glaucon calls it a "city of pigs" (372d). Socrates responds by presenting a "city with a fever" (373a-383c). This is large scale and caters to refined desires with various luxuries. Maintaining this fever will require constant expansion into neighboring territories, so he adds a professional military called guardians. Along the way, Socrates introduces a principle of specialization: since it is impossible for one person to practice many crafts well, each person should do what he or she is best suited to by nature (369d-370c). Glaucon agrees, so Socrates concludes that the guardians should constitute a professional army (374c).

Plato's Early Curriculum: *Republic* 2 and 3 (374–417)

The rest of book 2 and most of book 3 are occupied with the education of the guardian class. The first thing they need to be is brave and spirited (375b). In English, the lines between *spiritual*, *spirited*, and *spirit* can be blurry. In Greek, the terms *psychē*, *thymos*, and *daimōn* are clearly distinct. To explain what is meant by "spirited," Socrates offers dogs as an example. When attacked, dogs will fight back as needed. This, however, creates a puzzle (375b-376b): a successful guardian will have to be gentle toward the people he protects and high-spirited (*megalothymos*) toward his enemies. How can these opposing character traits exist in the same person at once? Dogs prove another useful example, as they can be fiercely loyal but also fierce toward attackers. Furthermore, dogs tend to be gentle toward people they know and aggressive toward people they do not know. Socrates sees this as a love of knowledge, which clearly marks out dogs as the most philosophical of animals. While he is likely joking, Socrates here makes the serious point that guardians must be raised to behave like his furry philosophers.

For the guardians' training, Socrates looks to Greece's traditional form of early education: music (*musikē*) and gym training (*gymnastikē*; 376e).

Music in this context includes anything involving a Muse: singing, playing instruments, poetry, theater, literature, and so on.[5] The rest of book 2 (376e-383c) is taken up with what the content of this musical education should be. In particular, it sets out what poets should not say about the gods: that they act immorally or that they change their forms. Anyone familiar with Greek mythology knows that the traditional gods do a lot of both. Zeus, for instance, pursues extramarital affairs by changing into a bull, swan, eagle, cloud, and shower of gold. Socrates's discussion of poetry spills over into book 3, as he discusses what we should not say about mortals: that death is evil and ought to be feared (386a-388a), that excess and indulgence are good (389d-392a), and that unjust people are happy (392b-c). The goal of all this is to raise children to be brave, disciplined, and just. While that sounds like a fine thing, it rules out the vast majority of Homer's and Hesiod's poetry, which were the foundation of Greece's traditional musical education.

Having dealt with content, Socrates moves on to style. The first point is that young people acting in plays should portray only suitable role models. If such roles are not available, they should merely narrate actions (392c-398c). Socrates then turns to questions of music theory (398c-403c). Rather than getting bogged down in technical details, he looks to the moral point: children should be raised listening to whatever rhythms and harmonies will make them brave and disciplined. Furthermore, music will help children develop a sense of grace and wholeness. That way, when they encounter something that is malformed, even if they cannot articulate what is wrong with it (that comes later in the curriculum), they will have an intuitive sense that something is off (401e-402a). This goes beyond just music to include instances of virtue and vice. The truly musical person, it turns out, will be a lover of the fine and beautiful (402d), which is the real point of all of this.

Athletic training also pursues a moral goal, as it arouses the spirited aspect of the soul, which will make people brave (410). This, in turn, "harmonizes" with the sense of grace imbued by music (411a). Socrates warns against pursuing one to the exclusion of the other: music alone can make people too soft; athletics alone can make them brutish and harsh. What we need is a balance of the two (410a-412b): the harmony of grace and power that rowers like to talk about.[6] While we might assume that athletic training is for the body and music for the soul (376e), it turns out that the main aim of both is character formation (410b-c). A healthy body does not make a healthy soul but vice versa (403d). What kind of athletic regimen creates a healthy soul? Socrates warns against overspecialization. Professional athletes, he argues, sleep their lives away, and do not deal well with changes in diet (404a). Wartime conditions are better: soldiers have simple diets and are generally fit, even if they occasionally need medical treatment (404b-405a). Thus, just as music has two parts (content and style), so too does athletic training (exercise and diet).[7] All four work together to get children's characters into shape.

US culture has come to see education as a private commodity rather than a public good. It was not always that way. Thomas Jefferson argued that the United States needed a school within walking distance of any house. His rationale was that the country needed a "natural aristocracy," in which the people who were best suited to rule would. For this to happen, children needed access to education. The alternative, he warned, was an "unnatural aristocracy," in which rulers were chosen on the basis of birth or their parents' wealth, as in the case of the upper classes of Europe. Given college admission scandals (to say nothing of the SAT prep classes that wealthy parents use to help their children get ahead), it is unclear how well we are living up to Jefferson's ideal.[8]

Socrates ends on a Jeffersonian note, arguing that certain members of the future guardian class will rise to the top as being particularly good at always doing what they believe to be best for the city. These will be elevated as the "complete guardians," while their classmates will be assigned as their "helpers/auxiliaries" (412b-417a). With this, the city will settle into three classes: the producers (farmers, shoemakers, merchants, and so on), the auxiliaries (army/police), and the "complete guardians" (rulers). To buttress these class divisions, Socrates invents a myth according to which people have various metals in their blood: gold, silver, iron, and bronze. Guardians will be raised to think that since they have gold in their blood, it is wrong for them to have it in their pockets. This bit of social engineering is meant to raise a class of rulers who shun personal monetary gain and think first about the good of the whole.

Justice as Civic and Mental Health: *Republic* 4

In looking for justice, Socrates reiterates that the goal in building the ideal city is to make the city as a whole, not just a part of it, as happy as possible (420). This will make it "one city" rather than what we usually find: a city in which the rich and the poor are effectively distinct political entities set against each other (421-427). Socrates suggests that we can avoid this problem through the ruling classes' voluntary poverty and commitment to the values instilled by their early education. They must always put the city first. To help ensure this, the city will devise marriage contracts within the ruling class and provide for the education of future generations (423e-424a).

What then is the justice of this city? Plato approaches this question holistically, looking to his ideal city for four of the virtues that Socrates called into question in his dialogues set in gyms. The wisdom of a city sits in the knowledge of guardians, who make decisions based on a holistic view of the city's well-being. The bravery of a city sits in its auxiliaries, who hold to the values instilled by their early education. What is the virtue particular to the productive class? It does not have one. Rather, discipline/moderation is obtained by the three classes working together harmoniously: the guardians rule, the auxiliaries help them rule, and the productive class submits to being ruled. Justice, it turns out, has been on the table for some time in the principle of specialization, that each person should do what he or she is best suited to by nature: guardians should rule, auxiliaries should assist the guardians, and producers should submit to their rulers' orders.

Is this remotely plausible? Socrates does not seem to mind if people move around within the productive class: if you start out a farmer but learn you would rather be a blacksmith, then do it. Similarly, there are mechanisms for moving around people who have been incorrectly classed—for instance, a potential guardian born to parents of the productive class. For a city to flourish, however, the people making money must be distinct from the people making policy. If you want to make money, that is fine. You can do that, but you will not be put in charge of the government. If you want to be in charge, that is fine too. You will simply take a vow of poverty. If you want to be in the army, that is also fine. You will take a vow of poverty and a vow of obedience to those higher up the chain.

With this account of civic virtue set out, Socrates is ready to examine justice in the individual soul. The account of civic justice suggests that it will have something to do with how the parts of one's soul relate to one another. The first step, then, is to look for analogous parts within the soul. For this, Socrates looks to instances of inner conflict.

Recall a time when you knew better but did something anyway. Perhaps it is the one more round you know you will regret in the morning or that piece of cake that will cost you sprints the next day. Why do we act against our own best judgment? Socrates's analysis is that the rational part of your soul is in conflict with its appetitive part. Most of us will accept the idea that we have appetites for physical pleasure, which sometimes conflict with our rational understanding of overall goods. But what about times when you do something that is just tasteless, and get mad at yourself for it? Socrates's example is looking at corpses. While this might have sexual overtones in an Athenian context, we could think about rubbernecks on the interstate who stare at car crashes. Such ogling is not wrong or harmful, just tasteless. Socrates concludes that in such cases the conflict is between appetite and our "spirited" part. To back his conclusion that this is not another instance of appetite or reason, he points to dogs and babies, who lack reason but abound in spirit. The dog example is, once again, informative. As pack animals, dogs care about issues of social standing: alphas, betas, protecting one's own, avenging slights, and so on. On Socrates's analysis, our spirited part is similarly keyed to issues of social standing and honor.[9]

If reason, spirit, and appetite are the soul's parts, what are its virtues? Using civic virtue as a model, Socrates suggests individual wisdom is the rational part's knowledge of the soul's overall good. Individual courage is the spirited part's holding to the mandates of reason. Individual discipline/moderation comes about when reason rules appetite, and spirit assists. Individual justice is each part doing its own work: reason ruling, spirit helping, appetites submitting to being ruled. What does this look like in practice? When you think clearly about the consequences of that extra round (reason), then you should not give in to your desire for it (appetite); rather, you should feel ashamed of being the sort of person who does that sort of thing, and take pride in doing what is best for you overall (spirit).

What is the alternative? If you put spirit in charge over reason, you become a hothead who flies off the handle at any perceived social slight. If you put appetite in charge, you will go for short-term and easy pleasures at the expense of what is best for you overall, appetites included. According to this line of thought, the way to balance our various desires and live our best lives is to use our reason and live like human beings. That is what justice is. At this point, Socrates has everything he needs to construct a response to Glaucon's challenge: justice is a kind of mental health understood in Hippocratic terms of harmony and balance. While all agree that justice is good for its consequences, Socrates must show that it is also good in itself. His definition of justice and the other virtues effectively reframes the question: If you did not have to worry about the consequences, would you rather be mentally healthy or mentally ill?[10]

CHAPTER 9

Women at the Gym
Republic 5–7

> Then women among the guardians must strip naked and wear virtue instead of clothes.
>
> —Socrates in Plato, *Republic* 457a

Megan Rapinoe has made headlines both on and off the field. With her signature ever-changing hair color, she led the US Women's National Soccer Team to a World Cup win in 2015. The next year, she garnered national attention for joining Colin Kaepernick in taking a knee to protest racial injustice. As an out lesbian, Rapinoe speaks openly about the struggles faced by the queer community and people of color in the United States. Her biggest impact as an activist so far came to a head in 2022 as years of protest and chants of "Equal Pay!" led to the Equal Pay for Team USA Act, ensuring that members of all US teams competing globally, including World Cup and Olympic teams, receive equal compensation and benefits regardless of gender. In all of this, Rapinoe has become the current face of a much older movement.

For much of the twentieth century, women athletes struggled to obtain equal footing with men. The first modern Olympic Games, held in Athens in 1896, hosted exclusively male athletes. The next games, held in Paris in 1900, opened the doors to women competitors, who made up twenty-one of the thousand athletes present. Numbers have inched higher over the years, reaching 48 percent in the 2020 Games in Tokyo.[1] Mere access is one thing; actual support is another. The biggest stride, within the United States, came with the passing of Title IX of the Education Amendments of 1972. Title IX ensured that any school receiving federal funding provide equal access to athletics for students regardless of gender: hence the paired men's and women's teams familiar from today's universities. Equal Pay for Team USA marks Title IX's fiftieth anniversary.

The place of Title XI in this progression is significant. Over the last fifty years, women have taken on ever higher leadership positions in the United States and in other countries have risen to the highest elected offices. Insofar as leaders need to be educated to rule, and athletics are an important element of education, it is fitting that advances in politics, sports, and education have occurred at the same time. While Rapinoe has not yet held an elected office, many retired athletes do, including Sharice Davids, a professional mixed martial artist currently serving as a congresswoman from Kansas, and Gerald Ford, who played football for the University of Michigan and coached for Yale before becoming president. This interconnection of leadership, education, and sports sets the stage for the philosophical heart of *Republic*'s middle books.

Philosopher Kings and Queens: *Republic* 5

Socrates is ready to conclude his argument that justice is valuable in itself when his companions object, wanting to know more about his proposal to cede marriage contracts and child-rearing to the state (see 423e-424a). This represents the first of three "waves" of objections. Socrates's response will take up the next three books of *Republic*. Along the way, we get some of antiquity's most progressive thinking about gender equality, an argument for eugenics, reflections on the nature of work, and the later stages of Plato's liberal arts curriculum.

Socrates spells out the first wave of objections in terms of his comment that guardian men and women should have everything "in common" (449a-457c). This idea rests on the principle of specialization, which was used in building the ideal city and ended up being the foundation for Socrates's account of justice. In this context, however, it raises a puzzle. Socrates is committed to the following three claims (453b-c):

a. Each person should perform the task he or she is best suited to by nature.
b. Certain men and women should perform the task of guardian.
c. Men and women are different by nature.

How can a single person hold all three ideas at once? Once again, questions of education are driving the discussion. In this case, it is the question of whether women should share in the combination of music and athletics devised to train young men to become guardians. Wouldn't it be ridiculous for women to strip naked and exercise alongside men?

Our knowledge of women's athletics in antiquity is limited by the fragmentary nature of the sources.[2] Women did compete in athletic festivals, such as the festival of Hera, which took place at Olympia during the off years of the main Olympic celebrations, and at the all-female gymnasium dedicated to Artemis at Brauron.[3] At such sites, women and girls competed in footraces, either naked or wearing knee-length tunics, and used tracks slightly shorter than the men's. Such events likely reenacted the story of Atalanta, a mythical runner whose hand in marriage was promised to anyone who could beat her on the track (someone finally did, but only by resorting to tricks). In this story, Atalanta, like the goddesses Athena and Artemis, presents the virtues of a maiden (*parthenos*).[4] The Greek term *parthenos*, which underlies the name of Athena's most famous temple, refers to a period of life beginning with the onset of menstruation, when a young woman was seen as a potential bride, and ending with her eventual marriage. The Greek love of competition (*agōn*) is seen here as young women play hard to get by literally running away from potential suitors. The point was not to escape marriage but to weed out unworthy suitors while demonstrating independence, bravery, and discipline. It was at roughly the same period of life that young men would take on male lovers in relationships that in some ways mirrored heterosexual marriage. For young women, these rites of passage were wrapped up in religious celebrations that, like the main Olympic Games, were closed to members of the opposite sex. The exception to this gender segregation was Sparta. Building a society around military prowess, Sparta's semi-mythical lawgiver, Lycurgus, dictated that young women should join men to compete naked in running, wrestling, discus, and javelin. This would remove softness and make them fit mothers of strong men. If Socrates's companions are scandalized by the idea of women working out naked, the subtext is that this is a very Spartan idea. Socrates, in a bit of historical anthropology, points out that Greeks once thought it was ridiculous for men to work out naked. It was only thanks to the Spartans that the custom caught on. Once it did, the Greeks accepted that it is better to exercise stark naked, and dismissed as barbarous any foreign peoples who worked out wearing clothes.[5]

CHAPTER 9

Whether or not we accept the idea that working out naked is natural, this discussion of naked exercise gives Socrates a springboard for making a bigger point: when nature and convention clash, then let go of convention, even if people laugh at you. As Socrates puts it, female guardians will "clothe themselves in virtue rather than cloaks" (457a). The implications of this are huge. Over the course of history, human beings have adopted many unnatural conventions that became so ingrained that the thought of changing them has seemed ridiculous: slavery, sexism, racism, homophobia, abuse of natural resources, and so on. People have even defended all of these as part of the natural order. Others have called for change. In time, we have come to see such unnatural conventions for what they are. In this, activists in recent times and the distant past have followed the lead of Hippocrates, who looked to social and environmental causes for disparities between different demographics, and suggested novel ways of changing the status quo.[6] As Socrates puts it, we should never laugh at those who act "for the sake of what is good" (452d-e).[7]

When it comes to the puzzle at hand, Socrates concludes that he and his companions did not argue "according to forms/kinds" (*eidos*). Plato's concept of forms will be central to the lofty theory of knowledge set out in *Republic* 6-7. For the moment, the point is that when talking about what people are suited to "by nature," Socrates and his companions latched onto a superficial observation—that men impregnate women and women bear children (454d)—and they treated it as though it gave deep insight into differences relevant to questions of ruling. That is pretty much how all prejudice works: focus on the color of someone's skin and draw conclusions about their intelligence; focus on someone's sexual preferences and draw conclusions about their character. In this case, Socrates argues, issues of procreation are irrelevant to ruling a state. Even if women tend not to match men in bodily strength (455e), they should not be barred from leading roles in government.

To get a sense of just how progressive this suggestion is, we can look to another student of Socrates, Xenophon. In his book *Oikonomikos* (Household Management), Xenophon devotes chapter 7 to how a husband should train his wife. He suggests a man should find a wife when she is young and impressionable so that he can train her however he likes. In an ideal marriage, the wife is given great authority over the running of a household: overseeing the use and upkeep of property, managing the slaves, and so on. This reflects a division of responsibility: the husband works outside the home to bring wealth into the home; the wife works within the home to manage that wealth. While it was a slave economy that made all this possible, we find here a kind of equal footing between husband and wife at least. Still, according to Xenophon, the ideal bride is a blank slate. Plato, by contrast, seeks out women who are fit by nature to rule whole states, and he sets them on an educational regimen of music and athletics to help them develop their innate capacities.

The second wave of objections emerges from this education program. All the co-ed naked wrestling will eventually lead men and women to have sex (457c-471e). We cannot, however, have guardians bearing children at random. Like dog breeders and horse breeders, the ideal city will make sure it has "the best people" breeding at "the right time." To make this happen, elaborate religious ceremonies and a carefully rigged lottery will ensure the most outstanding men will father children from as many mothers as possible. The most outstanding women will, likewise, most often be put to the task of bearing children. (The role of ritual footraces in the marriage process provides a cultural context that would make all of this sound less strange to Plato's original readers.) These children, in turn, will be immediately taken from their parents and sent to a "rearing pen."

The goal of all this is to make the city as unified as possible. Within the guardian class, people will refer to their elders as mother and father, and their peers as sister and brother. These will not be empty titles: given that no one knows who his or her actual parents are, there is a legitimate chance that anyone of the right age could actually be one's parent. In the ultimate affront to ideals of private property, Socrates imagines his guardian class to be one big family. The rest of Socrates's response details how women and children will join men on the battlefield (466e-471e), and what precautions to take to ensure children do not get killed.

It may seem that Socrates is trying to dissolve the bonds that bind a family together, but his real goal is to stretch that intimacy across the entire guardian class. Given the size of ancient Greek city-states, that might include a couple thousand people. The point of all this is to make the city as a whole as healthy as possible. That said, Socrates argues that his guardians are happier than even Olympic victors (265d-266c). While the latter get to eat for free the rest of their lives as a reward for their athletic victories (compare Socrates's proposed "penalty" in *Apology*), the guardians have their whole lives taken care of as a reward for much more important victories on the battlefield and in the legislature.[8]

The third wave of objections is the most difficult to overcome: none of this will happen until philosophers are put in charge of the government. Glaucon is incredulous. Socrates's response takes up the rest of book 5 (472a-480a) and spills over into books 6 and 7. The first step is to define what makes a philosopher. Socrates offers an analogy: just as lovers of young men are attracted to anyone in the "bloom of youth," and wine lovers will happily drink any wine, philosophers are lovers of wisdom as a whole. Anyone who gets picky about learning, particularly when he or she is too young to see the purpose of a study, should not be considered a philosopher.

Glaucon pushes back (475d-e). By this definition, people who love to look at things and those who love to listen (*philēkoos*) are philosophers because they love learning through seeing and hearing.[9] But that includes people who fill their days with frivolous things. To respond, Socrates builds on an insight from the first wave of argument. There, he criticized people for latching onto superficial observations rather than making distinctions according to forms/kinds. Knowledge, properly speaking, gets at the real nature of things: the form that ultimately explains something. People who love sights and sounds just ride along the surface. It is one thing to know what songs or paintings you like; it is another thing to understand harmonic progressions or color theory. People who merely know what they like are not, however, totally ignorant. Sounds and sights are something. Still, these people do not get at the deep principles. What are these deep principles? We will turn to that shortly. For the moment, Socrates merely carves out three categories: *knowledge* grasps what each thing really is; *ignorance* grasps nothing at all; *opinion* sits in between, grasping the surface features of particular objects.

While *Republic* 5's three waves may look like a laundry list of complaints, the first wave's puzzle about whether women are fit to rule "by nature" sets up the definition of knowledge that is the key to resolving Glaucon's critique of the third wave of criticism about philosopher kings and queens. This, in turn, provides the setup for the subject of *Republic*'s most famous and philosophically hard-hitting passage: Plato's cave. As we turn to this, keep in mind that Plato introduces it through the question of whether women should work out at the gym, and the implications of that for education, society, and fundamental questions about knowledge.

It has taken millennia for the world to start making real *Republic*'s vision of opportunities shared equally between the sexes for sports, leadership, and education. We still have a way to go. Progress was made during antiquity, though. In the Hellenistic period, as Roman power expanded and Athens became a college town with a glorious past, the Roman elite, looking to display their Greek learning, started building gyms and founding games. By this point, Plato's works had become a pillar of the Greek canon. The same period saw an upsurge of athletic contests between girls and maidens. Women such as Thalassia of Ephesus, winner of the Sebastà Games in Naples, Italy, in 82 CE, were now publicly recognized as international champions.[10] While we cannot be certain of *Republic*'s role in all this, the Hellenistic period represents an early stage in a process that is still unfolding today.[11]

Educating Future Rulers: *Republic* 6 and 7

Republic 6 and 7 set out a series of three images: sun, line, and cave. The last of these, commonly known as Plato's cave, is excerpted and used in high-school curricula for a range of purposes. Within *Republic*, these interlocking images present a systematic reflection on the nature of knowledge. What has this to do with working out naked? If we step back, we find that these three images provide Plato's reflection on the sort of philosophical exercise Socrates pursued in dialogues set in gyms. Its account of education as a painful ordeal of being dragged into the light gives a new context for the tough-love approach Socrates advocated in *Lysis*. While there is much to be said about *Republic*'s central images, we will focus on them insofar as (a) they provide a rationale for Socrates's activities at the gym and (b) they help us understand *Republic*'s main argument that justice, along with virtue in general, is a form of mental health.

The Challenge of Raising Philosophers: *Republic* 6 (484a-503e)

From the perspective of most twentieth- and twenty-first-century philosophers, there is not much of interest in this portion of *Republic* 6, which is mostly taken up with Socrates complaining about how philosophy is practiced in his day. But if we hold it up against Socrates's dialogues set in gyms, certain ideas jump off the page.[12] First is the account of what kind of person is well suited to study philosophy. The pursuit of wisdom will draw students' appetites away from other things that could lead to vice; they will thus be disciplined, brave, and just. They will have to be fast learners, with a good memory and a sense of what is musical and proportionate (485–487). In *Republic* 2 and 3, it was music, taught in gyms, that nurtured this sense of proportionality. In *Republic* 6, Socrates points out that truth is akin to what is proportionate: when you experience that lightbulb moment, you realize that everything is in its place.[13] In this way, *Republic* 6 provides a rationale for the role of music in the early curriculum of *Republic* 2 and 3. In terms of modern developmental and positive psychology, this passage is a protracted discussion of aligning interests (what you like) with strengths (what you are good at) and developing them through practice (exploring your interests and developing your strengths). Ideally, the final stage of this process is finding purpose (aligning your strengths and interests with some need in the broader world).[14]

Would-be philosophers, however, are often undone by their own potential. If they happen to be well-born, good-looking, and tall like Charmides, they will likely be fawned over by all those around them. This flattery will give them impractical expectations, and make it hard for them to hear those who would point out the work they still have to do (494). As they grow older, love songs from admirers, such as Hippothales wrote for Lysis, are replaced by the praise of the mob, to which Socrates's beloved, Alcibiades, is too attached. Athenians loved public speaking, and Socrates identifies the most dangerous threat to would-be philosophers: the sophists. These teachers of public speaking, such as Thrasymachus, learn how to please the mob, telling it whatever it wants to hear. They call that skill wisdom, and sell it to students at a great price (492–493). Young people would be better off staying out of politics through exile, disinterest, or physical illness (496).

The second thing to note about this passage is that it challenges our conceptions of what a true philosopher is. Philosophy is not something you can merely pick up as a hobby or study in college. Plato calls for a complete overhaul of society. Only in this way, he argues, can we raise people who pursue wisdom with the erotic passion described by Diotima, and demonstrate their unwavering commitment to the city that raised them (503a). It is one thing to be committed to wisdom and the city; it is another to have the wisdom to rule the state as is actually best. To become full-fledged philosopher kings and queens, promising individuals must come to understand "the form of the good" (505a).

Sun, Line, Cave: *Republic* 6 and 7 (504a-518b)

To spell out what this means, Socrates offers three images: sun, line, and cave. The sun was the most famous of the three in antiquity, and it sits behind images of knowledge as illumination that are found in various Western religions. Today, it is the cave that has caught people's imaginations, inspiring movies such as *The Matrix* with its grand conspiracy theory. All three images present education as a process in which people are moved from shadows into the light. The sun spells out the stages of this process in a static way. The line and cave set out what it is like to move through such a process. Let us therefore start with the cave, which presents the goal of all this, and then loop back to the sun and line to fill in the details.

Socrates imagines prisoners chained in a cave since birth (*Republic* 7). All they have ever known are shadows on a wall. While this might seem far-fetched, our digital world with its media distortion and increasingly convincing AI artwork could rightly be seen as wrapping us in shadows and blinding us to reality. In Plato's scheme, there are four objects of experience, each with its own type of experience; there are also transitions between them, each of which is upsetting. If a prisoner is freed, he can come to see puppets moving in front of a fire. While this is painful and disorienting, he can eventually realize that the puppets are what created the shadows and that these puppets are more real than the shadows they cast. From here, he can be dragged out of the cave and into the sunlight. For someone who has spent his whole life in a cave, this is even more disorienting. At first all he can see are reflections of things. Over time, he can look at things themselves, which are the models after which the cave's puppets were fashioned. Eventually, he can look at the sun, the brightest thing of all. At this point, he can realize that it is the sun's light that makes the things of the world above visible and causes their growth and nourishment.

The sun analogy (*Republic* 6) provides a context for the journey out of the cave. The sun we see in the sky is the source of light, which connects visible things to our sense of sight and thus makes seeing possible. This visible sun, however, ends up being an analogy for the invisible, intelligible sun, which is the form of the good. The form of the good is the ultimate source of knowledge and truth, which constitute the light by which we can understand whether any particular thing is good. If we apply this to the cave allegory, then the visible sun, which we see with our eyes, corresponds to the fire in the cave, while the intelligible sun, which we grasp with our minds, is the true sun on the surface, that is, the intelligible world. With this, we arrive at something like *The Matrix*: the world we have known our entire lives is not the real one. If that is the case, how do we escape?

The line offers the final piece of the puzzle. Take a line and divide it in two. On the one side are the objects we grasp with our senses; on the other side are the objects we grasp with our intellect—for instance, apples with which we learn to count versus numbers themselves. Having divided the line into two sides, divide each side into two again. On the sensible side are images of things and the sensible things themselves (pictures of apples vs. actual apples). On the intelligible side are ideas (the form of apple and numbers themselves) and insight into how all these ideas fit together in a whole that is organic and good.[15] Socrates labels these four modes of grasping the world imagination, opinion, knowledge, and understanding (see table 2). According to this scheme, social media, which gives us images of things that can be sensed, is at the absolute bottom of the pile. How do we get from there to the form of the good?

Through the sun, the line, and the cave, Plato invites us to think about the world from new perspectives. Just as our teachers used apples to help us learn actual numbers, we can use actual numbers (and anything else we have real knowledge of) to learn the form of the good. The key is how we deal with hypotheses. When studying geometry, as developed by the Greeks, we lay out axioms that we do not question, and we use them to draw conclusions about other ideas and objects of sense experience. In Plato's terms, we start at knowledge (level 3 of the line) and either move around within knowledge or use knowledge to judge opinion and imagination (levels 2 and 1). Socrates suggests that we can also turn the other way and use these same hypotheses as "stepping stones" on our way to something better: nonhypothetical understanding of the good (level 4). How to do so takes up the rest of book 7.

Let us pause for a moment to note a couple of connections. While *Republic* 6 and 7 present lofty ideas, the process of moving out of the cave sounds a lot like conversational wrestling with Socrates: it is painful, disorienting, and people on the outside see it as ruining students' eyesight and "corrupting the youth" (*Apology*). Plato, speaking through Socrates, goes so far as to say that a person who returned from the surface to the cave would likely be killed by those living in the cave, as the historical Socrates actually was. For those who have seen the light,

Table 2

SENSIBLE		INTELLIGIBLE	
1. Imagination	2. Opinion	3. Knowledge	4. Understanding

however, none of the things that occupy the cave dwellers' attentions is worth taking all that seriously. This account of forms is generally agreed to be Plato's innovation, not something he picked up from the historical Socrates. There is a question, therefore, about how far we should go in trying to fit Socrates's activities at the gym into this framework. That said, even the Socrates character in *Republic* claims not to know whether any of this is true (506). If what we are dealing with are Plato's texts, it is an open question how we are to fit the educational program of *Republic* 6 and 7, *Symposium*'s ascent to beauty, and Socrates's aporetic debates in *Laches, Lysis, Charmides,* and *Republic* 1 into a coherent whole.

Plato's Advanced Curriculum: *Republic* 7 (518b-541b)

In *Republic* 2 and 3, a combination of music and gym exercise prepares the soul. Given the psychological theory of *Republic* 4, we can now say how: gym work nurtures the spirited part of the soul, while music imparts a sense of order and wholeness, priming the soul for discipline/moderation and justice, which work together to produce psychic harmony. But these gym-bound activities merely prepare the way (521d-522b). True virtue requires wisdom to rule, and that requires understanding. In particular, it requires understanding of the form of the good. As discussion of the sun, line, and cave has shown, this is "not a matter of putting knowledge into souls that lack it . . . but of turning the whole soul" (518b). Socrates outlines a fifty-year curriculum for leading people out of the cave.

The early stages of this curriculum in music and gym exercise are presented as a kind of "play" (536d-537b), which children engage in freely up to age seventeen.[16] Between seventeen and twenty years of age, they undertake the military training set out in *Republic* 5 (537b-c). Throughout, they will pick up bits of information in an unsystematic way. From twenty to thirty, they critically examine what they have learned, mostly by studying math: arithmetic, plain geometry, solid geometry, astronomy, and music theory (522c-531d). According to Plato, certain experiences can be explained simply in terms of themselves, while others "summon" us to look beyond sense experience and think in purely intellectual ways (523a-525c)—for instance, through mathematical modeling. Let us use an example from the gym to show how the earlier and later stages of this curriculum connect.

Socrates once said that makeup will make someone seem beautiful, but gym training will make him be beautiful (Plato, *Gorgias* 465b).

CHAPTER 9

As we have seen in Plato's *Charmides*, the Greeks had plenty of opinions about male beauty, which were not simply "the bigger, the better." While conventions of bodybuilding have changed over the centuries, they all make use of proportions: waist to shoulders, biceps to calves, and so on.[17] Prior to any philosophical inquiry, Greek sculptors saw the human form as echoing the divine. The Greek statues that line museums, which are mostly Roman copies in marble of Greek originals in bronze, still take our breath away. Such statues embody ratios that we find in musical instruments in the relative lengths of pipes or strings. The same can be said for Greek architecture, much of which is based on the golden ratio, which can also be found everywhere from ferns and conch shells to spiral galaxies.

In short, music, geometry, and the other mathematical sciences allow us to understand experiences that students encountered in the early curriculum through play.[18] The point here is that human beings instinctively find numerical ratios beautiful, whether they are heard or seen. These same ratios structure elements of the natural world that are as disparate as the sound of a string, the curve of a conch shell, and the shape of a human body. In Plato's curriculum, philosophers spend their twenties figuring out the mathematical models behind everyday experience. The goal is to study each branch to its completion. Here the sense of order instilled by one's early education takes center stage. The real philosophers will not stop until they have that final lightbulb moment described by Diotima in *Symposium*, as they track each field to its basic principles.

That, however, is merely "prelude" (531d). Philosophers will spend their next five years, age thirty to thirty-five, studying pure dialectic. Through it, they leave the senses behind entirely and figure out how the basic principles they found in these different fields all fit together in a single, overarching system. In today's terms, this would be a grand unified theory. In Plato's terms, it is the vision of the form of the good. What does such a vision entail? To answer this, we would need to move beyond images and think via pure thought. Socrates tells his companions he can take them no further and ends this part of the discussion by merely pointing the way.

The true philosophers, having made it to this vision of the good, will then go back into the cave to work as soldiers for the next fifteen years, from age thirty-five to fifty. At this point, they will find out whether they can apply their learning to politics without compromising their principles. Those who succeed will become philosopher kings and queens. Unlike most rulers, they will approach ruling as a burden by comparison to the delights of philosophy, yet one that they must shoulder for the sake of the city that raised them.[19] While the masses will be left to chase shadows, people with a sense of how the world actually works will keep the masses in line as best they can. Having an army at their disposal will help. The goal is for the city as a whole to flourish.[20]

The Method of Hypothesis in *Republic* 1–7

Republic's exploration of justice hangs on the philosopher's understanding of the form of the good, yet it is this key detail that Socrates says he cannot explain. What should we make of this gaping hole at the heart of *Republic*'s argument? In chapters 7 and 8, I argued that *Symposium* is structured by Plato's method of hypothesis. This method proceeds as investigators keep identifying the question behind the question, until they arrive at a most basic question. The result is a string of hypotheses that eventually ends at a nonhypothetical first principle. At this point, they move into confirming (a) that all of these hypotheses in fact follow from the first principle, and (b) the truth of the first principle itself. We find the same process at work in *Republic*.[21] In *Republic* 1, Socrates sets out the initial hypothesis, that justice is profitable, which in *Republic* 2 he refines to justice is profitable in itself. To explain why, Socrates sets out an account of justice for the city and for the individual (*Republic* 2–4). Book 4's accounts of both civic and personal justice turn on the rule of wisdom, raising the further question, What is wisdom? *Republic* 5 refines the question, as the three waves of objections, following from the account of civic justice, clarify the need to grasp forms, and raise the new question: Knowledge of which form constitutes wisdom? *Republic* 6 and 7 answers: knowledge of the form of the good. This raises the final question: What is the form of the good? To answer, Socrates lays out his fifty-year curriculum. At this point, we might undertake his fifty-year course of study and see what it gets us. If all goes according to Socrates's plan, the result will be an understanding of a nonhypothetical first principle grounded in the basic structure of reality.[22] Alternatively, we could treat Socrates's account of the good as a hypothesis and confirm how well it answers all the questions that came before. Given this curriculum's emphasis on mathematics and concepts of balance borrowed from medicine and music, we can assume that the form of the good is somehow related to ideas of harmony, and the bringing together of disparate parts into balanced, organic wholes. By critically applying this idea to the questions raised since book 1, we can come to a provisional/hypothetical answer to Thrasymachus's initial question, Is justice profitable? This is Socrates's main task for *Republic*'s remaining three books.[23]

CHAPTER 10

Justice as Civic and Mental Health
Republic 8–10

> Like a wrestler, give me the same hold again.
> —Glaucon in Plato, *Republic* 544b

Is justice good in itself, and not merely for its consequences? After several twists and turns, with digressions on education and selective breeding programs, and with Glaucon's encouragement here to give him "the same hold," Socrates finally returns to Glaucon's challenge from book 2. Central to Socrates's elaborate response is the fusion of music and gymnastics laid out in *Republic* 2 and 3. People raised in this way will have their souls in order and a clear sense of how the world actually works. They will make decisions with long-term, overall goods in mind. They will not be particularly concerned with power, fame, or money, so they will not be tempted to abuse their power. In short, they will be mentally healthy and embody *Republic*'s four central virtues. The ideal state, by analogy, will be ruled by these ideal people, who then will keep everyone else in line. If this is what justice is, is it not attractive simply in itself?[1] In *Republic* 8 and 9, Socrates drives home this point, first, by comparing justice to its various alternatives, both in the state and in the individual soul (545c-576b). This, in turn, sets the stage for four arguments that justice is, in fact, preferable to all other ways of being (576b-580c).

Civic and Spiritual Decay: *Republic* 8 and 9 (545c-576b)

As Aristotle would later put it, there are many ways to miss a target, but only one way to hit it (*Nichomachean Ethics* 1106c). If we agree with Socrates that both the soul and the city are divided into three parts, and that when it comes to both city and soul, one of these parts must rule, then there is one way to hit the target of justice (putting reason/philosophers in charge), and two ways to miss it (putting spirit/auxiliaries in charge or putting appetite/moneymakers in charge). To say that a part of the soul rules is to say what takes priority. Athletes tend to be spirited people, who like to win. They will sacrifice bodily pleasure through grueling training in the pursuit of victory. Socrates sees this as putting spirit before appetite, and he finds it commendable. But what about someone who puts a desire for winning ahead of a desire for truth, for instance, by using steroids? It is not that such a person is uninterested in truth or bodily pleasures, he is simply more interested in winning. He lets his desire for winning rule.

Things get more complicated as Socrates lays out his argument. Appetite, it turns out, is internally complex. (Socrates refers to it as a many-headed chimera.) The first division is between necessary and unnecessary appetites. We saw this in *Republic* 2's distinction between a modest city, where the basic needs for food, shelter, and sex are met, and the city with a fever that goes beyond basic needs by bringing in prostitutes, luxuries, and pork. The athletic training of book 2 responded to this division through its emphasis on a moderate diet, which helps young souls educate their appetites through moderation/discipline.[2] Unnecessary desires are further divided into the lawful and the lawless. The Greek for "lawless," *paranomos*, does not mean just "illegal" but "outside the norm."[3] We might say "taboo" or "gross." Socrates gives the example of having sex with animals. Wanting a big house is one thing; bestiality is another. Given the divisions within appetite, it turns out there are five classes of goods that one may seek, and five analogous classes that could rule a soul or city. Socrates refers to them as constitutions (see table 3).

Rather than merely laying these out for comparison, Socrates arranges them in a process of decay. Nothing lasts forever, and he sets out how over the course of generations an aristocratic city/person will give birth to a timocratic city/person, and so on.[4]

While *Republic* 1 was frustratingly brief in throwing around big ideas without defining them, *Republic* 8–9 can seem somewhat plodding as

Table 3

CONSTI-TUTION	CITY RULED BY	PERSON RULED BY	GOOD SOUGHT	DISCUSSED IN
Aristocracy	Philosophers	Reason	Wisdom and good of whole	Republic 4-7
Timocracy	Warriors/Auxiliaries	Spirit	Honor	Republic 8 (545c-550c)
Oligarchy	The rich	Necessary appetites	Money	Republic 8 (550c-555b)
Democracy	The masses	Unnecessary, lawful appetites	Freedom	Republic 8 (555b-562a)
Tyranny	Tyrant	Unnecessary, unlawful appetites	Passion	Republic 8 (562a)-9 (576b)

Socrates and his companions dutifully walk through these various options. The main point, for present purposes, is that decay comes about when people do not hold to the proper curriculum of music and gym training. This leads to "unmusical" people who care more for reputation than learning, thus prompting the slip from aristocracy to timocracy. Such people/states, who thanks to their gym training still live highly disciplined lives, eventually start hoarding money. This prompts the slip from timocracy into oligarchy. When this discipline gives out, people turn from necessary appetites to unnecessary ones, prompting the slip from oligarchy to democracy.[5] Such people see themselves as "free." Socrates sees them as flighty. They have neither the discipline nor the grace brought about by rigorous training in music and athletics, so they float from one thing to another, following trends and chasing shadows. Having such people set policy is a recipe for disaster.

In political terms, Socrates sees tyrants as people who can successfully play a crowd, capitalizing on political and economic instability, to grab power. If successful, a tyrant eliminates anyone smart enough or strong enough to oppose him, surrounding himself with yes-men and keeping everyone else distracted via smear campaigns and fearmongering. In an ironic twist, democracy, which celebrates freedom, gives way to tyranny in which basically everyone is enslaved. The tyrannical individual, meanwhile, is someone who lives his life for unlawful, unnecessary desires. Socrates refers to this kind of desire as passion. The Greek term for "passion," *erōs*, is the subject of Plato's *Symposium*. Here it means something more like "lust."

If Socrates's division of the state and the soul are correct, then aristocracy, timocracy, oligarchy, democracy, and tyranny are the options for structuring a city or soul.[6] Which state would you want to live in? Which kind of person would you want to be? Where would you place today's societies within this scheme?

Comparing Constitutions: *Republic* 9 (576b-580c)

Modern readers, particularly in the United States, are often baffled by Plato's attack on democracy, and its denigration of freedom. Karl Popper famously dedicated the first volume of his work *The Open Society and Its Enemies* to Plato.[7] Such critiques, I suggest, stem from running together two differing conceptions of freedom. People today tend to think of freedom in terms of freedom from external restraints. The more options you have, the freer you are. We see this kind of freedom at play in *Republic* 8's presentation of democracy. But there is also the freedom to pursue the good. We find this in Socrates's presentation of the aristocracy, where each member of society is free to pursue whatever he or she is best at by nature. Understood this way, the freer you are, the fewer options you have. Perfect freedom is found in reducing your options to the one right one.[8] In practical terms, what would you rather have: the one job that is perfect for you or a choice between a bunch of jobs, none of which you will ever be satisfied with? If you are a typical American, you will probably want both: unrestrained options and the perfect job. Socrates's point is that this is not realistic. Some restraints are good. Finding out what you are not good at can be a useful step toward finding what you should be doing.[9]

The tyrant, Socrates argues, is an extreme example of someone who strives for freedom but ends up enslaving himself in the process (576b-580c). On the outside, he lives surrounded by bodyguards in constant fear of people challenging his rule. On the inside, the parts of his soul are in full-out civil war. His passion drives him to ignore truth or reputation. As a result, he will take ill-informed actions and then regret them. Lacking both musical grace and athletic discipline, he has no consistency and is constantly unsettled. In *Republic*'s terms, this person is severely mentally ill.

The truly free person is the one with a just, aristocratic soul, for whom reason rules over appetites with the aid of spirit. He enjoys mental health.[10] Even if we accept this argument, having a just soul may still not sound like much fun. Socrates responds to this worry with two arguments that make use of the fact that each part of the soul has its characteristic pleasure. Everyone is familiar with the sensual pleasures of appetite. Athletes are well familiar with the spirited pleasure of victory. Anyone who has worked through a problem and come to a lightbulb moment has experienced the rational pleasure of discovering truth. Socrates's first argument is that since (a) philosophers prefer rational pleasures to the pleasures of spirit and appetite and (b) philosophers are unique in being familiar with all three kinds of pleasure, rational pleasures are, therefore, the best pleasures (580d-583a). Socrates's second argument is that the only way to get all three kinds of pleasure is by putting reason in charge (583a-588b). Sensory pleasures are fleeting. To live your life going for nothing more than sensual pleasures is not a recipe for satisfaction. Likewise, spirited pleasures of honor and reputation can be a good thing. They can also get ugly. While it is fine to want a good reputation, we want to be known for the right things. How can you tell what the right things are? Use your reason to perform periodic reality checks. That is what reason is for: it looks for the good overall and works out ways to satisfy each of the soul's three parts. In short, philosophers have the most fun.

At this point, the two tracks of Socrates's city/individual analogy come close to colliding. On the one hand, the ideal city needs people to occupy each of the three classes; yet according to book 9's argument, only philosophers lead the best lives. Would the auxiliaries and productive classes be content with second- or third-best? Even worse, if wisdom is required for happiness, and only philosophers are able to attain knowledge of holistic goods, is it not the case that philosophers will be the only people with harmonious souls and happy lives? Kevin Crotty responds to this worry by suggesting that individuals' pursuit of whatever profession best fits them is what generates virtue for both the individual and the state. Philosophy/governance is one profession, which is driven by understanding of the form of the good. Carpentry is another profession, within the productive class, which is driven by knowledge of the form of, say, the couch.[11] In either case, professionals use reason to look to forms and guide their work. Furthermore, people sincerely invested in their work, whether it be statecraft or carpentry, will take pride in it and not cut corners even when they can get away with doing so (compare Gyges's ring in *Republic* 2). Such people set spirited desires above appetitive ones. Pouring oneself into a career that fits one's own talents and interests becomes a recipe for developing an ordered, virtuous soul.[12] It also makes for competent professionals who make useful contributions to society. Here, we find a mutual dependence between the virtue and flourishing of the individual and the virtue and flourishing of the state. Rather than see a zero-sum game, where the philosophers get the best lives and everyone else gets scraps, Plato presents a picture of mutual dependence, encouraging us to set aside concerns for comparative ranking and to look honestly at how each of us can create a meaningful life by contributing to the community.

Socrates closes *Republic* 9 with another image: inside each of us is a human, a lion, and a chimera (588b-592b). The human, which he calls the most godlike, represents our reason; the lion represents our spirit; and the chimera, with its many heads, represents our appetite. Giving in to unnecessary passions merely feeds the chimera, which proceeds to enslave our inner lion and human. Without anyone holding it in check, the chimera (particularly its most bestial heads) grows to the point that not even it is satisfied. It is bad enough to have unlawful desires. Acting on them just makes things worse. The worst case is when you act on them and get away with it. The point of punishment is to tame the inner beast. In a complete inversion of Thrasymachus's argument from *Republic* 1, getting away with injustice is the worst thing possible for the unjust person. It is much better to have one's inner lion keep the chimera in check. Best of all is for one's inner human to act as the master animal-handler, taming both the lion and the chimera. In this way, the individual can act on necessary, and perhaps even unnecessary yet lawful, passions, albeit within reason. He may also care about status within reason. This is the image of justice as psychic harmony and mental health that Socrates has been building for the last eight books.[13]

Afterword: *Republic* 10

Having come full circle and tied a neat bow on the argument, Socrates keeps going. The first half of *Republic* 10 ties together the discussions of poetry that are scattered throughout books 2-9.[14] The second half looks to the rewards of justice after death, recalling Socrates's discussion with Cephalus at the start of *Republic* 1. This section opens with a somewhat convoluted argument for the soul's immortality, which makes ample use of the body/soul parallels Socrates has used throughout *Republic* (608c-612b). Perhaps more convincing is the argument that, despite what was agreed to in addressing Glaucon's challenge, just people typically do receive the benefit of justice while alive (612b-614a). Unjust people, as Socrates sees it, are like runners who sprint ahead at the start but fall apart before completing a race. Just people, by contrast, are like distance runners whose steady pace and long-term goals make them victorious in the end.

Socrates drives the point home by offering a myth (614a-621b).[15] Er, so the story goes, died, traveled to the underworld, and then returned to life without drinking from the river of forgetfulness. His story serves as a cautionary tale about the postmortem consequences of our actions during life. Each soul spends one thousand years being rewarded, punished, or chastised for its actions on earth. At the end of each cycle, souls are brought together by the Fates and given a choice of lives (617d-621a). Er observes a number of mythological figures, including the female athlete, Atalanta, who decides to come back as a man. The philosophical point is that people with souls out of balance make bad life choices. Er watched one soul dazzled by wealth choose the life of a tyrant, only to learn that he will end up eating his own children. Even those who get the last pick can find a life that will be satisfactory. As *Republic* 2-9 have shown through the psychology of the three-part soul, what we value most, what rules within our soul, will shape the kind of life we lead.

Plato's Response to Socrates

Socrates's approach to philosophy is famously summed up at *Apology* 38a: "The unexamined life is not worth living for a human being." In *Apology*, Socrates embodies human wisdom: not thinking that one knows things that one does not know is the virtue associated with the examined life. In living such a life, one embraces perplexity (*aporia*) and continues the search for knowledge. The end goal, however, is divine wisdom, whose robust content allows the gods to live lives far beyond any human happiness. *Republic* sits somewhere between these two extremes. Socrates, here speaking for Plato, moves beyond the *aporia* of book 1, grounding an account of civic and personal virtue in more fundamental accounts of human nature, and how human beings relate to one another and to the fundamental structures of the world. All of this, however, is explicitly presented as an elaborate hypothesis, not yet anchored in nonhypothetical knowledge of the form of the good. The theory is provisional. If Socratic cross-examination (*elenchos*) ends with a mostly negative "It turns out we don't know what we thought we did: let us keep inquiring," then *Republic*'s method of hypothesis ends with a more positive "We still lack knowledge, but let us treat this theory as provisional, and see where it takes us." In short, neither *Republic* nor *Symposium* offers final, set-in-stone answers to Socrates's questions. Rather, both works point beyond themselves to more fundamental realities and provide regimes of spiritual exercise for pursuing them, be they *Symposium*'s erotic pursuit of immortal beauty or *Republic*'s fifty-year curriculum of music, gymnastics, math, and dialectic. The nature of the exercise has shifted from Socratic *elenchos* to Platonic hypothesis. In both cases, though, Socrates, his companions in dialogue, and Plato's readers are all left with quite a lot of work to do.

This work-in-progress reading plays out in the lives of *Republic*'s hypothetical philosopher kings and queens. While it takes fifty years for them to come to knowledge of the form of the good, this learning is merely a prelude to the real task of governance. Such knowledge does not constitute an answer key or how-to manual for statecraft. Rather, philosophical rulers will move constantly between the form of the good and concrete political situations, much like the carpenter checking his work against the form of the couch. Here again, Eryximachus's image of *erōs* as a process of filling and emptying provides a fitting image for the philosophical life, as philosopher rulers bring mortal systems in line with immortal models through a process that continues for as long as the city lasts.

In reading *Republic* and *Symposium* against the background of the ancient gym, I have highlighted their debt to Hippocratic medicine. Plato scholars routinely recognize the holistic nature of such ideas insofar as bodily, mental, and civic health are understood in terms of internal balance. However, Hippocratic thinking is holistic also in how individual people and even demographic groups are conceptualized as belonging to larger systems. Hippocratic doctors are forerunners of current movements in preventative medicine, which make social and environmental determinants of health central to regimens of care. The size and complexity of our modern population, global economy, and information systems make systemic thinking even more necessary than it was for Plato's original readers. We see this in social justice movements, which call attention to entrenched inequalities such as the effects of social determinants of health on different racial groups (see the introduction to part 2). *Republic*, for all its complexity, provides a streamlined version of Plato's own world. And several centuries later, *Republic* gives modern readers an opportunity to practice systemic thinking.

In approaching *Symposium* and *Republic* through the lens of the gymnasium, we have also highlighted the importance of purpose in the educational programs they set out. This focus on purpose has been largely ignored by scholars.[16] Or, worse, people like Popper read *Republic* as an attempt to crush individual autonomy in service of an authoritarian state. Parallels between *Republic*'s sorting mechanisms and current work in developmental and positive psychology show Popper's thinking to be backward. A good deal of the systemic thinking advanced in *Republic* involves identifying individuals' strengths and interests and finding ways to nurture those in service of the greater community's needs. Helping individuals find purpose does not crush autonomy; it enables it. Today, talk of purpose is too often associated with religion. Outside of schools with religious affiliations, questions of purpose tend to be addressed in career offices and not as part of the academic curriculum. Plato bridges the gap between academics and career counseling. Via the method of hypothesis, *Republic* and *Symposium* invite readers to separate and explore different aspects of their inner lives and broader contexts, and then to step back and think creatively about how they might fit all these pieces together.

Yet Plato goes beyond today's psychologists. For him, it is not enough merely to pursue purpose (aligning one's skills and interests with broader needs): this purpose must also be grounded in a sense of transcendence.[17] We must bring mortal life into sync with immortal models. This can sound otherworldly when compared to a typical career-office conversation. Athletics and music, once again, bring Plato's thinking back to earth. For many of us, finding a rhythm is a key experience of bringing the mortal and immortal into sync.[18] Whether or not we go on to pursue formal study in mathematics and physiology, Plato's bigger point is that immortal realities permeate the world around us. In the political realm, *Symposium*'s striving after immortality is captured in today's concerns for sustainability.[19] As human beings, we straddle the mortal/immortal divide: the secret to happiness is the constant pursuit of excellence as we continually and creatively shape our daily lives around eternal standards in our professional pursuits, whatever they may be. We might disagree with the particulars of *Republic*'s class system or the way Plato divides the soul, but by engaging in such disagreements we draw closer to ourselves and closer to the world we live in. With this, we are set on our way to building our own best lives.

PART III

Aristotle's Elite Performers

> In the Olympic Games, it is not the finest and the strongest who are crowned victor, but those who compete: for it is from this group that winners come. The same is true in life.
>
> —Aristotle, *Nicomachean Ethics* 1.8, 1099a3-6

Aristotle studied at Plato's Academy and went on to establish his own school in another gym, the Lyceum. His followers are known as the Peripatetics, thanks to their habit of discussing ideas while walking around. Aristotle was also a Greek speaker, working in the shadow of Socrates and Plato, so when he turned to spelling out the good life, he used terms and ideas that had been forged in the *palaistra*. Like these earlier figures, Aristotle understood flourishing (*eudaimonia*) to be the goal of human life, virtue (*aretē*) to be central to that flourishing, and education to be vital for pursuing both. He even followed his teachers in focusing on bravery, moderation, justice, wisdom, and friendship as the core of this virtue theory.

Aristotle opens *Nicomachean Ethics* (*NE*) with a sketch of happiness as a life of excellent activity, using elite performers—in athletics, music, and intellectual pursuits—as models, and then spends the rest of *NE*'s ten books filling out the details of this opening account.[1] Athletic concepts are scattered throughout. Some of these have been widely acknowledged, such as his account of character formation based on regimens of strength conditioning (chapter 12). Others have been passed over without comment, such as the competitive aspect of the term "excellence" (*aretē*) in both English and Greek (chapter 11). Scholars have discussed other terms, such as "ornament" (*kosmos*), at length without acknowledging their athletic connotation as relevant to *NE* (chapter 13). The athletic resonances of *kalon* are further obscured for English readers, given the term is often translated as "noble" or "fine" rather than "beautiful."[2] Meanwhile, scholars have outright rejected Aristotle's claim that friends will compete and strive to outperform each other in performing virtuous acts (chapter 16).

The problem is not merely that current scholarship has some gaps when it comes to Aristotle's use of athletic concepts. Rather, by suppressing some and ignoring others, current scholarship has made it impossible to see how these scattered pieces fit together in a single, unified system that binds *NE* into a coherent project and offers fresh perspectives on standing debates—for instance, whether human happiness consists in "becoming immortal" through the pursuit of many valuable activities or a single most valuable activity (chapter 17). As a first step in remedying this situation, I will use this introduction to lay out relevant aspects of Greek athletic culture that would have been common knowledge among Aristotle's original readers.

Herakles and the Olympic Games

Olympia, along with Delphi, Nemea, and Isthmia, was host of one of the stephanic games, at which victors were crowned with a wreath (*stephanos*). The Pythian Games at Delphi honored Apollo and awarded crowns woven from his sacred tree, the laurel. The Olympic Games honored Zeus and used crowns of olive branches. These were awarded in the temple of Zeus, as athletes stood in front of a forty-one-foot, gold-and-ivory statue of Zeus, who was himself wearing an olive crown and holding his eagle staff in one hand and the goddess Nikē (Victory) in the other. The parallel headgear was no accident: Greek gods were seen as ideals of perfection to aspire to. A winner in the Olympic Games came as close to this ideal as a mortal could manage. This ideology was communicated through both art and literature.

The exterior of Zeus's temple provided context for the crowning ceremony. The eastern pediment, situated in the triangular space under the temple's roofline, tells the mythical story of the local king, Oinomaos, who offered his daughter's hand in marriage to anyone who could beat him in chariot racing. Losers were executed on the spot. One contestant, Pelops, finally won by switching the linchpin in Oinomaos's chariot for one made of wax. Pelops won the girl, Hippodamaia, and became king of the southern region of the Greek mainland, whose name incorporates his: the Peloponnesus. The story of Pelops served as the archetype for the chariot races at the Olympic Games. The western pediment of the temple of Zeus depicts a local tribe, the Lapiths, who invited their centaur neighbors to a wedding. The centaurs, being only half human, got drunk and start abducting Lapith women. Fighting ensued. This scene, also prominently depicted on the Parthenon, in Athens, provides an allegory for the triumph of fully human civilization (Greeks) over half-human barbarism (non-Greeks). The Olympic Games were crucial to this self-understanding, as every four years Greek city-states, which were often at war with one another, would declare a sacred truce and gather in Olympia for an event so revered that the Greeks used the names of its victors as a way of telling time.[3]

Situated below the two pediments were groups of six sculptural scenes, called metopes, that depicted the twelve labors of Herakles. As the son of Zeus and the mortal woman Alkmene, Herakles roused the envy of Zeus's wife, Hera, and was sentenced to perform a series of labors (*athla, ponoi*) for the king Eurystheus.[4] These labors include slaying and capturing monsters, fetching objects, holding up the sky, and cleaning stables by diverting the course of a river. Like the Lapiths, who overcame the half-human, half-civilized centaurs, Herakles's battles with monsters embody a triumph of enlightened civilization over the forces of chaos and barbarism. As a reward for his labors, Herakles ascended to Mount Olympus upon his death, where he became a god and took Hēbē (Youth) as his immortal wife.

According to myth, Herakles also founded the Olympic Games. His heroic labors (*athla*) were replaced by competitions (*agōnes*) in pentathlon, wrestling, boxing, and chariot racing, for which victors earned rewards (*athla*) in the form of olive crowns (*stephanoi*). As Herakles became immortal through his labors, athletes (people who compete for *athla*) sought to embody the divine through competition. This, however, was not a matter of merely brute force. Just as Herakles outsmarted various opponents, and Pelops won Hippodamia through cunning, Olympic competitions required rigorous training, refined technique, and thinking on one's feet.[5]

These connections between Olympian artwork and Aristotelian ethics are made explicit in the victory odes of the poet Pindar. Born half a century before Socrates, Pindar weaves together many of the key terms that Socrates would come to question. Pindar's *Odes*, therefore, help us see the default assumptions *NE*'s original readers would have made regarding ideas such as *aretē, kalon, athlon, stephanos,* and *eudaimonia*. Aristotle tells us that virtues aim at the *kalon*, for which Pindar gives us Olympic victory as a model. This slices through the disagreement over whether to translate *kalon* as "noble" or "beautiful" by presenting certain activities as obviously worthy of pursuit simply because they are awesome.

Pindar also helps us understand a term that readers of *NE* have for the most part gotten backward: *kosmos*. The basic meaning is "order," such as the way a general would put troops in order.[6] In Aristotle's hands, this sense of the word comes to mean "universe" or "cosmos" (in the English sense).[7] Yet there are another two meanings built on this one. One has to do with imposing order on something from outside through clothes, makeup, or other adornments. This is the root of our term *cosmetics*. This meaning shows up in Hesiod's *Theogony* 586-588 and *Works and Days* 72-76 as the poet describes the creation of Pandora, whose name means "All-Gift," since she was adorned by various goddesses and made into a trap for mankind. A *kosmos* in this sense conceals one's true nature in a deceptive way. Pindar, by contrast, uses *kosmos* in the *Odes* to refer to victory crowns or to the victory ode itself.[8] In this sense, a *kosmos* draws attention to inner virtue that has been made manifest through competition. While a *kosmos*, in the Pandora sense, conceals one's true nature by covering a woman's body, a *kosmos* in the athletic case reveals one's true nature as men compete in the nude.[9] Scholars across the board have assumed the cosmetic reading in Aristotle. In doing so they get key passages of *NE* backward, as I will argue in the chapters to follow.

As a poet for hire, Pindar composed poems to commemorate victories in all four stephanic games. In each ode, he weaves the individual's victory into a larger context of family history and mythological models, often conveyed through obscure references. Ideas now familiar from philosophy are ubiquitous. *Olympian* 3 sets these ideas out in a way that is particularly useful for our purposes. The dedicatee is Theron, tyrant of the city of Akragas in Sicily, whose team won the chariot race in 476 BCE. As owner of the team, Theron did not physically compete. Still, his entry into the games, as in many of Pindar's *Odes*, is seen as a labor (*ponos*), since it is voluntary, competitive in spirit, and exposes one to the danger of defeat.[10] The original performance of *Olympian* 3 was likely at a feast in honor of the children of Leda and Tyndareus: the twin gods, Castor and Pollux, and their more famous sister, Helen of Troy.[11] The work begins with a nod to this occasion.

> To please the hospitable sons of Tyndareus
> and Helen of the beautiful hair,

> and to honor famous Akragas is my prayer,
> as I begin a hymn to Theron for his Olympic victory;
> this is the finest reward
> for horses with never-wearying hoofs.
> This is why, I believe, the Muse stood before me
> as I composed in a brilliant new way
> to fit my voice of glorious celebration to the Dorian measure;
> since the victory wreaths (*stephanoi*) woven in his hair
> exact payment from me of this god-inspired debt:
> to combine in due harmony the many-voiced lyre, the cry of pipes,
> and the placement of words in honor of Aenesidamus' son [Theron].

Before her abduction, Helen was queen of Sparta in the Peloponnesus, where Greek was spoken in the Doric dialect. Hence Pindar's use of it for this poem, where he likens the weaving of a victor's crown to his poetic weaving of words and music. The poem continues as he turns to the origin of the practice of bestowing victory crowns.

> Pisa too instructs me to speak out:
> for from there come god-given songs to men,
> whenever the unswerving Hellene judge, an Elean of Aetolian stock,
> fulfilling Herakles' ancient orders, sets above a man's brow
> the glory (*kosmos*) of the grey-green olive in his hair,
> which once Amphitryon's son [Herakles] brought from Istrus' shadowed springs
> to be the most beautiful (*kalon*) reminder of contests (*agōnes*) at Olympia.[12]

Here we have *kosmos* used interchangeably with *stephanos* (crown). While it is "a most beautiful reminder" (Pindar uses the superlative form of *kalon*), the beauty comes from what it reminds one of: competition. Pindar explains:

> Herakles had by his eloquence won over
> the people living beyond the North Wind, Apollo's servants.
> With honorable intent, he begged from them
> for the all-welcoming grove of Zeus
> a tree to furnish shade for all,
> and to be a crown (*stephanos*) for deeds of virtue (*aretai*).
> For by now altars had been dedicated to his father [Zeus],

> and the gold-charioted moon at mid-month evening
> had shown her eye full upon him.
> He had laid down the great games' holy principle of judgement,
> and had established the four-year cycle for his festival,
> to be held beside the sacred banks of Alpheus;
> but the land of Pelops grew no lovely trees
> in the dales of the son of Cronus [Zeus].

Here, Pindar credits Herakles for introducing the olive tree to the Peloponnesus and for establishing the Olympic Games. Meanwhile, *aretē* in its plural form, *aretai*, can mean not only virtues but deeds of virtue. Pindar specifies that it is the latter for which a crown is given.[13] From here, Pindar recounts Herakles's travels in service to Eurystheus, which eventually brought him face-to-face with an olive grove. The passage concludes:

> There he stood and marveled at the trees,
> and a sweet desire seized him to plant some
> around the point in the twelve-lap course where horses turn.
> And so today he gladly attends this his festival
> with the godlike twins, sons of deep-girdled Leda.

By invoking Herakles's presence at their celebration, Pindar highlights the capacity for athletic competition to bring mortals in contact with the divine. This provides the kernel of the idea behind the Olympic Games as formal undertakings:

> Departing for Olympus he instructs them
> to take charge of the admired games (*agōna*),
> where men compete in virtue (*aretē*) and swift chariots are driven.
> And so, I believe, my spirit urges me to tell Theron
> and the Emmenidae that glory (*kudos*) has come to them
> through the gift of the sons of Tyndareus [Castor and Pollux],
>   expert horsemen,
> because of all mortals they honor them
> with the most numerous hospitable feasts,
> preserving by their pious intention the rites of the blessed
>   (*makaros*) gods.

By calling the gods blessed (*makaros*), Pindar introduces an idea that figures periodically in *NE*, either as a synonym for happiness (*eudaimonia*) or for a state beyond it (chapter 11). Pindar draws the poem to a close by first quoting himself (*Olympian* 1.1 opens with the phrase "Water is best") and then drawing all this back to Theron, whose victory is being celebrated.

> If water is best (*aristeuō*), and gold the most revered of all possessions,
> now Theron in his turn, by his deeds of virtue (*aretai*),
> has travelled from his home to the world's limits
> and lays hold of the pillars of Herakles [the Strait of Gibraltar].
> Further than this neither simpletons nor wise should go.
> I shall not venture there; I should be a fool to try.

In short, winning at the Olympics is the best thing a human being can strive for. In the process, Theron, like Herakles, approaches the blessed (*makaros*) gods and becomes immortal. Crowns (*stephanoi*), meanwhile, are not mere decoration (*kosmos* in its cosmetic sense): their beauty (*kalon*) comes from being won through contests of virtuous deeds (*aretai*). They are a way to reveal one's inner worth (thus functioning as a *kosmos* in its athletic sense). While Pindar does not differentiate between virtues and deeds of virtue as clearly as a philosopher might like, his stress on competition, like Herakles putting his strength to use through twelve grueling labors, captures something close to Aristotle's insistence that virtue must be put into action. The end result is an aspirational ethic as individuals strive to become more than merely human.

Each of these ideas appears in *NE*, though it is only by holding Aristotle's text up against an athletic background that we can see how they fit together in an organic whole.[14]

Chapter 11

A Sketch of the Good Life
NE 1

> The work of a kithara player is to play the kithara. The work of a good kithara player is to play it well.
>
> —*NE* 1.7, 1098a8–10

What do you want to do with your life, not just in the short term, but as a whole? In a 2021 survey of seventeen developed economies, Pew Research turned up five top answers for what people found most meaningful in life: family and children, career and occupation, material well-being, friends and community, physical and mental health.[1] There is variation within this set. Most European countries rank career ahead of material well-being, while the United States and Japan rank material well-being ahead of career. In the United States, liberals tend to find meaning in nature, and conservatives tend to find meaning in religion. Hobbies, including sports, show up in eighth place. Pets are sixteenth.

Aristotle parts ways with his predecessors insofar as he begins his inquiry into the good life by taking a poll. After all, "it is reasonable for each group not to be completely wrong" (*NE* 1.8, 1098b28–29). In this inquiry, he follows his typical endoxic method: laying out opinions (*endoxa*), spinning out puzzles (*aporiai*), and working through those puzzles as a means of articulating philosophical theory. Assuming everyone has a partial grasp of what constitutes happiness, Aristotle sees it as the task of philosophy to fit those pieces into a single, systematic whole.² When it comes to what we want out of life, the uncontroversial answer, as Aristotle sees it, is that everyone is ultimately after *eudaimonia*, which we might translate as "happiness," "flourishing," or "the best life for a human being" (*NE* 1.4, 1095a18–20). Yet people disagree about what *eudaimonia* consists in. Aristotle's strategy is to provide a theory of *eudaimonia* that will accommodate people's differing opinions by setting them within a broader context.

Polling Opinions and Setting Out Puzzles: *NE* 1.5

Aristotle distills people's opinions about *eudaimonia* into four general categories and points out the shortcomings of three of them (*NE* 1.5). Aristotle's now lost *Protrepticus* illustrates a similar choice of lives via the different kinds of people who attend the Olympic Games: some to make money, some to compete for glory, and some simply to watch the spectacle.³ The *NE* version lacks these narrative details. The text we have is more or less lecture notes, so perhaps Aristotle added them on the fly. In any event, as is often the case with Aristotle, his line of thought is easily captured in a table (see table 4).

English speakers often think of happiness as a feeling. Aristotle's word for this is "pleasure" (*hēdonē*). It might be that happiness (*eudaimonia*) does ultimately consist in pleasure (*hēdonē*). The somewhat later philosopher, Epicurus, thought so and worked out an elaborate hedonist theory. Aristotle calls this a life "fit for cows." In this, he is not merely being insulting; his point is that aiming for nothing in life beyond physical pleasure sets the bar too low, since human beings are capable of more than cows and other nonrational animals.

In speaking of honor (*timē*), Aristotle likely has in mind athletes, soldiers, and politicians. The trouble with such a life is that it relies

Table 4

LIFE OF...	GOOD SOUGHT	SHORTCOMING
Gratification	Pleasure	It is fit for cows.
Political activity	Honor	It relies on others.
	Virtue	It is present when asleep.
Study	Study	(More on this later.)
Moneymaking	Money	It is merely instrumental.

too much on others. If your self-worth is based on whether others are fawning over you, Aristotle rightly points out, you are setting yourself up for a fall. This has become a huge problem in the age of social media.[4] Rather than being honored or liked, perhaps what we should shoot for is to be honorable or worthy of being liked. What does that mean? Being good at being human, which is to say virtuous. Aristotle is not content with this either, though, as someone could be brave, smart, fast, and so on but never put those virtues to use. The student who is smart but never applies himself is not leading his best life.

Outside of philosophical contexts, the Greek word for "study," *theōria*, refers to the practice of sending officials to observe oracles and/or religious festivals (there was considerable overlap).[5] While this background would have been obvious to *NE*'s original readers, particularly those familiar with his *Protrepticus*, Aristotle seems to have a different meaning of *theōria* in mind. What exactly that is, he puts off discussing until the very end of *NE*.

Seeing happiness as moneymaking, finally, is simply confused. Money is a means to some further end: to understand happiness, we must know what that end is.

If Aristotle's list is meant to be exhaustive, its omission of interpersonal relationships seems problematic. Given the priority given to family, friends, and even pets in the Pew survey, we may wonder how much human needs have changed since Aristotle's time. Aristotle's response is to ask what exactly we want in such relationships: pleasure, honor, material support, support in developing virtue? In *NE* 8–9, he will argue that we should think about relationships by looking at what they are based on. The options he gives there—pleasure, utility, virtue—fit easily within *NE* 1.5's survey of lives. So, barring further opinions about *eudaimonia*, the question on the table is how to choose between these main options, nearly all of which Aristotle has found problematic. With this, the puzzles have been set out.

Working through the Puzzles: *NE* 1.7, 1097a15-b21

While individuals disagree about what happiness consists in, Aristotle suggests that we can agree on some general features of how we structure our lives around happiness. His first step toward resolving our puzzles is to lay out two general criteria for happiness.

Aristotle's first criterion is that happiness is *teleion*. English editions tend to translate this as "complete" or "final." The Greek is derived from *telos* (end) in the sense of the ultimate goal to which other aspects of our lives lead. In the spirit of Aristotle's somewhat awkward Greek, let us use the equally awkward term "endy." Aristotle spells this out: we pursue happiness for its own sake; we pursue other things for the sake of happiness; we do not pursue happiness for the sake of anything else (*NE* 1.7, 1097a31–36). In short, happiness is the "endiest" end. There are a number of things to note here.

First, endiness comes in degrees. Goods such as health may be desirable for themselves and for their consequences. In *Republic* 2, Plato declares such things to be the highest goods and argues that justice belongs to this category (chapter 8). Aristotle disagrees. He finds such goods second-best. The endiest end is the one for which goods such as health serve as a means. This disagreement may simply reflect that Plato and Aristotle are pursuing different projects in these works. *Republic* is an inquiry into the nature and value of justice. *NE* is an inquiry into the nature of happiness. If Aristotle sets the bar higher, it may simply be that his current topic (*eudaimonia*) is broader than Plato's (justice). I suspect, however, and the subsequent philosophical tradition seems to bear me out, that there is a deeper disagreement going on here. In reading *Republic* and *Symposium*, I argued that purpose—finding self-worth through contributing to the well-being of others—is central to Plato's moral thought. If asked directly about his ideas of *eudaimonia*, Plato may very well hold to *Republic* 2's scheme and declare that the best life is one that is useful for ends beyond itself. This might simply move the discussion back a step, for instance, by making the good of one's community the highest good. It may also lead to a more nuanced situation in which my well-being is tied up in contributing to the well-being of my friends and family, whose well-being is tied up in contributing to the well-being of their friends and family, and so on. This idea fits nicely with the culture of cooperative competition, which was put on display in Socrates's conversations in gyms, hinted at in *Lysis*'s discussion of friendship, and more fully embraced in *Symposium*'s account of erotic love as a striving toward immortality. In short, Plato finds happiness in being useful. Aristotle seems to turn this on its head. At least on one reading, his ranking seems to place useless goods ahead of useful ones simply because of their uselessness.[6]

Second, it is unclear what Aristotle means by saying one end is "for the sake of" another. One reading looks at this instrumentally.

Advocates of this view tend to translate *teleion* as "final." For example, I go to the supermarket to buy walnuts to cook with my morning oatmeal, to eat as breakfast, to have energy for the day, to do well at school, to get a good job, to make money, and so on. If asked why I do any of these things, the next item in the list provides the answer. Aristotle's idea is that we will eventually arrive at an item where my response will be just "because." On this reading, all actions converge on a final, endiest end: happiness. This gives us a narrow view of happiness as a singular end and everything that leads to it as a means that lacks worth in itself.[7] What single thing could serve as such an end? Aristotle's pleasure, virtue, study, and money seem a plausible list of candidates. But if pleasure is all that matters, winning by cheating would be fine, provided one does not get caught. If study is all that matters, you could neglect family and friends, so long as they stayed out of your way. If money is all that matters, you could enter a career you hate, provided it comes with a large paycheck. To be honest, people do these things all the time. But are they really living their best lives? Proponents of the narrow view have responses to these various worries (chapter 17). Still, by understanding "for the sake of" instrumentally, we relegate large stretches of life to a crass means/ends calculus.

Because of these problems, many scholars recommend reading Aristotle in noninstrumental terms.[8] On this reading, to say that we want pleasure "for the sake of" happiness means that pleasure is a component of happiness. We could say the same for virtue, moneymaking, study, or any other good that is valuable in itself and contributes to a well-lived life. Proponents of this view tend to translate *teleion* as "complete." Such thinking leaves space for means/ends reasoning: even if playing lacrosse is part of my happiness, the bus ride I take to a game is still merely a means. This expansive view of happiness seems better to capture everyday intuitions about a well-lived life. There are some things we do simply for what they get us; yet a well-lived life will include several different things all of which are valuable in themselves. This approach, however, raises its own problems. If happiness is a composite whole of several intrinsically valuable things, then how many valuable things are enough? If sports, family, and study are all valuable, how do we deal with conflicting demands on our time? Such questions bring us to Aristotle's second criterion for happiness.

Happiness, according to Aristotle, is also self-sufficient (*autarkēs*). Sometimes he uses this term to refer to a person who needs nothing he does not already have. Sometimes he uses it to refer to a life that needs nothing it does not already have. Either way, this seems a demanding standard. When given the choice between a life as a pro athlete and the same life as a pro athlete plus a cookie, who would pass up the cookie? What if we add a second cookie? A second home? A sports car? Where do we draw the line and say, This is enough? One useful, albeit morbid, way to approach this question is from the perspective of someone on their deathbed. A self-sufficient person can look back on life and say, I would not change a thing. This shifts the perspective away from cookies and sports cars. Put starkly, Aristotle asks: Would you trade your life for someone else's? The self-sufficient person will answer no. While this may be inspiring, it does not give much guidance to those of us who are still building our lives. What is it that makes one life self-sufficient, and another not?

NE 1.1–2 suggests that goods fall into hierarchies. Aristotle uses the example of bridle making, which is valuable for the sake of riding horses, which is valuable for the sake of attacking enemies, which is valuable for politics, which is useful for a well-ordered state, which is valuable for the happiness of everyone living in it. Echoing a strategy employed in Plato's *Republic*, this particular example zooms out from the individual to the state as a whole. Yet it still suggests a way of approaching an expansive reading of happiness. Could the bridle maker suddenly stop his craft and become an olive farmer? Of course. But what the state needs from him is bridles not olives. Likewise for an individual: there are many goods that we could pursue, but what matters is that the ones we do pursue fit into a coherent structure. When I look back on my life, what matters is not how many goods I amassed but whether those goods fit meaningfully into a life with which I can be content.

This reading of Aristotle finds support in contemporary psychology. In *Grit*, Angela Duckworth sets out to see what a number of high-performing individuals have in common.[9] The majority of professional athletes, musicians, and soldiers in her study fit easily into the agonistic spirit of ancient Greece. What do people who excel in competitive contexts have in common? According to Duckworth, they all display high levels of grit, which she defines as the combination of passion and perseverance. Our culture tends to romanticize passion as a flame that burns hot and fast. The passion that underlies grit, however, is a "slow burn" that involves getting one's goals in order.[10] Duckworth quotes Seattle Seahawks coach Pete Carroll on the need for a single overarching goal or life philosophy. In Carroll's case, it is "Do things better than they have ever been done before."[11] We all have short-term goals: crew practice, eating breakfast, writing papers, reading articles, hitting legs, calculus homework, calling mom, choir practice, going out, sleep, and so on. Modern life can be overwhelming in terms of the sheer number of goals we pursue in a day. Duckworth's advice is to start grouping these individual goals into broader projects—for instance, school, family, friends, health. The next step is to fit those middle-level goals into a single overriding goal. Ideally, we can align all our various goals into a single hierarchy. Few of us have lives this tidy. What we usually find, instead, is a lot of mid-level goals that do not form a coherent whole. At other times, we find people who have a high-level goal—becoming a doctor, for instance—but no realistic conception of what it takes to get there. I have met several premed students who arrived at college without the algebra skills necessary to make it through the chemistry course they need to even begin studying biology. Given their professional aspirations, these students are not on track to live the best lives available to them.

According to Richard Arum's 2011 study *Academically Adrift*, about 50 percent of US college students fall into the two classes of dabblers and dreamers. The other half of US students are split evenly between the unengaged, who are just going through the motions of school, and the motivated but directionless.[12] This last group is good at doing school. They study hard, get good marks, put in service hours, and pad their college applications with sports, arts, and other extracurriculars. Their motivation for all this is most often to get into a good college, which is a step to getting a good job, which is a step to being successful. But when asked about the end goal of all this, most students fumble.[13] Does happiness come with landing a good job? Buying a house? Financial independence? Retirement? The trouble with all of this, according to Aristotle and Duckworth, is that students today do not think hard enough about the structure of their goals. As Arum has shown, some students do not think about such things at all. Some may have bucket lists, but a bucket does not lend itself to prioritizing. Others are on the fast track, though they cannot say to where. In short, Aristotle would agree with contemporary psychologists who find that our society is failing to prepare young people to live their best lives. At this point in our discussion of *NE*, however, we are still laying out general criteria for judging what a best life actually consists in. Aristotle's self-sufficiency criterion, read against the start of *NE* and Duckworth's study of high-performing individuals, suggests that the best lives will be structured in coherent ways. On a narrow understanding of happiness, this ensures that any means lead effectively to a single end. On the expansive view of happiness, this ensures that structured goals hold together multiple intrinsic goods in coherent wholes and provide a way to say when those goods are enough.

The final puzzle is how to fit family and friends into all this. If a happy person is self-sufficient, then he has everything he needs, and thus seems to have no need for other people. This sounds like a rather lonely life. Aristotle, however, takes it as a brute fact of our nature that "humans are political animals" (*NE* 1.7, 1097b12). A self-sufficient person is still a human being. His life will thus include immediate family, friends, and fellow citizens. As the Pew survey suggests, the best life involves meaningful relationships with other people.

In sum, we all seek *eudaimonia*, and we can all agree that *eudaimonia* is both endy and self-sufficient. There is some disagreement on how to understand these two criteria. A narrow view sees the best life as containing one most-valuable thing. An expansive view sees it as a compound of multiple valuable things. Either way, the best life will be coherently structured and somehow involve relationships with other people. Lives devoted to pleasure, honor, virtue, and moneymaking have been suggested as candidates for this best life, though each has been found lacking. With this, the stage is set for Aristotle's own theory of what constitutes the best life for a human being.

Aristotle's Account of *Eudaimonia*: *NE* 1.7, 1097b22–1098b7

Aristotle argues that human happiness amounts to living well, given the kind of thing a human being is. Socrates suggested such an idea at the end of *Republic* 1. Put briefly, human happiness is doing the human thing well. Spelling out what "the human thing" means is one of *NE*'s central contributions to Western ethics. Aristotle's official view is that happiness is a life of virtuous activity expressing reason. This definition ties together several elements of Aristotle's larger inquiry into biology, psychology, ethics, and politics. Let us walk through each part of this definition as laid out by Aristotle in *NE* 1.7. We will start with "expressing reason."

Aristotle approaches human happiness by thinking about what it means for a thing to have an *ergon* (1097b23–33). The Greek term literally means "work" and can refer to an activity or a product. A sculptor, for instance, produces a work of art, a statue, through his work on a piece of stone, sculpting. Some activities, however, do not produce anything beyond themselves. The work of a dancer is to dance. Unlike the sculptor, a dancer does not produce anything beyond the dancing. Because of this, scholars often translate *ergon* in *NE* 1.7 as "characteristic activity or function." The *ergon* of an artifact is easy to identify: the *ergon* of a knife is to cut; the *ergon* of an ergometer is to measure a rower's work. But Aristotle thinks that living things have an *ergon* as well (1097b33–1098a7).[14] The *ergon* of a plant is to grow and reproduce. Whatever it is about a plant that lets it do this, Aristotle calls its soul (*psychē*). The life functions of plants are limited to nutrition, growth, and reproduction. Aristotle sums these up by referring to plants' nutritive souls. Nonhuman animals, let us say dogs, also engage in nutrition, growth, and reproduction, but in ways distinctive to themselves. They do not, like plants, simply wait for food to come to them: they hunt it. They do not just cast their seed to the wind: they spot mates and chase them. Given this new layer of complexity, Aristotle concludes that dogs, and all other animals, have sensory souls. We humans, likewise, do everything plants and dogs do, but in our own characteristic way. We neither wait for food to come to us nor simply chase things when hungry: we work out mealtimes, count calories, and so on. Likewise for reproduction, we neither cast our seed to the wind nor chase whatever catches our eye: we go through a complicated courtship process and join intentional relationships with long-term commitments. The thread tying all of these together is that we think about what we are doing. Aristotle thus concludes that humans have rational souls. As with dogs' sensations, our reasoning is tied up in our lower life functions: nutrition, growth, reproduction, sensation, and the rest. When it comes to performing the human *ergon*, the human thing, Aristotle concludes that reason must take center stage.[15]

But simply having an *ergon* is not enough. As Aristotle puts it, "In the Olympic Games, it is not the finest and the strongest who are crowned victor, but those who compete: for it is from these that winners come. The same is true of life" (*NE* 1.8, 1099a3–6). This is one of the most explicit pieces of athletic thinking in Aristotle's account: talent that is never applied scores no points. Happiness thus consists of a certain sort of activity. The question is, What sort of activity?

Aristotle argues that an *ergon* (work, function, characteristic activity) carries its own standards (*NE* 1.7, 1098a8–18). If your goal is to play the kithara, an ancient forerunner of the guitar, what that really means is that you should pursue excellence/superiority (*hyperochē*) in your kithara playing.[16] The same goes for any undertaking. The Greek word for "excellence" is *aretē* (virtue). At this point, Aristotle relies rather heavily on his teachers' list of human excellences: justice, moderation, bravery, and so on. He will spell out his own account of these virtues in the books to follow. For the moment, he grounds the role of virtue in the well-lived life via the agonistic idea that the point of doing anything is doing it better than other people. To the victor goes the crown. Pulling these pieces together gives us an account of happiness as virtuous activity that expresses reason.

The final piece is to point out that *eudaimonia* extends across an entire life. While our moods might change over the course of the day, it makes no sense to say, "I woke up this morning living the objectively best life for a human being, but then I stubbed my toe, so I stopped living the objectively best life for a human being, but then someone complimented my new haircut, so I was back to living the objectively best life." As Aristotle puts it, "A single swallow does not make a spring" (1098a18–20). With this, we have his entire account: happiness is a life of virtuous activity expressing reason.

What does this look like in practice? Given all the passage's talk of athletic crowns and superior kithara playing, the lives of an Olympic victor and a virtuoso musician are the most obvious candidates. Given that the Pythian Games awarded crowns for kithara playing in a *musikos agōn*, there is a good reason for treating these as a single candidate. Such lives are active and embody human excellence. One scholar highlights this point by translating *aretē* not as "virtue" but as "virtuosity."[17] Furthermore, reaching a top level of performance takes both time and the use of reason as competitors develop their technique. Duckworth cites psychologist Anders Ericsson for the "ten-thousand-hour rule," which specifies the amount of deliberate practice it takes to master various skills in athletics, the arts, and other areas of life.[18] The Greeks, however, saw Olympic victors as attaining godlike status. To attribute happiness only to this elite and quite small group surely sets the bar too high. We might downplay the text's athletic imagery and say that the crown of happiness belongs to those who are the best in any endeavor. This would open the door to outstanding florists, weavers, sanitation workers, and philosophers. Yet it would still open it only to the best of them. By presenting virtue in agonistic terms, Aristotle gives a picture of *eudaimonia* at home with Plato's aristocratic individual and our own ideas of meritocracy.[19] Little wonder it lines up well with Duckworth's study of high-performing individuals. Still, we may rightly ask, Just how excellent does someone need to be for Aristotle to count him happy?[20] If Aristotle looks to elite performers as models of happiness, is this a form of elitism we are willing to accept? To get a better sense of this, we can look at how Aristotle puts his theory of happiness to work.

Back to the Opinions: *NE* 1.8–10

Having set out happiness in its entirety, Aristotle argues, we are now in a position to see how the people he initially polled each grasped a part of the whole.

Those who think happiness is pleasure are not completely wrong: excellent activity is, in fact, enjoyable. There is simple delight in a well-played game. The pleasure that comes with excellent activity is its own reward, thus making a life of excellent activity self-sufficient. This is in contrast to things that we do not enjoy, which need to have pleasure added "like a charm bracelet" (*NE* 1.8, 1099a16). The point is that pleasure in virtuous activity is not like jewelry, which has no necessary connection to the body it is set upon.[21]

Those who think that happiness is honor have already been addressed: the real point is not to be honored but to be honorable, which is to say virtuous or virtuosic. But, as we saw above, it is possible to have virtue but never act on it. The point of virtue is to get yourself into (moral) shape so that you can outperform other people. Virtue may be endy but it is not the endiest end, since it is desirable both for itself and for the excellent activity that it makes possible. In this, Aristotle accepts Plato's classification of justice in *Republic* but downplays the elevated status Plato affords justice and other virtues. The main argument of *Republic* 2–10 is that justice is a form of mental health, that, like bodily health, is valuable all by itself. In invoking Olympic victors, Aristotle argues that Plato does not go far enough: the ultimate point of virtue is not to have virtue but to use it.

As for money, Aristotle has already argued that it is not endy at all. Nevertheless, money has a place in the good life. Aristotle's account of virtuous activity shows what money, in the best-case scenario, is a means to. The point of having money, and resources generally, is that they permit one to engage in excellent activity. Even if the Greek athletes competed naked, the time, food, trainers, and facilities needed to achieve Olympic levels required considerable resources.[22] Likewise for virtuoso musicians. Surprisingly, Aristotle classes friends along with money and political power as things one "uses" for the sake of fine actions (*NE* 1.8, 1099a29-b1). Whether we use friends in the same way we use wealth remains to be seen (chapter 16). The fact that this is virtuous activity suggests that we will, at least, not be abusing our friends.

As for Aristotle's two criteria for happiness, a life of virtuous activity ends up being self-sufficient by integrating into itself all the broad classes of goods identified in Aristotle's initial poll. It is also endiest insofar as we can tell a coherent story about how people desire money, virtue, and so on for the sake of happiness but not the other way around. But which way should we understand "for the sake of" in this context? The example of money suggests an instrumental relationship. This would support a narrow view of happiness as a most final end, and distinct from the means that lead to it. Money, however, was the only item on Aristotle's list to be rejected for not being endy at all. It makes little sense to claim that we desire pleasure as a means to virtuous activity. Aristotle's point seems to be, rather, that pleasure is a component of virtuous activity.[23] This would support an expansive view of happiness, in which these various goods are component parts of a most complete end. How, finally, does virtue fit into this? It seems fine to say that a vase painter's virtuosic skills in painting are a means to producing a vase that is distinct from those skills. Yet there is an inherent confusion in talk of painting, which could refer to either the action or its product. Aristotle's examples of Olympic victors and virtuoso kithara players remove this ambiguity: in either case, there is no product beyond the performance. Aristotle concludes that it is the activity and not its product that is the end aimed at. In sum, the narrow view of happiness makes good sense of money's place in a good life, while the expansive view of happiness makes sense of the whole list.

Having neatly fitted each of the initial survey of lives into his own account of happiness, Aristotle moves on to a messier question: If happiness is a kind of excellent activity, and excellent activity requires resources, to what extent is our own happiness outside our control? He starts out with another bit of *endoxa* (*NE* 1.8, 1099b2–6), saying, "Lack of good birth, good children, and beauty spoils our blessedness (*makarios*)." He cites, by way of example, Priam, the mythic king of Troy (*NE* 1.9). According to various legends, Priam's city was burned to the ground, his sons were slaughtered, his wives and daughters were sold into slavery, and Priam himself was beaten to death by Achilles's son, Neoptolemus, using Priam's grandson, Astyanax, as a club.[24] Priam offers an important caveat to Aristotle's account of happiness (*NE* 1.10, 1100b22–30):

> Many things come about by chance (*tychē*); some small, some great. Minor strokes of good or bad fortune clearly don't carry any weight in life. But many and great things turning out well will make life more blessed (*makarios*), for they naturally add an ornament (*sunepikosmeō*) and his use of them is beautiful (*kalon*) and excellent (*spoudaios*). On the other hand, [many and great] things turning out badly will oppress and spoil his blessedness (*makarios*), for they bring pain and impede many activities.

This is the first instance in *NE* of *kosmos*, here in its verb form, *sunepikosmein*. In the introduction to part 3, I argued that *kosmos* has three senses: strategic, cosmetic, and athletic. The vast majority of scholars read this passage in the cosmetic sense, treating goods of fortune as something imposed from the outside and bearing no close relationship to the individual's character. But Aristotle has a term for that: "charm bracelet" (*NE* 1.8), and he treats it with suspicion, just as Hesiod does in describing the adorning of Pandora. This seems out of keeping in the present passage, which invokes religious language to speak of an adornment that makes someone "more blessed." The strategic reading of *kosmos* avoids this problem, yet it still seems odd to say that good fortune will put someone's life into order. Good birth, good looks, friends, money, and so on do not give structure but call for structure.

This leaves the athletic reading in which things going well for an individual reflect that individual's virtuous activity. From this perspective, *kosmos* is a synonym not for "charm bracelet" but for the "crown" (*stephanos*) given to Olympic victors. On this reading, good fortune is the outward manifestation of a person's inner virtue, which has been brought about through excellent activity. But this runs into an obvious problem, which I suspect is what motivates the standard cosmetic reading, that such a good would be the result of the individual's activity and not of fortune. The solution, I suggest, sits in Aristotle's idea that when it comes to matters of ethics, the best we can aim for is what "usually" happens.[25] The athletic parallel is apt. People who put in no effort get nothing. People who put in excellent effort naturally get crowned. Winning, however, is not guaranteed. The passage concludes: "But even in these circumstances, beauty (*kalon*) shines through (*dialampō*) when someone bears many and great misfortunes with good temper, not because he is not distressed but because he is noble and great-spirited (*megalopsychos*)"

(*NE* 1.10, 1100b30–33). This conclusion to our passage easily fits an athletic mindset: the image of beauty shining through could be straight from Pindar, who speaks of "shining fame" (*lampei kleos*) and "a crown glistening with olive oil" (*liparos kosmos*) like an anointed athlete.[26] The athletic context also helps us make sense of the religious language: competing well is great, but being crowned victor is "blessed." It is a way for humans to share in the life of the gods. Aristotle concludes, "If this is right, a happy person will never become miserable, but he will not be blessed if he falls into a fate like Priam's" (*NE* 1.10, 1101a7–8).[27]

Is our happiness outside of our control? Aristotle's answer seems to be yes and no. On the one hand, happiness consists in virtuous activity, and Aristotle claims that a person can engage in that even amid disasters like Priam's. Such a person is happy (*eudaimōn*) but not blessed (*makarios*). Blessedness requires excellent activity to be crowned with the natural reward of actually accomplishing things—having friends, family, wealth, honor—which, in turn, provide the means for an individual to engage in further virtuous activity. Beauty may shine through in defeat, but it usually shines through in success. The result is a virtuous cycle in which success breeds success, albeit only usually. External goods have a place in this cycle as both means and reward. Granted such things are not entirely within the individual's control (chance plays a role), but they usually are. In the end, the Priam example adds a layer of complexity to Aristotle's attempt to integrate the opening catalogue of lives into his account of excellent activity, yet it leaves the basics of that integration in place while admitting that in life, as in sports, there are no guarantees.[28]

The question remains, Just how elitist is this view? Aristotle gives examples of top performers in athletics and music. I suggested above that we might broaden this to include top performers in any field. But is happiness really limited only to the best of the best? We can find an answer, I suggest, in the way *NE* 1.8 integrates other goods into virtuous activity. Aristotle's virtuosic individuals build whole lives around putting virtues into activity, taking pleasure in that activity, making themselves worthy of honor, and putting material resources (and friends) to good use along the way. Any life that can do that, I suggest, will meet Aristotle's standard of excellence.

"More Blessed"

Aristotle's original audience had a ready model for a life dedicated to the pursuit of excellence: Herakles. Modern scholars tend to downplay

NE's religious language.²⁹ *NE* 1.9, however, expressly connects human happiness with divinity, as either a gift from the gods or as something intimately connected to the most divine thing within us. *NE* 1.12 likens happiness to the god's blessedness as something worthy of honor (*timē*) rather than merely congratulations (*epeinos*). Born a demigod, Herakles held divinity within him. Through his labors (*athla, agōnes, ponoi*), he reached his full potential and became a god. Olympic athletes imitated this by seeking prizes (*athla*) through competitions (*agōnes*) with the ultimate goal of receiving the ornament (*kosmos*) of an olive crown (*stephanos*; see *NE* 1.7) as they stood before the massive statue of Zeus wearing the same crown.³⁰ *NE*'s discussions of athletes and blessedness are not just a handful of ways of speaking of happiness: they are part of a single aspirational ethos that was already extensively developed in art, literature, and religious practice.

What do such aspirations require? According to Aristotle and Duckworth, nothing short of organizing one's life around central goals. Here too, Herakles provides a helpful model, as the core of his myth—the twelve labors—boils down to an organizational principle. While this might not sound very exciting, the episodic nature of this list has deep roots. One possible origin of the Herakles myth is the Egyptian *Book of Gates*.³¹ Here the sun god, Ra, makes a nightly boat voyage through the underworld, passing through a series of twelve chambers, corresponding to the twelve hours of the night, before ascending again into Heaven/the sky. From a religious perspective, *Book of Gates* holds out hope for the souls of the deceased that they may travel through the underworld with Ra and take their place in Heaven at the end. Herakles's labor-structured life also fits nicely with the hierarchies of goals set out by Aristotle and Duckworth, as an overarching quest is broken down into twelve mid-level goals, which define the shape of Herakles's life.

Given his hard-earned transformation into divinity, it should come as no surprise that Herakles was a patron deity of Greek gyms. His statues and altars adorned these sites where men gathered through the whole of their lives to strive through blood and sweat to be the best versions of themselves. Did Aristotle have Herakles in mind when he wrote *NE* 1? We cannot know. But, given the popularity of the myth and the pride of place *NE* 1 gives to elite performers, people striving for the divine, and Olympic competitors (not to mention that the Lyceum was a functioning gym that likely contained altars to Herakles), Aristotle would hardly have been surprised if a student had brought Herakles up in response to *NE* 1. Either way, as Aristotle turns to flesh out *NE* 1's sketch of happiness, he introduces another famous strongman, the wrestler Milo of Kroton, as he presents his account of what virtues are and how we obtain them. With this, we have our first indication that ideas about elite athletes provide connective tissue holding the sections of *NE* together.

Chapter 12

Training
NE 2–3

> Ten pounds of food . . . may be too little for Milo but too much for someone new to working out.
>
> —*NE* 2.6, 1106b1–4

Milo of Kroton, son-in-law of the philosopher/mathematician Pythagoras, was famous in antiquity for three things. First was his athletic prowess. Ancient wrestling matches were won by the first contestant to throw his opponent to the ground three times. Milo won this event seven times at the Pythian Games and seven times at the Olympic Games.[1] On one occasion at Olympia (ca. 520 BCE), it appears that no one dared compete with him, since he was the only person to enter the match. As he made his way to be crowned, however, he slipped and fell. The crowd called for him not to be crowned since he fell all by himself. Never one to back down, Milo responded, "I fell once. Let someone else throw me another two times."[2] Second was his appetite. According to the ancient food critic Athenaeus, "Milo of Kroton used to eat twenty pounds of meat and twenty pounds of bread and wash it down with eight quarts of wine. At Olympia he hoisted a four-year-old ox on his shoulders and carried it around the stadium. He then butchered it and ate it all alone in a day."[3] Third was his training regimen. Milo's present-day fame, and occasional appearance on athletic wear, come from his practice of what is now known as progressive resistance training. The story goes that Milo lifted a newborn ox over his head every day until it was a full-grown ox.[4] Whether it was the same ox he ate at Olympia, we can only speculate.[5]

When Aristotle turns to filling out the details of *NE* 1's sketch of happiness, he invokes Milo as a model for thinking about the nature of virtue. Socrates, as Plato presents him in various dialogues and Aristotle will present him in *NE* 7, entertained the idea that virtue is ultimately a form of knowledge. Plato, as we saw in *Republic*, argued that virtues are ultimately states of one's soul, which constitute a form of mental health. Aristotle accommodates both ideas by distinguishing between virtues of thought, which are acquired by learning, and "virtues of character, which are acquired through training" (*NE* 2.1, 1103a17). In fact, Aristotle argues, the latter, which are called *ēthos* in Greek, derive their name from *ethos* (training).[6] Aristotle uses the rest of *NE* 2 and the start of *NE* 3 to give a general definition of virtues of character, and then explores particular instances, one by one, in *NE* 3–5. In *NE* 6, he turns to virtues of thought, where he makes a similar distinction between practical wisdom (*phronēsis*), which, he argues, is intimately wrapped up in the virtues of character, and theoretical reason (*sophia*), which finds its fulfillment in theoretical study (*theōria*). With this, Aristotle accommodates ideas from his teachers in a holistic theory, laying out in great detail not only what virtues are but also how we acquire them. Given the centrality of training to character virtue, *NE* 2 is full of images drawn from the gym.

Training and the Mean: *NE* 2

For Aristotle, training (*ethos*) sits somewhere between a mere capacity and an actual action. He calls this middle ground a condition (*hexis*; *NE* 2.5), which is the end result of a conditioning regimen.[7] In particular, it is a condition that leads one to decide in certain ways (*hexis proairetikos*; *NE* 2.6). All people, for instance, have the ability to drink too much (capacity). And there are times when people actually do drink too much (action). Those who overdrink time after time are alcoholics (condition).

Conditions do not arise in us automatically. They are the result of training/conditioning. Aristotle introduces the idea via one of *NE*'s few jokes: you can throw a stone in the air as many times as you like, but you will never train it to stay up (*NE* 2.1, 1103a20–22). Humans are different. Our character is the result of training. This works for both good and bad character. By performing just actions, we become just. By performing unjust actions, we become unjust. Aristotle looks to the gym to illustrate this point: "Strength arises from eating a lot and withstanding much hard labor (*ponos*), and it is the strong person who is most capable of these very actions" (*NE* 2.2, 1104a30–33). So too with virtues of character. But how do we distinguish between just and unjust acts so that we can make sure children are trained the right way?

As a first step, Aristotle notes that both overtraining and undertraining ruin bodily health (*NE* 2.2). What we should shoot for is a sort of Goldilocks zone, which he calls the mean.[8] Does that suggest that there is a correct amount for each person to eat, drink, fear, and so on? Aristotle clarifies by comparing Milo with a newcomer to the gym: "Ten pounds of food . . . may be too little for Milo but too much for someone new to working out" (*NE* 2.6, 1106b1–4). The mean is relative to the particular situation of the individual. This is not to say that Aristotle endorses what is today called moral relativism, that whatever a person or culture thinks is right actually is right for them. Aristotle's point is merely that the mean varies from one situation to another, so we should be smart about what we are trying to accomplish. When bulking, load up on carbs. When cutting, go into caloric deficit. If you have never squatted before, start with just the bar. This is also not to say that a trainer applies one body of knowledge to advise Milo and another body of knowledge to advise the first-time gym-goer. Rather, the trainer has one body of knowledge—that is, knowledge of training—which leads him to make different recommendations to individuals in different circumstances. By analogy, to speak of an ethical virtue as a mean state (*mesotēs*) does not imply that the state itself is somehow positioned between extremes, but merely that it results in feelings and actions that hit the mean (*meson*). The virtue of moderation, the acquired disposition to eat neither too much nor too little, is the same for everyone, even if it dictates that Milo eats more than most other people.[9]

The next piece of Aristotle's account is emotion: we hit the mean when we reliably feel pleasure and pain in the right way (*NE* 2.3). Someone who enjoys eating moderately is moderate. Someone who pines for empty carbs is not. Someone who feels shame at the thought of hazing people is just. Someone who thinks it sounds like fun is not. At *NE* 2.7, Aristotle combines these two sets of ideas -deficiency/mean/excess and pleasure/pain—to give a rough list of the ethical virtues, running through cases of fear, confidence, bodily pleasures, monetary exchanges, donating to causes, popularity, anger, honesty, jokes, interacting with friends, and being offended. In each case, he argues, there is a way to go overboard, a way to fall short, and a way to hit a happy medium.

At the end of the day, Aristotle's thinking about virtue is thoroughly practical: "The purpose of our present examination is not to know what virtue is, but to become good" (*NE* 2.2). We should therefore not be "like a sick person who listens attentively to a doctor, but acts on none of his instructions" (*NE* 2.4, 1105b13-16). How do we obtain a healthy character? The first step is to have had parents and teachers who raised us the right way, using rewards and punishments to steer us as children toward feeling pleasure in the mean and pain in things that fall outside the mean, with the ultimate goal that we come to feel correctly without interventions from external authorities. Short of that, take a good hard look at your character, be honest with yourself about your bad habits, and try to push in the other direction (*NE* 2.9): if you enjoy drinking too much, then cut yourself off short of what would be your healthy mean. If you have weak shoulders, then program more shoulder work into your routine than you will ultimately need. Over time, you can come to enjoy a healthy medium.

A Trainer's Handbook: *NE* 3.1–5

In sum, trainers can shape children's characters through a mix of repeated actions, punishments, and rewards. Aristotle takes it for granted that such practices exist. In *NE* 3.1–5, he sets out to understand why and in what cases they are successful. In short, *NE* 3.1–5 is a handbook to guide trainers in meting out pleasures and pains. The passage is thick with puzzles and technical terms. I will go quickly over the first four chapters, which set the stage for the main discussion of training, which comes at the end.[10]

NE 3.1 sets out puzzles about which actions are performed willingly and which are not. A few cases are quickly dismissed: actions under compulsion and actions done in ignorance. What does this leave? *NE* 3.2 carves out a class of actions that are distinctive of rational, adult humans: those performed via decision (*proairesis*). The idea was introduced in *NE* 2.6, where Aristotle defined virtue as a *hexis proairetikos*, that is, a condition that leads one to decide in certain ways. *NE* 3.2 explains that decision is the result of deliberation (*bouleusis*), which *NE* 3.3 presents as a rational process about things that are up to us but do not always turn out the same way. We do not deliberate about policies in foreign countries because they are not up to us. We do not deliberate about how to do long division because it always comes out the same way. Deliberation ends up being a kind of thinking on our feet when we have to deal with unscripted problems.[11] Aristotle illustrates the point: "We deliberate about navigation more than about gym training because navigation is less exactly worked out" (1112b5-7). In an age of GPS, we might chuckle at the thought that gym training was once a more exact science than navigation. Aristotle's point, though, is that we can tell a lot about a person's character by seeing how she thinks on her feet. Nevertheless, deliberation is merely means/end reasoning: it takes a goal as given and works out the series of lower-level goals through which to meet it.[12] Wish (*boulēsis*; *NE* 3.4) is what determines which goals provide starting points for our deliberation and decision on any particular occasion. It provides the motive for an action.

According to Aristotle, these three activities—wish, deliberation, decision—are rational processes that reflect a person's character. By showing motive, wish shows whether a person is brave, cowardly, petty, generous, and so on. By picking certain goals for the sake of other goals, deliberation shows the relative worth a person assigns to various things. Decision, finally, shows how much conviction a person has regarding the product of his rational wishing and deliberations. All of these give insight into a person's character. Trainers, therefore, should take all of this into account when assigning praise and blame, punishment and reward, with an eye to helping children under their care wish, deliberate, and decide in ways that are in line with the mean.

This analysis of individual actions and the thought processes behind them lays the groundwork for the passage's final question: Do we willingly have virtue or vice (*NE* 3.5)? Today, we might think of someone struggling to overcome alcoholism or a drug addiction. Does it make any sense to say that such people willingly have vices that they actively want to escape? On this score, antiquity was not so different from today. Aristotle argues that alcoholics are, in fact, responsible because they have lived carelessly (*NE* 3.5, 1114a4-5). They are like people who train incorrectly for a contest (*agōn*; 1114a7-9). Giving his own spin on male beauty contests, Aristotle concludes, "While we would never blame someone for being naturally ugly, we *do* blame people for not going to the gym (*agymnasia*) and for lack of care (*ameleia*)" (1114a23-25). In short, a person's character, like a person's physique, is the result of a lifetime of choices. By improperly training either body or mind, people freely give up their freedom (1114a19-21). Yet, insofar as they freely got themselves into these binds, they are responsible for their vices and should be held accountable.[13]

This trainer's handbook has two main takeaways for our understanding of what virtues of character are and how we acquire them. First, *NE* 2 may have left the impression that virtues of character are fairly mechanical states, which we acquire through repetition and then act on without thinking. Granted, it might take careful reasoning to figure out just what the mean is in a particular situation, but *NE* 2 left open the possibility that such thinking is carried out by the trainer, not the trainee.[14] *NE* 3.1–5 corrects this potential misreading by showing how virtues and vices are infused with rational processes of wish, deliberation, and decision. As Aristotle set out in *NE* 1.7, human virtue is intimately tied up with rationality. A human being who thoughtlessly performs virtuous deeds is no better than a well-trained dog.

Second, *NE* 3.5's emphasis on rational processes in character formation shows that not only the end goal, virtue, but also the processes through which people develop virtue involve rational thought on the part of the trainee. This corrects the black-and-white picture implied by Aristotle's depictions of adults as rational and children as lacking reason. Instead, we find a developmental scheme in which simple repetition, reinforced by praise, blame, punishment, and reward, is gradually supplanted, as children are called to think on their feet in situations when the correct way forward is not immediately clear. If this reading is right, Aristotelian training is not merely a matter of rote memorization and drilling but makes room for what is today known as experiential learning. Since the goal of moral development is to enable people to navigate unscripted problems, then training for that goal should involve as much thinking on one's feet as is appropriate for the trainee's developmental stage.

Having set out a general account of what character virtues are and how we acquire them, Aristotle spends the rest of *NE* 3 presenting two paradigm virtues: bravery and moderation.

Bravery: *NE* 3.6–9

Plato's *Laches* brought bravery to the table through a discussion of fighting in armor. While today we think of people in many circumstances being brave (from children skinning knees to cancer patients stepping up for chemo), the Greek term *andreia* (literally, "manliness") has strong military associations. In setting out a definition of bravery, Aristotle's first step is to distinguish it from closely related virtues. He concludes that bravery is most often seen in war (*NE* 3.6). Is that to say that children on the playground and patients in the oncology ward are not brave in our sense? Not necessarily. But Aristotle is talking about something else.[15]

A brave act, according to Aristotle, ends up hitting a mean of both confidence and fear while aiming at the *kalon* (what is fine, beautiful, noble; *NE* 3.7). The variables can be neatly shown in a table (see table 5).[16] On one axis, we have fear. While we might think of brave people as fearless, Aristotle points out that there are some things that you should fear: those that are actually dangerous. Playing chicken with a freight train is not brave; it is just stupid. People who do so are deficient in fear. More common are people who are excessive in fear and shrink from things that are not actually dangerous. The brave person, then, is one who fears things that are actually dangerous and does not fear things that are not. We find a similar range of attitudes regarding confidence. It is not that brave people are really confident. As with any ethical mean, confidence is relative to the individual. Someone with excessive confidence overestimates his own abilities to perform as the situation demands. Someone deficient in confidence underestimates his own abilities. The brave person has a realistic sense of what he is capable of.[17]

Our first two axes, of fear and confidence, amount to a reality check: the brave person has a realistic sense of the situation and her own abilities. Still, it is possible to have all that in place and still be prone to taking pointless risks.[18] It is one thing to run out into traffic to save a child chasing a ball. It is another thing to do it simply for the thrill. Aristotle's final criterion looks to whether an action is done for the sake of the *kalon*.

The term *kalon* sits somewhere on a continuum between moral and beautiful, though scholars disagree about where Aristotle situates it in *NE*.[19] When it comes to risking death on the battlefield for a good cause, such as defending one's home and family, the moral reading

Table 5

	DEFICIENT FEAR	**MEAN OF FEAR**	**EXCESSIVE FEAR**
EXCESSIVE CONFIDENCE	Dangerously reckless	Overconfident	Showing bravado*
MEAN OF CONFIDENCE	Reckless	Brave	Cowardly
DEFICIENT CONFIDENCE	Numb	Underconfident	Paralyzed with fear

* Aristotle does not discuss the corners of this table. In two cases, the two axes combine to form extreme cowardice and extreme recklessness. Someone deficient in both fear and confidence would take a very passive approach to life. Extreme fear and extreme confidence seem harder to combine in a single person. My students have suggested we see these combined in the bravado displayed by bullies.

is easy to make. Such an act is noble and fine. To call it beautiful is much harder. There is nothing pretty about being mowed down in battle, particularly for the person being killed. But perhaps pretty simply aims too low. We are more likely to refer to death on the battlefield as glorious. This English term, derived from a Latin root, has to do with light and calls to mind Pindar's heroic language of "shining fame" and a "crown glistening with olive oil."[20] Aristotle makes a similar point by likening the battlefield to a contest at the gym (*gymnikos agōn*) in which boxers suffer physical pain and great labor (*ponos*) for the sake of a crown (*stephanos*) and honor (*timē*; *NE* 3.9). Death may seem a steep price for a reputation one will not be around to enjoy. Such a critique is in line with a cosmetic reading, in which a *kosmos* or *stephanos* bestows beauty. In the athletic context, which Aristotle explicitly invokes, a crown reveals or acknowledges one's inner worth.[21] If we set these ideas against the backdrop of hero worship in general and Herakles in particular, then all this talk of labor, crowns, and facing death provides a way for human beings to overcome their merely human nature and realize their divine potential. Why would someone want to win an Olympic crown for boxing or die defending his home? Because these are among the most awesome (*kalon*) things you can do with your life![22] Anyone who thinks otherwise is likely too concerned with physical comfort.

In the end, where should we place the *kalon* on the moral/beautiful continuum? Rather than argue for a particular spot on the continuum, our discussion of *NE*'s heroic context suggests we take a harder look at how we think of morality and beauty. In justifying a soldier's sacrifice, Aristotle invokes neither the greater good served nor one's duty to the state. What he does talk about is honors and crowns. As we saw in *NE* 1, however, the real point of honor in a well-lived life is not to be honored but to be worthy of honor, that is, to be virtuous. With this, we run the risk of circularity: in singling out a certain action as for the sake of the *kalon*, we are attempting to define what counts as virtuous. Aristotle, however, seems to take a certain set of *kalon* actions for granted, and he connects these with divinity. At *NE* 1.12, he states that we give honor (*timē*) to the gods for their blessedness but we do not give them congratulations (*epainos*). Similarly, in *NE* 3, honor is given to athletes and soldiers. The idea of morality at play, then, is an aspirational one as human beings seek to live their best lives, through heroic striving. The resulting actions are beautiful not because they are pretty but because they approximate divine models.[23]

Moderation and the Pleasures of Touch: *NE* 3.10–12

What do eating, drinking, and sex have in common? According to Aristotle, they all involve touching something (*NE* 3.10). To illustrate the point, he cites a glutton who wished that his neck were longer so that he could take more time swallowing food. What is more, we naturally derive pleasure from each of these forms of touching (*NE* 3.11). It is therefore right and good for us to engage in them, provided we hold to the mean. The condition (*hexis*) to do so is the virtue *sōphrosunē* (moderation/discipline).[24] This is the virtue that Charmides, who seems to have suffered from hangovers, supposedly embodied but could not define. As with bravery, Aristotle applies his account of the mean by looking to the gym: "Whatever is pleasant and conducive to health and wellbeing, the moderate/disciplined person will desire moderately and as is necessary; likewise for other pleasures, provided they are not obstacles to health or contrary to the *kalon*" (*NE* 3.14). In short, Aristotle sets our pursuit of the natural pleasures of touch within two boundaries: health and the *kalon*. The first of these has already been explained through *NE* 2's discussion of Milo: what is healthy depends on a number of circumstances relative to the individual. Aristotle likens the second to getting rubbed down with oil at the gym, a pleasure that is "most fitting for free people (*eleutheriōtatai*), involving all of the body, not just a part of it" (3.10).

While Aristotle's rationale for massages is not the most informative, it shows that both biological and cultural considerations are relevant to determining the mean relative to the individual. Pork provides an excellent source of protein, but there is no right amount for someone keeping kosher. Far from giving a simple continuum of too little or too much, *sōphrosunē* requires us to pursue "the right things, in the right ways, at the right times" (1119b17; 1106b21 adds "with the right people").[25] When it comes to sex, then, the question is not simply, How much is the right amount? We must ask, rather: When, with whom, for what reason, and in what manner? These questions, in turn, force us to look at the particulars of an individual's situation: age, relationship status, religious commitments, and even scheduling may come into play. The end result is a balancing act as we integrate natural pleasures into our lives, enjoying eating, drinking, and sex, but not to the point that they interfere with our health, role in society, or other commitments.

What counts as moderate for an individual is thus not exclusively a matter of biology. General cultural norms impose guidelines, and an individual's own choices play a role. Again, this is not a matter of relativism in the sense that whatever I think is right is right for me. Rather, by choosing to commit to certain projects, we limit what we may do in other areas of life. As Hall of Fame pitcher Tom Seaver put it,

> Pitching . . . determines what I eat, when I go to bed, what I do when I'm awake. It determines how I spend my life when I'm not pitching. If it means I have to come to Florida and can't get tanned because I might get a burn that would keep me from throwing for a few days, then I never go shirtless in the sun. . . . If it means I have to remind myself to pet dogs with my left hand or throw logs on the fire with my left hand, then I do that, too. If it means in winter I eat cottage cheese instead of chocolate chip cookies in order to keep my weight down, then I eat cottage cheese.[26]

These reflections from an elite athlete help us see how we may pursue natural pleasures, "as is necessary" and "provided they are not contrary to the *kalon*" (1119a17–18). When we enjoy eating a piece of cake, we might call it beautiful. Aristotle would call it pleasant. He certainly would not call it noble. The same goes for drinking and sex. If we are to find the *kalon* in such things, it will not be in the pleasure we take from them but in how they are integrated into our lives overall. For a professional chef, a piece of cake might actually be a thing of beauty, but this is because it makes visible the excellent activity around which that chef has structured his life. For the rest of us, as for Tom Seaver, cake is something we may enjoy, provided it does not interfere with whatever hierarchy of goals we have chosen to pursue. In this way, they will not be "contrary to the *kalon*" but something we engage with "as is necessary."[27]

Students are often surprised to find Aristotle chiding people for not engaging in enough drinking or sex. For him, not all virtuous activity involves noble sacrifice and self-denial. Simply having the right relationship with food has its place in the well-lived life. And while the ancient Greeks were no puritans, Aristotle does admit that when it comes to natural pleasures, people are more often prone to excess than deficiency. If anything, he has trouble coming up with a Greek term for someone who enjoys pleasures too little (1119a5–11). Still, he is aware that some people "drift too easily into natural pleasures." Such people would do best to drag themselves in the opposite direction (*NE* 2.9).[28] He holds this out as a second-best option for those who struggle to find a stable mean. As in all things, though, the best option is to hit the mean in these pleasures. And we should raise our children to take pleasure in doing so (*NE* 3.12).[29]

For the moment, we have reached a stopping point in *NE*'s discussion of virtue. *NE* 2 lays out Aristotle's account of character virtues as conditions that aim at the *kalon* and are arrived at through training involving repetition, pleasure, and pain. *NE* 3.1-5 clarifies the role that thinking plays in all this, first and foremost through deliberation. Through the examples of bravery and moderation, *NE* 3.6-12 specifies that the mean is always relative to some *kalon* end. With this, Aristotle's basic account of what virtues are and how they are acquired is in place. The next three books of *NE* turn to questions of how particular virtues fit together in a life of virtuous activity.

Chapter 13

Greatness of Spirit
NE 4

> Greatness of spirit is a kind of ornament of the virtues, for it makes them greater, and it does not come to be without them. For this reason, it is difficult to be truly great-spirited, since it is impossible without beautiful goodness.
>
> —*NE* 4.3, 1124a1–4

> I'm not concerned with your liking or disliking me. All I ask is that you respect me as a human being.
>
> —Jackie Robinson

Of all the virtues of character laid out in *NE*, the most controversial is *megalopsychia*. The term means "greatness of spirit" and is sometimes translated as "magnanimity."[1] Aristotle defines the great-spirited person as "someone who thinks himself worthy of great things and really is worthy of them" (*NE* 4.3, 1123b2). The particular thing he is worthy of is honor (*timē*), and the worthiness of the great-spirited person is rooted in his having all the virtues. This person "is at the extreme in making great claims but at the mean insofar as he makes them accurately" (*NE* 4.3, 1123b13–14). Aristotle's presentation of this virtue is unusual in that it contains an extended sketch of what a great-spirited person is like: he will be tall, have a deep voice, move slowly, refrain from engaging in actions of small importance, reserve his efforts for grand acts, not care much what most people think, look for the approval of good people but not care too much if he does not receive it. Aristotle's presentation of the great-spirited person has struck some as so ridiculous that scholars spent the better part of the twentieth century trying to explain it away as either a joke or a form of elitism contrary to Christian humility and modern egalitarianism.[2] Around 1990, however, scholars started to defend

Aristotle's great-spirited person by taking a more critical view of their own cultural contexts and looking afresh at how greatness of spirit fits within *NE* as a whole.³ Given that *NE* 4-6 opens with greatness of spirit and closes with practical wisdom (*sōphrosunē*), both of which ensure that virtues, in their full form, come as a complete set, the two passages serve as bookends, giving unity to these three books of *NE*.

Aristotle's MVPs: *NE* 4.1–4

If we were to look for great-spirited people in our own times, the sporting world would be a good place to start, as Aristotle's description of such a person sounds a lot like a most valuable player (MVP) or a greatest of all time (GOAT). Jackie Robinson, for instance, broke the color barrier in 1947 when he became the first African American to play Major League Baseball. With his sights set on this lofty goal, he had little concern for whether people liked him, as one of this chapter's epigraphs shows.⁴ Eunshil Bae presents the great-spirited person as a "mental athlete," who is like an "Olympic champion runner [who] shows little interest in competing with ordinary, untrained runners."⁵ The sporting world of antiquity was also a promising source of models, as *NE* 4.1-4's talk of prizes and crowns attests. Aristotle first introduces greatness of spirit at *NE* 1.10 in the context of a person's virtue "shining through" in times of ill fortune. In that passage, external goods were said to be a *kosmos* (ornament) of virtue. The discussion in *NE* 4.1-4 contains *NE*'s remaining three controversial instances of *kosmos*. In what follows, I will contribute to the effort to defend greatness of spirit against its twentieth-century critics. My approach builds on existing work, by situating controversial virtue within the nexus of athletic/heroic ideas running throughout *NE*.

Greatness of spirit is presented as the third in a set of four virtues. The set itself is structured as a pair of pairs, each of which has an everyday and a grand form. Generosity (*eleutheriotēs*; *NE* 4.1) is a virtue concerned with spending everyday sums of money. It strikes a mean between stinginess (deficient spending) and squandering (excessive spending).⁶ Like any virtue of character, this is done for the sake of the *kalon*, "giving to the right people, the right amounts, at the right time" (1120a23-25). As with discipline/moderation, I take "right" here to be defined by the virtuous person's overarching goals, which structure his *kalon* activity. And, as with any virtue of character, Aristotle is clear that this spending is relative to the individual's particular context and resources (1120b7–11).

The grand form of generosity is *megaloprepeia*. This term, Aristotle explains, comes from "great" (*megas*) and "fitting" (*prepon*; NE 4.2, 1122a24–25). While it is normally translated as "magnificence," I will use the more current term for such a person, "big spender," with the understanding that this is meant as a positive attribute. Like a generous person, a big spender must strike a middle way between stinginess and tasteless squandering, yet he does so on a grand scale. Aristotle illustrates this by invoking ancient liturgies, or public offices, by which rich citizens voluntarily decorated public temples, outfitted war ships, or underwrote religious festivals. He calls these instances of "good love of honor (*euphilotimētos*) for the common good" (1122b21–22). These examples seem to suggest that big spending is a virtue only for the rich.[7] Aristotle, however, states that one may also exhibit the virtue of big spending in expenses that come up only once in one's private life—for instance, buying a house or hosting a wedding banquet (1123a6–9). In fact, one may be a big spender by giving the most beautiful (*kalon*) ball or oil flask (*lēkythos*) to a child (1123a14–16). The latter is one of the few bits of kit one would bring to an ancient gym. Aristotle is clear that its cost is minimal. The big spender, however, will find just the right oil flask to give to a child, getting the best value for his money without going overboard into excess and extravagance. Given these examples, it seems that what makes an act of spending big is not how it compares to the resources that most people have but how it compares to the resources of the individual spender. From this perspective, generosity and big spending are virtues concerned with "ordinary" and "extraordinary" spending.[8] While this still places big spending beyond the reach of the poor, it opens up the possibility for people of moderate means, who are Aristotle's target audience in the first place.

Aristotle claims, "The big spender will be furnished with a house (*oikos*) befitting his wealth, for this is a kind of ornament (*kosmos*)" (1123a6–7). On the cosmetic reading, this amounts to wealthy people merely showing off by buying big houses. Aristotle's emphasis, however, is on what is fitting (*prepon*). The passage continues that what "befits" a temple is different from what befits a house or a tomb. If a house is a means of showing off, then it must do so the right way: rather than impose beauty from outside, the wealthy person's house should be an accurate reflection of his own fiscal worth.[9] What is more, even in private matters the big spender "is not lavish for his own sake but for the common good" (1123a-45). An Athenian house (*oikos*) is not only a building but also the land and people that go with it. As Plato's dialogues illustrate, the house provides a venue for symposia and sophistic demonstrations. Like public gyms, the house provides a vital space for education and networking. Aristotle himself speaks of entertaining ambassadors from abroad (1123a3-4). So, as with liturgies, the big spender's house also serves the common good, albeit on a smaller scale. Even the gift of an oil flask has some public significance, as it helps a child pursue his civic education by way of something like the ancient equivalent of back-to-school shopping.[10]

In sum, the big spender's house is a *kosmos* in the athletic sense, in that it expresses its owner's inner worth through external prosperity, while serving as a resource for further virtuous activity in service of the public good. As with the goods of fortune in *NE* 1.10, we find a virtuous cycle as the big spender's house serves both as an outward manifestation of his virtuous activity and as a means to virtuous activity in the future. The person in *NE* 1.10 was said to show greatness of spirit in times of ill fortune. I argued, however, that this was the exception, whereas a virtuous cycle was the norm, as goods of fortune are "usually" the ornament of virtuous activity. The real test of this reading is whether it holds up for the extended discussion of greatness of spirit in *NE* 4.3-4.

Aristotle presents greatness of spirit as the grand form of a virtue that lacks a name in Greek but we might call healthy pride (*NE* 4.4). Both the common and the grand form strike a mean between the small-spirited person (*mikropsychos*), who seeks less than he is worth, and the vain person (*chaunos*), who thinks himself worth more than he is. Vain people "adorn themselves (*kosmeō*) in clothes, ostentatious style and that sort of thing" (1125a30). With this, we finally have a clear use of *kosmos* in its cosmetic sense. Note, however, that it is connected to a vice not a virtue. The vain (literally, spongy) person lacks self-knowledge and thus aims to express outwardly more worth than he actually has within. This is a textbook example of a deceptive, cosmetic *kosmos*.[11] Great-spirited and properly proud people, by contrast, seek the honor they actually deserve. This aligns with the athletic sense of *kosmos*.

Aristotle stipulates that greatness in this discussion refers to "greatness in each virtue" that "seems to belong to the great-spirited person" (1123b30). But what exactly does "greatness in virtue" mean? Most scholars take this to refer to the degree of one's virtue.[12] It makes intuitive sense to refer to one person as more virtuous than another. Perhaps for this reason, this assumption has gone largely unquestioned in the scholarship. According to Aristotle's theory as laid out across *NE* 2–3, however, virtues of character are acquired conditions (1) to act in ways that strike various means, (2) which involve correct feelings of pleasure and pain, and (3) which aim at the *kalon*. The three parts of this account suggest at least three ways in which virtues may be great. The first is that one person may outdo another in hitting the mean. This is the least promising option.[13] Is the surpassingly virtuous person someone who always eats exactly the right amount of carbs or tells jokes at just the right time? While admirable, this hardly sets someone apart from the crowd in the ways Aristotle speaks about the person of great spirit.[14] If we focus on feelings, we might say that virtues are made greater insofar as people come better to enjoy virtuous activity. Aristotle will elaborate on this idea in *NE* 7's discussion of discipline, where he sees the transition from grudging compliance to willing enjoyment of moderate behavior as marking the final stage of moral development. *NE* 10's account of pleasure, in turn, sets this idea within a virtuous cycle akin to what modern athletes refer to as flow. None of these ideas, however, are explicitly stated in the present context. This leaves the final option: virtues may be made greater by coordinating their activity toward ever more *kalon* ends. But would this entail putting one's best possible effort into pursuing beautiful ends or actually accomplishing those beautiful ends?[15] Our passage continues (1123b31–1124a4):

> In no way would it suit a great-spirited person to run away with his arms flailing or to commit an injustice. Why would someone for whom nothing is great commit shameful acts? And if we examine each case, it will be completely ridiculous to find that the great-spirited person is not actually good. Nor would he be worthy of honor if he were vicious (*phaulos*), for honor (*timē*) is the prize (*athlon*) of virtue (*aretē*) and it is awarded to the good. It seems therefore that greatness of spirit is a kind of ornament (*kosmos*) of the virtues (*aretai*), for it makes them greater, and it does not come to be without them. For this reason, it is difficult to be truly great-spirited, since it is impossible without beautiful goodness (*kalokagathia*).

The phrase "prize of virtue" immediately preceding "ornament of the virtues" could hardly make the athletic context clearer. Yet in what sense of virtue? It is uncontroversial that *aretē* in the plural can mean virtuous deeds. We saw this in Pindar, *Olympian* 3.18's "crown for virtuous deeds."[16] Could this be the sense at play in *NE* 4.3? That Aristotle uses an article, "the virtues," where Pindar does not, may count against this as a translation. That said, Aristotle is explicit at *NE* 1.8: "In the Olympic games, it is not the finest and the strongest who are crowned victor, but those who compete: for it is from this group that winners come." So, whether we translate *kosmos tōn aretōn* as "crown for virtuous deeds" or "crown for virtues," there is explicit reason within *NE* for thinking that it is not merely having virtues but actively using them that makes one worthy of praise. If we continue the thought, then this *kosmos* increases activities that put those virtues to use.[17]

If this is right, we find a third virtuous cycle: like the happy person's good fortune (*NE* 1.10) and the big spender's house (*NE* 4.2), the great-spirited person's attitude toward great honor makes outwardly visible the worth of his virtuous activity, while also serving as a means for further virtuous activity (*NE* 4.3). At least, usually. It is fairly easy to see how goods of fortune, houses included, may contribute to one's virtuous activity. It is not immediately clear how one's relationship to honor plays an analogous role. Some scholars think that the great-spirited person's sense of self-worth emboldens him to undertake great deeds in ways that the small-spirited person would not.[18] That seems right, but it only explains the individual's self-worth, not the honor others pay him. Why should the person of great spirit care what others think of him? I have two responses.

First, we may embrace the practical spirit of *NE* and recognize that honor and resources often go together. Athletic scholarships are given only to those students whose talent is recognized. Promotions recognize good work, at least in theory, and bring increased income and responsibilities. The link between recognition and resources is built into the Greek word for "honor," *timē*, which has as much to do with positions of public office as it does with conferring praise. From this perspective, it is little wonder that greatness of spirit first appears in *NE* in connection with external resources.

Second, recall that when buying a house, the big spender "is not lavish for his own sake but for the common good." If the big spender and the great-spirited person are meant to parallel each other, what would it mean to care about one's reputation "for the common good"? In his work on logic, *Posterior Analytics*, Aristotle presents Socrates as an example of a great-spirited individual. The context is a general discussion of crafting definitions through identifying features that members of a group have in common. Aristotle illustrates this process by identifying

Socrates's boyfriend, Alcibiades, as an additional example of a great-spirited person, as well as the Homeric heroes Achilles and Ajax, each of whom "does not endure insults, for one waged war, another gave into rage, and the third killed himself." By contrast, Socrates and the Spartan commander Lysander are said to have greatness of spirit in their "indifference to good and bad fortune" (Aristotle, *Posterior Analytics* 97b17-25). Some scholars use the passage from *Posterior Analytics* to read *NE* 4.3 as Aristotle's not terribly successful attempt to combine Homeric love of honor with Socratic indifference by cutting out their extremes. The end result, on this reading, is a person who cares about honor more than other external goods but does not care about it too much.[19]

I suggest that we can make better sense of this fusion of intolerance of insults and indifference to fortune through the somewhat paradoxical idea that an individual's concern for his own honor may rest on his concern for the common good. Let us begin with Socrates. In Plato's *Apology*, Socrates makes light of a death sentence (29d-c), calls himself god's gift to the city (30e), insults jury members who care about anything other than virtue (29e-30b) and—after having been found guilty—suggests that he deserves to be fed for life at public expense like an Olympic victor (36d-e). It is easy to see Socrates as indifferent to the whims of fortune. It is therefore something of a surprise when, in the midst of all this brazen "come what may," Socrates expresses concern for his own reputation. Most people in his situation would resort to rhetorical tricks: begging, crying, and dragging their children into court in hopes of winning sympathy votes. Socrates takes the opposite approach: "With regard to my reputation and yours and that of the whole city, it does not seem right to me to do these things, especially at my age and with my reputation. For it is generally believed, whether truly or falsely, that in certain respects Socrates is superior to the majority of mankind" (Plato, *Apology* 34e-35a). What should we make of this death-before-dishonor mentality? Given that Socrates in *Apology* presents himself as pursuing a divine mission to make people care for virtue above all else, the most obvious explanation is that Socrates is willing to die to preserve his reputation, because his reputation allows him to serve as a role model for others in the pursuit of virtue. To do otherwise would be to show that death matters more to him than his divine mission. Viewed from this perspective, Socrates's concern for his own reputation is based on his concern for the common good. We might make a similar case for Achilles's intolerance of insults, insofar as one's reputation for superiority is key to one's ability to rule within Homer's heroic context. Meanwhile, Achilles's willingness to risk his life in battle, even in the face of a prophecy about his untimely demise, shows an indifference to goods of fortune that is not so dissimilar to Socrates's. While Socrates and Achilles are cited in *Posterior Analytics* but not *NE*, I suggest that we can find something that Achilles and Socrates do have in common: each leads a life that is tightly structured around overarching goals that contribute to the common good, and each values his reputation insofar as it makes visible his life's work and serves as a means of pursuing that work. We find a similar use of one's reputation to serve the common good in modern athletes from Jackie Robinson to Megan Rapinoe, who have successfully used their position in the public consciousness to fight for the rights of marginalized groups. In short, all of these figures treat their reputation as a *kosmos* of virtuous activity.

For Aristotle, the highest human end is excellent activity. Greatness of spirit, I suggest, determines the attitude one takes toward choosing high-level goals and arranging mid- and low-level goals in service of them. Healthy pride, by contrast, determines the attitude one takes toward low-level goals, working within the parameters set by higher-level goals.[20] As we saw in *NE* 1, the place of honor in *eudaimonia* is not merely to be honored but to be honored for the right reason: excellent activity. This is why the person of great spirit cares more about the approval of good people than of the crowd. Yet, provided that his actions are worthy of honor, he will not be overly troubled if those actions go unappreciated.[21]

When it comes to making virtues greater, this reading sidesteps the oddity of increasing a mean. It is not the moderate nature of an action that greatness of spirit increases. It is the agent's overall activity, his life's work, insofar as greatness of spirit provides a structure of motivation and purpose for everything an individual does.[22] This structuring activity also explains the role greatness of spirit plays in unifying the virtues. Organizing one's entire life around a single overarching goal is a huge challenge. It takes tremendous discipline, practice, care, and thinking on one's feet. If an individual is missing any of the virtues of character, he runs the risk of undermining his own efforts: backing down from challenging situations, overindulging in natural pleasures to the detriment of other goals, failing to navigate social situations, and so on. This is why greatness of spirit manifests itself only once all the other virtues of character are in place, and serves as the outward expression of this inward worth.²³ It is a *kosmos* of the virtues. Meanwhile, the attitudes and behaviors that constitute greatness of spirit are what allow an individual to navigate this hierarchy of low- and mid-level goals in service of his high-level goal. As we have seen, Tom Seaver pets dogs with his left hand to avoid injury to his pitching hand. To expand on Bae's suggestion, an Olympic runner may decline to race amateurs both to avoid unnecessary injury but also to avoid humiliating those amateurs. In short, greatness of spirit allows a person to keep his "eyes on the prize."

Soft Skills: *NE* 4.5–9

The second half of *NE* 4 introduces a set of virtues to guide how individuals interact with each other. These serve to contextualize greatness of spirit within other aspects of one's social life.²⁴ Today we call these soft skills. Unlike one's abilities in math, language, or athleticism (hard skills), soft skills are hard to quantify but help individuals navigate work with others. Aristotle's list includes evenness of temper (4.5), friendliness (4.6), honesty (4.7) and wit (4.8). While he does not quantify them exactly, he does suggest that each may fit a scale of excess, mean, and deficiency. There are times when jokes, for instance, are called for, such as roasting someone at an awards banquet. The individual who does not appreciate the roast is too stiff. But there are other times when jokes or banter are not called for, such as funerals. Someone who makes crass jokes on solemn occasions is tasteless. A witty person hits the mean by his ability to read the room and engage or not engage in humor as it is called for. So too for the other skills, which involve how we respond to offensive behavior (evenness of temper), how we present ourselves to people we meet for the first time (friendliness), and how we talk about our own accomplishments (truthfulness). While this section of *NE* is useful, particularly for people headed into job interviews, it is possibly the least controversial portion of the work. It clarifies what other factors must be in place for a person to pursue a life of great spirit and big spending. Aristotle continues this contextualizing project in book 5.

Chapter 14

Sportsmanship and Thinking on One's Feet
NE 5–6

> The decent person is not a stickler for justice in a bad way but takes less than he might even if he has the law on his side.
>
> —*NE* 5.10, 1138a1-2

> Virtue makes the target correct, and practical wisdom makes the things leading to the target correct.
>
> —*NE* 6.12, 1144a7-9

Homer's *Iliad* 23 is one of the West's earliest pieces of sports journalism. The context is a series of funeral games for Achilles's friend (and possibly lover) Patroclus. Unlike stephanic games, where winners were crowned and losers returned home in shame, these contests have prizes for people who come in second and third place. Achilles draws prizes from the treasures he has looted and people he has enslaved during the Trojan War. For the wrestling match (*Iliad* 23.700-739) he sets out for the winner "a large tripod to be set in a fire, worth twelve oxen," and for the loser, "a woman skilled at many crafts and worth four oxen." While this is hardly a victory for human rights, it gives a glimpse into economics at a point before monetary currencies have become the standard. This particular match, however, ends in a tie. Achilles therefore tells the competitors, Ajax and Odysseus, to "take equal prizes and go." There is an obvious problem with this conclusion: if the prizes on offer are not equal in value, how can Ajax and Odysseus take equal prizes? Questions such as this motivate *NE* 5's discussion of justice.

Justice: *NE* 5

NE 5.1-2 distinguishes between a general sense of justice (*dikaiosunē*), which amounts to "lawfulness" and "complete virtue," and particular justice, which is a virtue of character governing interactions between individuals involving resources.[1] *NE* 5.3-5 lays out the three spheres in which particular justice operates: distributing goods (5.3), correcting wrongs (5.4), and exchanging goods (5.5).[2] Aristotle presents these in terms of geometric proportions, arithmetic proportions, and something he calls a "diagonal combination."

Justice in distribution is accomplished by distributing honor, wealth, and other resources in ways that mirror the recipients' relative worth (*NE* 5.3). Worth (*axia*), in turn, is calculated in one of three ways. Democracy holds citizenship to be a person's mark of worth and thus assigns all citizens the same share of goods. Oligarchy holds wealth to be the marker of worth and assigns the greatest goods to the wealthy. Aristocracy, finally, assigns the greatest goods to the best (*aristos*) people. As we saw in *Republic*, "best" refers not to the inherited titles of European aristocrats—what Thomas Jefferson refers to as an unnatural aristocracy—but to virtues that can be tested and ranked through competition. *Iliad*'s wrestling match reflects this thinking, ranking the winner three times as valuable as the loser. Since the value of the prizes (a twelve-oxen tripod and a four-oxen woman) vary proportionately to the worth of the recipients, Aristotle calls this a geometric mean. This captures the competitive ethos we have seen at play in the person of great spirit's striving to accomplish great deeds and put his great virtue to use.

Justice in correction is used when the proper proportion between resources and individual worth is not met. Homer does not say how Achilles handled the tie, but let us suppose that Ajax takes the tripod and Odysseus takes the woman. To remedy this injustice, Aristotle's theory dictates that we must take the amount that Ajax exceeds the mean and give it to Odysseus. Since the tripod is worth three times what the woman is, removing one of its legs and giving it to Odysseus would make up the difference. Given that this would destroy the tripod, however, what Aristotle really means is that Ajax should give something of equivalent value—for instance, four oxen.[3] Since justice here is achieved through adding and subtracting, Aristotle calls this an arithmetic mean.

Aristotle claims that justice in exchanges works by a diagonal combination (*NE* 5.5). I suggest we think about this in terms of the rhetorical figure chiasmus. This figure is named after the Greek letter *chi*, which consists of two diagonal lines: X. This is how Greeks conceptualized strings of words that fall into an *abba* pattern, like the famous line from President John F. Kennedy's inaugural address:

Ask not what *your country* can do for *you*
X
ask what *you* can do for *your country*.

Aristotle applies this thinking by imagining a housebuilder and a shoemaker coming together to exchange shoes and a house. He concludes, "As a housebuilder is to a shoemaker, so must the number of shoes be to a house" (*NE* 5.5). Read carefully, this expresses a chiastic pattern: housebuilder, shoemaker, shoes, house. What brings all this together is need (*chreia*).[4] The carpenter's need for shoes is small relative to the cobbler's need for a house. What each person pays should, in turn, reflect the relative value of these goods (fig. 5).

While particular justice protects the rights of individuals, its larger goal is to promote the common good.[5] When distributive justice ranks an individual's worth, this worth is measured by his contribution

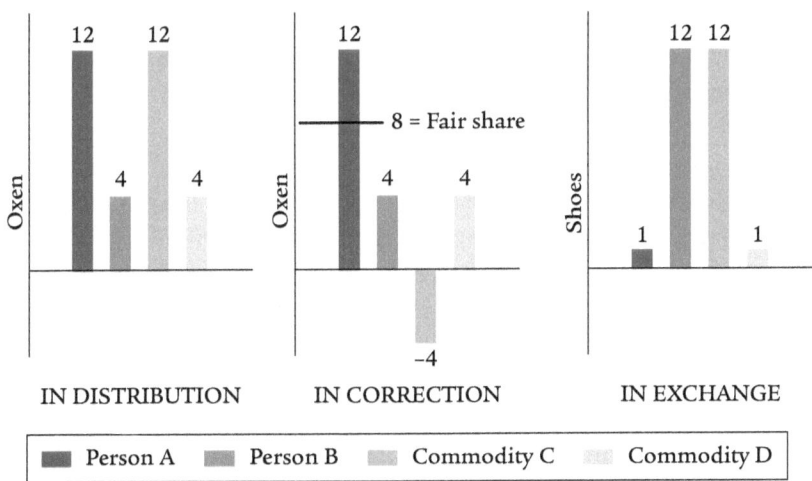

FIGURE 5. The relationship between Person A, Person B, Commodity C, and Commodity D in particular justice in *NE* 5.3–5.

to the common good: ruling, teaching, farming, racing, and so on. A person who embodies particular justice will be content with such judgments, since he sees how they contribute to the community as a whole, and he will not desire more than his fair share. The end result is to harmonize a competitive spirit for personal advancement with respect for others' contributions to one's community. In this, particular justice comes close to what we could call good sportsmanship. Those who fall short of this do so by desiring more than their fair share. This is the vice *pleonexia*, which we saw figuring prominently in Plato's *Republic*.

While it is wrong for someone to seek more than his fair share, it is fine for him voluntarily to accept less than what he is owed. If, for example, neither Ajax nor Odysseus had four oxen or equivalent goods to bring about justice in correction, then one of them could have simply accepted the woman and allowed the other to keep the much more valuable tripod. This insight underlies *NE* 5.9-11's question about whether one can be unjust to oneself.[6] Aristotle's answer is no, since voluntarily taking less than what one is due amounts to giving the other person a gift. It is also an instance of what Aristotle calls decency/equity (*epieikeia*). At *NE* 5.10, Aristotle explains that the purpose of the law is the common good, yet, since laws are written using universal terms, there will be particular instances when enforcing the law detracts from the common good. In those instances, the decent/equitable person will not enforce the full extent of what the law requires. Thus, by violating what the law's authors set down, the decent person promotes what the law's authors' intended, the common good, in circumstances that those authors could not have reasonably foreseen.

This idea of decency/equity presents another angle of good sportsmanship, which connects to the rest of *NE* two ways. First, it builds on *NE* 4.3's account of the great-spirited person who will overlook small honors and focus instead on large ones. This idea is elaborated in *NE* 8-9's discussion of friends who will spend their resources as they compete in virtue. If justice sets minimal requirements for holding a state together, friendship sets maximal, aspirational requirements and, in some sense, makes justice irrelevant (see chapter 16). Second, in calling on individuals to interpret what legislators intended but did not write, Aristotle's account of decency highlights the need for just individuals to think on their feet as they engage in civic life—for instance, by serving on juries. "A fully just person, then, is not merely a follower of rules, but is also a competent maker and adjudicator of the law."[7]

We find a prime example of decency and sportsmanship in Australian runner John Landy. In the 1965 Australian Championships, Landy narrowly avoided injury during the final mile of the race. Another runner had clipped the heel of Ron Clarke, also in the race. As Clarke went down, Landy jumped to avoid collision but scraped his spikes on Clarke's shoulder. This was clearly not Landy's fault, and there was no rule calling on him to do anything for Clarke. If anything, the general expectation of racing is that Landy would simply keep going. Instead, he stopped, apologized to Clarke, and helped him up before returning to the race. The people who laid down the rules for this event, and the Olympic Games to which its winners would advance, never covered an instance as specific as accidently scraping an opponent to avoid collision when someone else has caused him to fall. Landy, however, broke with what was expected to uphold the spirit of the event's rules in a situation no one had seen coming.

Thinking on One's Feet: *NE* 6

Student athletes often have a leg up when applying for jobs. As many employers recognize, balancing the demands of school and sports is a huge accomplishment that requires careful time management, discipline, and stamina. These are all excellent qualities in an employee. They also embody the spirit of Aristotelian virtues: by hitting the mean in all things, the virtuous student athlete approaches life as a grand balancing act. That all sounds lovely in the abstract. Yet, as student athletes will attest, people who actually live this way often confront competing demands calling for split-second decision making. In such cases, the balancing act of life can feel more like juggling while riding a bicycle. To take a slightly more athletic image, a life of excellent activity requires a lot of "thinking on one's feet."

NE 6 continues the line of thought set out in *NE* 3.1–5's trainer's manual by focusing on the virtues of thought. Along the way, Aristotle responds to Socrates's theory that all virtues are in reality forms of practical wisdom.[8] He opens by using an athletic image: "In all the states of character we have discussed, and in others as well, there is a target (*skopos*) at which the person having reason aims and either tightens or loosens, and this is the standard (*horos*) of mean states which we say are between excess and deficiency, since they align with correct reason (*orthos logos*)" (*NE* 6.1, 1138b21–25). Loosening and tightening hearkens back to talk of the mean, which is by now familiar. What the new image adds is the idea that all of this is in reference to a particular target one is attempting to hit. Without a particular target in mind, there is no right tension. Aristotle admits, "While all that is true, it is not clear." *NE* 6 thus sets out to clarify what this target is, how virtues of character relate to it, and what correct reason has to do with any of this.[9]

Aristotle's first step, which takes up the bulk of the book, is to differentiate between the various virtues of thought (*NE* 6.2–11). Central to this are theoretical wisdom (*sophia*), which studies things that are not up to us and always the same, such as math or physics, and practical wisdom (*phronēsis*), which studies things that change and are within our power to bring about. Theoretical wisdom is the virtue associated with study (*theoria*; see discussion at *NE* 1.7–8 and 10.6–8). Practical wisdom is the virtue associated with deliberation (*bouleusis*; cf. *NE* 3.2). The most important object of practical wisdom's deliberations is living well, and it operates "not in a piecemeal way, about how to bring about health or strength for instance, but about living well as a whole" (*NE* 6.5, 1140a27). In this, practical wisdom serves an "administrative ability," which prioritizes and organizes one's various activities within an ordered whole.[10]

At this point, practical wisdom sounds a lot like my presentation of greatness of spirit. This could be a particular problem for me, given that I have pushed against standard readings that see greatness of spirit as concerned with ordering *virtues*, and argued, instead, that it is primarily concerned with organizing *virtuous activities* into hierarchies of low-, mid-, and high-level goals. This seems to be precisely the task that *NE* 6 attributes to practical wisdom. So, while Aristotle must in general say "more clearly" how practical wisdom and the virtues of character fit together, clarity on the relation between practical wisdom and greatness of spirit is a particularly pressing need for my reading, which frames *NE*'s overall account in terms of elite performers. With this challenge in mind, let us turn to the heart of *NE* 6's discussion.

NE 6.12–13 returns to *NE* 6.1's demand for clarity by raising a series of puzzles about how theoretical and practical wisdom contribute to happiness. The philosophical payoff is to clarify the relationship between happiness, practical wisdom, and the virtues of character.

The first puzzle (1143b19–21) states: Theoretical wisdom is concerned with topics such as physics and math, but these seem to have nothing to do with human happiness. Aristotle's response (1144a1–6) is fairly straightforward. In the language of *NE* 1, the active engagement with theoretical wisdom is study: this is a complete/final (*teleion*) activity and thus a component, if not the entirety, of happiness: "Theoretical wisdom produces happiness not in the way that the medical art produces health but in the way that health produces health" (1144a5-6). In other words, it is not that theoretical wisdom is the study of human happiness but that human happiness is the study of theoretical wisdom. The next two puzzles use medical and athletic imagery to question practical wisdom's contribution to happiness.

The second puzzle states: If knowledge of medicine or gym training does not make an already healthy or fit person more healthy or fit, then practical wisdom, which is knowledge of the human good, does not make an already good person better (1143b21-28). Aristotle's response begins, "Our work (*ergon*) attains its end (*apoteleō*) according to practical wisdom and virtue of character" (1144a6-7). This verb form of "end" (*telos*) hearkens back to *NE* 1's idea that happiness consists in putting virtues to use.[11] The text continues, "For [character] virtue makes the target (*skopos*) correct, and practical wisdom makes the things leading to the target correct" (1144a7-9). How does this targeting work?

The third puzzle focuses not on being good but on becoming good. It states: If practical wisdom is necessary for becoming good, then it is enough for a person merely to follow the advice of others, as is the case with medicine and gym training (1143b28-33). To answer this, Aristotle responds, we must first "take a step back" (1144a11-1145a6). In *NE* 2's discussion of training, Aristotle argued that we become brave by performing brave actions. One result of this is that it is possible for someone who has not yet acquired a settled condition to act bravely to perform the same kind of act that a person in such a condition would engage in. *NE* 6 builds on this idea by distinguishing between "natural virtue," which is with us from birth and "full virtue," which is a mature and settled condition. How does one move from natural virtue to full virtue? Aristotle draws another distinction. Some people are clever (*deinos*) at means/end reasoning. Cleverness can be used for good or ill, though in its properly developed form it constitutes an integral part of practical wisdom. Putting these two distinctions together, Aristotle argues, "we cannot be fully good [have full virtues] without practical wisdom, and we cannot have practical wisdom without virtue of character" (1144b31-32). How should we understand this chiastic yet cryptic phrase?

Socrates toyed with the idea that all virtues are simply instances of practical wisdom. This idea raises various problems, as we saw in Plato's *Laches*. Aristotle responds that Socrates was half-right: virtues of character are not instances of practical wisdom, yet each requires practical wisdom. With this, Aristotle loops back to *NE* 6.1's request for clarity about practical wisdom, virtue of character, and correct reason: "People say that virtue is the state aligned with correct reason. Now the correct reason is the reason aligned with practical wisdom; they all seem to believe then that the state aligned with practical wisdom is virtue" (1144b21-24). The virtues of character dispose us to act in certain ways when confronted with pleasures, pains, expenses, and social interactions. Practical wisdom allows us to act according to those dispositions successfully by setting them within a holistic understanding of the human good. This involves not only reasoning about means of pursuing various ends but also "specifying" what those ends look like in concrete situations.[12] A person may, for instance, be disposed to be generous toward a friend who needs money. Yet there are times when giving a friend money would not be in that friend's best interest: Does he need money for drugs? Does he need money to pay off gambling debts? Would he be better off in the long run if he had to work to earn the money himself? In such instances, practical wisdom will step in and decide that giving a friend money is not the generous thing to do. Practical wisdom is a skill at reading circumstances, deciding what factors are relevant to action, and using them to adjust one's concept of what counts as the mean in that instance. It is the ethical equivalent of the archer's skill, which tightens and loosens for the sake of hitting a target (*skopos*). It is for this reason that no one may have any of the character virtues in their full form without having practical wisdom.

At the same time, we cannot have practical wisdom without having every virtue of character. As a result, it is impossible to have any virtue of character without having all of them. Why? Practical reasoning takes a holistic view of human action. In order for it to gain this holistic perspective, one needs an all-encompassing view of the human good, as is provided by the aims of the full range of the virtues of character. Because of this, practical wisdom does not emerge in its full state until fairly late in the process of moral development. This is not to say that no practical reasoning happens before then. As we saw in the trainer's manual of *NE* 3.1-5, the process of training in virtues of character is not purely mechanical but involves ever more rational reflection as students mature. *NE* 6 calls this thinking cleverness while the process of maturation is still underway. At some point, however, the scales tip, the student comes to see how the virtues of character, all of which aim at some *kalon* end, may be brought together into a holistic pursuit of all this *kalon*. Mere cleverness gives way to practical wisdom, and natural virtues become full virtues.

In sum, Aristotle's response to our final puzzle is no: it is not enough for a student merely to follow a trainer's instructions. Rational thought is integral to the process of training, and one cannot attain full virtues of character without attaining practical wisdom at the same time.

Final Thoughts: *NE* 4–6

Having worked through *NE* 6's string of puzzles, what can we say about the relationship between greatness of spirit and practical reason? If anything, the problem with my reading looks more serious, now that we can add further worries that both of these virtues are acquired only in presence of all the virtues of character, that both come at the end of the process of moral development, and that both ground the idea that one may not have any virtue of character in its full form without having all of them. Are practical wisdom and greatness of spirit simply the same thing?

To respond, I would point out that practical wisdom is intimately involved in every virtue of character. Granted, when it comes to greatness of spirit, that relationship seems to be particularly intimate. What differentiates the two, I suggest, is the concern for honor. I argued above that greatness of spirit provides the ability to keep one's "eyes on the prize," that is, to devote one's efforts to high-level goals and accept or dismiss mid- and low-level goals insofar as they align with or detract from them. Practical wisdom, with the aid of cleverness, approaches these hierarchies from a rational, calculating perspective. Greatness of spirit approaches the same hierarchies from an affective perspective: through it we embrace some undertaking as clearly awesome (*kalon*), while not getting sidetracked by undertakings that are worthy in themselves yet pose obstacles to a life built around a singular purpose. Virtues of character in general "make the target correct." Greatness of spirit is unique among the virtues of character insofar as it deals with targets for other targets.[13] If we want a metaphor, greatness of spirit "crowns" the virtues not so much by sitting on top of them like a medieval monarch's golden crown as by encircling them like an athlete's wreath and holding them all together.[14]

Aristotle's Olympic victors and Angela Duckworth's elite performers provided prime examples of individuals who organize their lives around such singular goals. It seems possible, though, that one could have a life of full virtue and practical wisdom while holding two or three mid-level goals in balance. Duckworth, who is herself a very gritty person, admits that she cannot align her commitments to family and career under a single overarching goal.[15] Perhaps greatness of spirit comes in degrees: elite performers provide the central case, while others organize their lives around a handful of mid-level goals, such as work, family, and hobbies. If I am right that greatness of spirit is a virtue for any happy person, not just the rich and powerful, then Aristotle requires us to give our lives some kind of overarching shape. This leads us to one final question.

Where should we place *NE*'s treatment of *kalon* on the scale from moral to beautiful. Here too, greatness of spirit, understood via Aristotle's elite performers, provides an answer. It is perfectly possible for a person with character virtues to lead a life with little overarching integration of goals. Such a person would eat moderately, step up bravely when called upon, engage justly in transactions, help out friends when needed, not get unduly angry, be funny enough, and so on. By checking each of these boxes, this person leads a perfectly moral life, but there is nothing particularly awesome about it. He is like William Deresiewicz's excellent sheep, who do everything that is expected of them but have little idea what their varied pursuits add up to. Such people do better on "resume virtues" than "eulogy virtues."[16] When it comes to summing up a person's life, no one wants to hear that she got decent grades and paid her bills on time. Such details are compelling only if they can be situated within a larger story. I have, for instance, taught a number of nontraditional students who are the first in their family to attend college. Some of them have young children and want to show them that college is for them. On top of full-time jobs and raising children, these students commute to campus at night for three-hour classes, schedule study times weeks in advance, give up on anything like sufficient sleep, and somehow find enough hours in a day. For these people, getting good grades is an awesome accomplishment. If such people do not embody greatness of spirit, I don't know who does. Aristotle's point, as I take it, is that hitting the mean is not enough. Our activities need to be moderated for something. They need to fit into overarching projects that we can look back on and say: I did something awesome with my life. Duckworth talks about this in terms of grit. Aristotle talks about it in terms of greatness of spirit and calls it a *kosmos* of the virtues.

Existing scholarship has ignored the athletic context of *NE*'s use of *kosmos* and actively shunned Homeric/heroic resonances within *NE* and Aristotle's *Posterior Analytics*. As a result, scholars were left with the cosmetic sense of *kosmos*, which made goods of fortune, houses, and greatness of spirit seem like strange afterthoughts and unnecessary additions to one's virtue. By stressing the athletic sense of *kosmos*, I have shown how all these pieces fit together as one's good fortunes, house, honor, and greatness of spirit make outwardly visible one's inner worth through a life of structured, virtuous activity. This beauty is not one imposed from without but shines forth from within and is ultimately a matter of organizing one's life around meaningful projects and having the grit to keep one's eyes on the prize. It is the beauty not of makeup but of a victor's crown.

CHAPTER 15

Enjoying Discipline
NE 7

> "Excuse me. How do I get to Carnegie Hall?"
>
> "Practice, man. Practice."
>
> —Author unknown

We talk about people playing an instrument or playing a sport, but the physical and intellectual work it takes to become a professional musician or athlete is nothing short of grueling. Children who pick up an instrument or ball for the first time do not automatically commit themselves to practicing for hours on end. If Aristotle is to model his account of happiness on elite performers in athletics and music, how can he explain the motivation required to attain such lofty goals? This question provides the context for *NE* 7.

We encountered discipline (*sōphrosunē*) in *NE* 3.10-12 as the virtue concerned with pleasures of touch. While that sense is still present, *NE* 7 takes a broader approach, exploring how discipline and various conditions falling short of it apply to any virtue of character. Parallels to athletics and music are woven throughout, suggesting that we may better understand how one becomes virtuous by thinking about how one becomes a virtuoso.

Discipline and Weakness of Will: *NE* 7.1–10

NE 7 is a textbook example of the endoxic method (*NE* 7.1). Aristotle canvases existing opinions (*endoxa*; *NE* 7.2), spins out puzzles (*aporiai*; *NE* 7.3), and works through those puzzles by drawing a slew of distinctions, looking back to the initial opinions (*NE* 7.4–14). The particular opinions he lays out rely on nuances of the Greek language that are hard to translate short of working through a text such as *NE* 7 itself. Let our opening reflections on practice therefore stand in as *endoxa*, so that we may jump straight into the puzzles.

Socrates famously argued that it was impossible for someone to know better but do something anyway. Aristotle sees Socrates's position as puzzling, simply because people do it all the time (*NE* 7.2). Plato agrees. In *Republic* Plato uses the inner conflict that comes about in moments of weak will (*akrasia*) to divide the soul into three. Aristotle sides with Plato on this, but he builds weakness of will into his broader theory in a different way.

In *NE* 2's account of character virtues, Aristotle argues that to have a virtue, one must know the mean, act on the mean, and enjoy acting on the mean. These three criteria, taken together, produce four options for how one might relate to the mean in any given sphere of action. These four options, which present Aristotle's attempt to systematize the *endoxa* laid out in *NE* 7.1, provide the underlying structure for *NE* 7.4–12's long list of distinctions (see table 6).

Let us walk through this list, using a key example provided by Aristotle that is applicable for anyone training for elite sports: avoiding excessive sweets (1147a24-b9). Offer a triple-frosted cupcake to the average four-year-old, and you will not run into conflicting motivations. He does not have any concept of sugar being bad and will wholeheartedly want to eat the cupcake. This child is undisciplined about avoiding sweets. At some point, perhaps through a combination of belly aches and parental explanation, he will develop the belief that he should not eat triple-frosted cupcakes. Despite this belief, he along with many adults will give in and eat them anyway. This child is now weak-willed about sweets. Given more time, and practice at turning down cupcakes, he may finally come to resist temptation. But he resents it. He is now

Table 6

	UNDISCIPLINED (*ASŌPHROSUNĒ*)	WEAK-WILLED (*AKRASIA*)	STRONG-WILLED (*ENKRASIA*)	DISCIPLINED (*SŌPHROSUNĒ*)
KNOW THE MEAN	–	+	+	+
ACT ON THE MEAN	–	–	+	+
ENJOY THE MEAN	–	–	–	+

strong-willed about sweets. Given even more time and practice, however, he can lose a taste for sweets and enjoy a low-sugar diet, happily eating fruit for dessert. He is, at last, disciplined about excessive sweets.

If you had to choose between these four stages, which one would you want to be at? Which presents the fullest life for a human being? Granted, there is a certain bad-boy attraction in knowing better and doing things anyway (weakness of will). But Aristotle's point is that such behavior is ultimately self-destructive. Likewise, what is the point of doing everything right but gritting your teeth while you do it (strength of will)? And while we might say that ignorance is bliss, do you really want to be so out of touch with reality that you are constantly acting against your own self-interest without realizing it (undisciplined)? While talk of virtue may sound dreary when held up against unbridled pleasures, Aristotle's point is that the ultimate goal of virtue is the most consistently pleasant life over the long haul. Meanwhile, cupcakes are just one example, one that actually involves a pleasure of touch. Aristotle applies this same four-stage scheme to the development of any virtue of character.[1]

What is going on in the mind of the weak-willed person? For Plato, this is a simple victory of the soul's appetitive part over its rational part. Cupcakes taste great: long-term, overall goods be damned! In *NE* 7, Aristotle spells out the mechanisms of inner conflict in more literal terms. Central to all of this is his account of conditions and training. Given that conditions are acquired through pleasure and pain (*NE* 2) but also involve rational calculation (*NE* 3.1–5 and *NE* 6), he approaches the matter from the perspectives of both emotion and reasoning.

From the perspective of rationality, Aristotle analyzes actions as conclusions to what he calls a "practical syllogism" (*NE* 7.3).[2] These consist of a general premise, a particular premise, and a particular conclusion. While the jargon is cumbersome, the point is fairly simple, as can be seen in the following example:

> General Premise: Human beings should not consume very sweet things.
> Particular Premise: I am a human being, and this cupcake is very sweet.
> Conclusion: I should not consume this cupcake.

Each premise here refers to the person performing the action (human/me) as well as the opportunity for action (sweet things/cupcake). This suggests at least four opportunities for error to slip in. I may, for instance, not realize that what I am consuming is a sweet: people looking to eat healthy will often opt for salad rather than fries without realizing that some salad dressings contain up to 12 grams of sugar. But unless I am somehow unaware of the sugar content of frosting, this does not explain our cupcake case. In such a case, perhaps, I know about the sugar in frosting or salad dressing, but for some reason I fail to call it to mind. While this may seem implausible, recall that practical reasoning often involves setting individual actions within our broader hierarchy of goals, as here:

> General Premise: People who want to stay lean should not consume very sweet things.
> Particular Premise: I want to stay lean, and this salad is very sweet.
> Conclusion: I should not consume this salad.[3]

Cupcakes wear their sweetness on their sleeves, so when I am confronted with a cupcake, my desire for washboard abs springs immediately to mind. By contrast, salads seem healthy, so I may let down my guard and not call to mind what I have learned about the sugar content of certain dressings. This makes even more sense if we bring in additional virtues, as here:

> General Premise: Job applicants should not post offensive content on social media.
> Particular Premise: I am a job applicant, and this political meme is offensive.
> Conclusion: I should not post this meme.

The general premise embodies the social virtue friendliness, which regulates how we interact with people we do not know well. Given that I do not know my potential employers, or their political leanings, I might not realize that what I find funny may be offensive to them. All I am thinking is that the meme is funny and that my friends will find it funny. Since I interact with my friends on social media, posting this meme is an instance of another social virtue: wit. Thus in pursuing one social virtue, wit, I transgress the boundaries of another, friendliness. This sort of thing is easier to imagine actually happening, particularly for people whose character is still under development. But it cannot account for people who actively think at the time, "I should not eat this cupcake," and do it, anyway.[4]

One way to salvage this line of thinking is to be more precise about what it means to know something. In our cupcake case, I might be aware of the relevant facts and have them all currently called to mind, yet I do not really understand the biology behind the general premise, and as a result I merely believe it. Knowledge, by contrast, requires that this premise is integrated into my overall body of knowledge in the holistic way that practical wisdom brings about.[5] Yet, as we have seen, no one obtains practical wisdom without also acquiring all the virtues of character, so we may rightly wonder whether it is the practically wise person's knowledge or his conditioned emotional response that is really at work here.

How do emotions figure into *NE* 7's account of weakness of will? While most scholars analyze Aristotle's account of habit in the context of developing virtues, Rachel Barney looks to the role of habit in the formation of vice.[6] On her reading, being undisciplined is not merely an absence of knowledge but a condition brought about through improper training. Vice, like virtue, requires practice.[7] What is more, she argues, the intemperate person's bad habits are not the result of following a flawed theory of virtue. Just the opposite: it is only after repeatedly engaging in immoderate acts that a person acquires immoderate character and then seeks to justify that immoderation through rationalizations that twist and pervert practical reasoning. By setting practical reasoning in the passenger's seat, so to speak, Barney highlights the nonrational forces that go into the formation of any condition, be it virtuous or vicious. First, there are pleasures inherent in the act itself, such as the natural pleasures of touch. Second, there are external rewards and punishments that coaches employ to guide habituation. Third, there is what Barney calls "pleasures of habit as such." If, as a child, I am given a candy every time I put my dirty clothes in the laundry bin, putting clothes in the bin will eventually become "second nature" for me. As an adult, well after the supply of candy rewards has dried up, I may simply enjoy having my dirty clothes neatly stored away and not in piles all over the floor. Conversely, I may develop my salad habit before learning about the perils of certain vinaigrettes and keep at it, simply because having a salad with a meal feels right to me.

Given all that, should we understand giving in to cupcakes as a failure of reason, a failure of emotional conditioning, or some combination of the two? Aristotle's answer, I suspect, is that it depends on the circumstances. The broader payoff, however, is a rich and varied account of human motivation. Having worked through these puzzles, let us return to our opening question: What does it take to become an elite performer or, more broadly, to become disciplined in any of the virtues of character?

Pleasure and Unimpeded Activity: *NE* 7.11–14

A standard reading of *NE* stresses the role of pleasure in acquiring virtues of character.[8] This approach looks to passages scattered throughout *NE* to create a context for understanding *NE* 7.11-14's discussion of pleasure. Here, Aristotle contrasts pleasures that result from need, such as drinking water when thirsty, with pleasures that arise from "unimpeded activity." While the terminology is new, this builds on *NE* 1's argument that excellent activity is pleasant, and people who think that happiness consists in pleasure are not completely mistaken. The idea of unimpeded activity returns in *NE* 10.3's more famous discussion of flow, where it sets the stage for the much-debated suggestion that happiness consists in study.[9] Here in *NE* 7, Aristotle presents the more general idea that by mastering new skills and putting that mastery to work in unimpeded activity, we expand our understanding of the range of pleasures we are capable of experiencing. This is clearest in music or sports, where people who have developed beyond the beginning stages take joy in actively engaging in their respective spheres of virtuosity. Likewise for the other virtues. A person who has a more-than-basic mastery of the social virtues takes pleasure in interacting with others. A brave person enjoys stepping up when called upon. A big spender or person of great spirit takes joy in pursuing their various projects. Such people have "acquired a taste for, a capacity to enjoy for their own sake, things that are in fact noble and enjoyable for their own sake."[10]

This standard reading, according to which moral development proceeds by experiencing higher-quality pleasures, has been criticized.[11] According to this rival reading of *NE*, "on Aristotle's considered view, virtuous acts are *not* typically overall pleasant even for the virtuous, let alone for the learners."[12] The standard reading compares learning virtue to learning to ski. The rival reading denies the sports analogy. Instead, it reads *NE* 2.1, which likens training in moral virtues to learning to play the kithara, in light of *Politics* 8.5, where Aristotle claims that learning to play music "is no amusement but is accompanied by pain."[13] I take issue with the rival reading for several reasons. First, to contrast sports as fun and music as hard work gets wrong both Greek culture and Aristotle's understanding of it (to say nothing of the truth!). Both sports and music, if pursued seriously, involve both pleasure and pain. If the standard reading goes too far by stressing pleasure over pain, the rival reading goes too far by stressing pain over pleasure.

The first point of disagreement, I suspect, is how to understand *kalon*. Miles Burnyeat, who defends the standard reading, translates *kalon* as "noble," yet his discussion of acquiring a taste for the noble suggests that he also embraces aesthetic dimensions of *kalon*. We, like Herakles or Olympic athletes, pursue certain things because they are just obviously awesome. Howard Curzer, who advances the rival reading, sees this line of thought as "residual elements of an older, Homeric value system, coexisting uneasily alongside Aristotle's newer system of values."[14] In short, what I see as the key to making sense of *NE*'s aspirational ethic modeled after elite performers, Curzer sees as an obstacle in need of removal. This leaves the rival reading a thoroughly moralistic understanding of *kalon*, in which not even virtuous people take much pleasure in acting on their virtue. While Curzer's rival reading downplays pleasure in moral development, it does make room for pleasure in two forms.[15] First is the "warm glow stemming from the belief that he or she is acting rightly," but this is merely an internalized version of external rewards. The second is "pleasures proper to virtuous acts," but the example given is a moderate meal, which Aristotle considers a pleasure of touch. By denying the sports analogies, the rival reading makes no room for people who come to experience new, higher-quality pleasures as they advance in their development. In short, Curzer's rival reading leaves out flow.

The second point of disagreement is how to understand the relative timing in how we develop emotionally and intellectually. The standard and rival readings agree that developing virtues of character comes first and developing virtues of thought comes second. Yet the standard reading takes this to mean that people begin developing character virtues before they begin developing virtues of thought.[16] This seems right to me. The rival reading argues that people must finish developing moral virtue before they can begin developing practical wisdom and the virtues of thought.[17] Curzer admits that this goes against the most obvious reading of various passages, yet he argues that it is the more "charitable" reading insofar as it supplies Aristotle with a more attractive view.[18] What is actually going on in *NE*, as I argued in my discussion of *NE* 3.1–5, is that after the very earliest stages, virtues of character and virtues of thought are developed in tandem. Sports and music provide helpful points of reference. Technique is developed through a sort of muscle memory arising from a combination of repeated actions and rational reflection. The cycle may begin with isolated elements: how to stand, how to breathe, how to position parts of one's body. Over time, these elements are coordinated into larger and larger skills as one gains mastery of an instrument or sport. This makes room for *NE* 7.3's exploration of people who in some sense know (or, more accurately, believe) what they should be doing but have not yet fully integrated this information and made it second nature.

As for the question of pleasure versus pain, contemporary psychology suggests that the question is not so much which as when. William Damon is a leading expert on how children develop a sense of vocation in life. His empirical studies have shown that in the earlier years, children make the most progress when given the ability to play around with ideas in supportive, low-stakes environments. It is only after a child has sufficiently advanced that constructive criticism is useful.[19] This criticism, however, is not negative but part of what Anders Ericsson calls deliberate practice.[20] This is not merely repeating an action, but identifying areas of improvement, setting specific goals, and pursuing them in systematic ways. At the very least, deliberate practice is something other than unimpeded activity and tends to be tiring. Angela Duckworth points to musicians who nap between practice sessions.

As a personal aside, I am a fairly accomplished organist/pianist, and decided during COVID-19 quarantine that it would be fun to learn to play classical guitar. While I have no trouble reading music, I did not appreciate how different the techniques would be. As a keyboard player, I am accustomed to pushing a key and getting a sound. With the guitar, to play any given note, I must figure out which spot at the intersection of six strings and twenty or so frets to depress with which of four fingers of my left hand, while simultaneously identifying which of five fingers of my right hand to use to pluck which of the six strings. All that to play a single note. Add to this that keyboard music numbers fingers of the left hand starting with the thumb, and guitar music starts with the index finger, and what was meant to be a relaxing diversion during quarantine ended up being an intellectually draining activity that I could manage for about twenty minutes before setting the guitar aside.

In contrast to my failed foray into guitar playing, Duckworth argues that in cases of elite performers across a range of fields we find a virtuous cycle as the pleasures of flow provide motivation for the pains of deliberate practice, which, in turn, unlock ever greater pleasures of flow.

As with virtuosos, so with virtues. So, in one sense, the rival reading is right to focus on the role of pain in moral development. Yet, if the parallel with elite performers is valid, the rival reading is wrong to focus on the pains of shame and punishment. Positive reinforcement works. In the right circumstances, critical feedback works. Punishment is, at best, a last resort. The main role of pain is the flip side of flow: it is the effort put in neither by the beginner nor by the expert but by someone at an intermediate stage, the strong-willed person who is still mastering the relevant virtue or skill, while having made sufficient progress to be motivated to push on further to disciplined, unimpeded activity. In this, the standard reading is right. But its defender, Burnyeat, could go further in embracing athletic notions, looking to the *kalon* not merely in moral terms of the noble but more clearly embracing the aesthetic aspects of some acts as simply awesome.

CHAPTER 16

Gym Buddies
NE 8–9

> Whatever someone has as the goal for which he chooses to exist and be alive, that is the activity he wishes to pursue in his friend's company. Hence some friends drink together, others play dice together, while others work out at the gym together and go hunting together, or do philosophy together.
>
> —*NE* 9.12, 1172a1–5

In an age of earbuds, the gym can be a solitary place. Even with other people around, many still find loneliness in the crowd. As we saw with Socrates, ancient gyms were quite social. Not only does wrestling require a partner, young men attended class in rooms surrounding a central sandpit in which that wrestling took place. This social aspect is seen today mostly in team sports, and it is through reflection on the nature of teamwork that we most easily see the intersection of athletics and ethics now. But, aside from relay races, the Greeks tended not to compete in teams. Wrestling, boxing, racing, discus, and long jump were all about testing the individual's athletic excellence. When it comes to making sense of *NE* 9.12's reference to people who "work out together" (*syngymnazō*), we must shift our attention from teams to gym buddies.

Let us play Socrates for a moment and ask: What are gym buddies, really, and how do such relationships contribute to a well-lived life? Gym buddies spend a huge chunk of time together and share at least one common interest, the gym. They tend to be of the same gender, share their thoughts and struggles, have a type of exclusive relationship, and, when it comes to spotting, literally trust each other with their lives, all in close, sweaty, physical proximity. While this does not typically include romantic forms of intimacy, how are such relationships so different from dating? How do they differ from other forms of friendship?

What is it that friendships in general contribute to the well-lived life in the first place? When I ask my students this last question, I tend to get two responses. On the one hand, people take a hard subjectivist line: "Friendship is whatever you want it to be. Don't judge me!" Some friends are similar in character and interests. Others illustrate that opposites attract. Often students will talk about best friends in terms of knowing each other since they were young. Students also speak of friendship in terms of unconditional love and acceptance. This response likely stems from our culture's Christian heritage, but its secular version is alive and well today. Still, if we think that friendship is an important part of a well-lived life and that it is possible for friendships to go bad (recall the "toxic" friendships discussed in *Lysis*), then both sets of responses leave us with little to go on when it comes to choosing our friends. Not all gym buddies are created equal. In the gym and friendships in general, what we want is to identify the right kind of relationship. This is the task Aristotle sets for himself in *NE* 8-9.

This chapter's epigraph, which is thick with "together" (*syn-*) verbs, is the final knot in the string of puzzles, distinctions, and arguments that make up *NE* 8-9's discussion of friendship. The parallel between gym buddies and philosophy buddies is established earlier in the text, as Aristotle borrows athletic terminology to speak of practice (*askēsis*) in virtue and competition (*hamillaomai*) for the *kalon*. While these explicit references to the gym take up a small fraction of *NE* 8-9's overall text, they come at key points in its argument. These same passages have struck some scholars as morally offensive and have sparked a surprisingly heated debate. In the spirit of *Jeopardy*, if gym buddies are the answer, then our task in reading the bulk of *NE* 8-9 that leads up to this will be to determine the question.

Aristotle opens his discussion of friendship (*philia*) claiming, "It is a virtue or involves virtue" (*NE* 8.1.1). This waffling gets back to his idea from *NE* 1.7 that happiness must be self-sufficient (*autarkēs*). If we are concerned with the *endoxa*, then clearly everyone agrees that the good life requires friends. Yet Aristotle's account of human flourishing, as we have laid it out so far, seems fairly individualistic. The challenge for Aristotle is to reconcile these two ideas, fitting friendship into his account of happiness as a life of excellent activity. His discussion proceeds in three stages. *NE* 8.1-6 classifies friendships by what they are based on: pleasure, usefulness, goodness. *NE* 8.7-9.3 fleshes out *NE* 1.7's claim that self-sufficiency should be understood "not for a single person, but for [one's] parents, children, spouse and in general for friends and fellow citizens." *NE* 9.4–12 invokes ideas from the gym to argue that the highest form of friendship plays a key role in happiness, as it encourages friends to practice and compete in virtue.

Types of Friends: *NE* 8.1–6

Given that living well is a form of activity, Aristotle suggests that we can categorize friendships based on what we do with our friends. He gives three broad categories of friendship based on pleasure, usefulness, and goodness/virtue (*NE* 8.3). Friendship based on pleasure may sound lurid. While he does speak of erotic relationships (1158a10–14, 1164a2–6), the category includes any relationship we may have simply because it is fun. He lumps children's relationships into this class, since children live primarily by their feelings. College students might think of their going-out friends. These are the people with whom we enjoy doing things, without thinking about them the rest of the time. While we would be upset if something happened to these people, should our parents die, we would probably not invite them to the funeral. In such relationships, Aristotle argues, the two people care not so much about each other as about what they get from each other: fun. These relationships are a sort of transaction that both parties get something out of.

Closely related to this are friendships based on usefulness. This category might sound odd to English speakers, but is captured by phrases such as "I have a friend in IT who can help with that." We all have relationships with people who can do something for us, whom we are generally pleasant around, but whom we stop thinking about the moment we do not need them. This type of friendship is even more clearly a transaction: it is not the person so much as what we get that we ultimately care about. As with friendships based on pleasure, friendships based on usefulness allow us to engage in various activities. In *NE* 1, Aristotle argued that pleasure and money—or resources generally—have a place in the good life, yet people who consider them to be the good life see only part of the picture. So too with friendships based on pleasure or usefulness: they are not bad; they are just incomplete.

Aristotle's third category of friendship is based on virtue or the good. *NE* 2–6 laid out how a virtuous person leads a full, active, and disciplined life. She is engaged in her community and happily fills her days with purposeful activity. Now imagine that two such people meet each other: Marilyn Monroe and Ella Fitzgerald; Barack Obama and Oprah Winfrey; Desmond Tutu and the Dalai Lama. Would each member of these pairs do things for the other? Of course. They would also enjoy spending time together. Nevertheless, their relationship would not be based on mere usefulness or pleasure but on the deep appreciation each has for the other's virtuous character and activity.

These three categories of friendship interrelate in various ways. Friendships based on virtue bring both pleasure and usefulness, yet friendships based on pleasure or usefulness do not of themselves bring virtue. As in *NE* 1's account of happiness as virtuous activity, which included roles for money, honor, pleasure, and study, friendships based on virtue are complete/perfect (*teleion*; 1156b7–17) in that they integrate pleasure and usefulness within a broader whole. Furthermore, *NE* 8's bases for friendship line up with *NE* 1's different understandings of happiness: pleasure to pleasure; virtue to virtue. Friendship based on usefulness is presented as a means to either pleasure or virtue, and Aristotle speaks of this category of friendship in value-neutral terms that mirror *NE* 1's discussion of money. Meanwhile, in friendships based on virtue, each person values the other's character and thus values the other for herself. Given that a virtuous character is a stable character, such friendships will be long-lasting. Friendships based on pleasure or usefulness, by contrast, will tend to dissolve when the fun or the benefit dries up.[1]

Self-Sufficiency and Political Animals: *NE* 8.7–9.3

Human happiness is a matter of living to our full human potential, and "humans," as Aristotle puts it, "are political animals" (1097b11, 1169b18–19). The second stage of Aristotle's discussion of friendship elaborates this idea by exploring the different relationships that hold a state (*polis*) together. The sheer diversity of relationships (parent-child, fellow citizen, master-slave, fellow dinner-club members, mercenaries for hire) and topics (inequality, gift-giving, constitutions, families, conflict) can make this section seem like a hodgepodge. We can pull the pieces together if we view *NE* 8.10–12 as Aristotle's response to Plato, *Republic* 8–9. In this earlier work, Plato uses his own account of justice to categorize political constitutions and relationships between the parts of an individual's soul through an elaborate series of parallels. Aristotle takes the different approach of using his account of humanity's political nature to categorize political constitutions and relationships within families. Aristotle's ranking of acceptable constitutions roughly matches Plato's in definition if not in name: monarchy (rule by one), aristocracy (rule by the few), and timocracy (rule by many). Yet, whereas Plato placed the worst constitution (tyranny) at the furthest remove from monarchy in his account of civic decay, Aristotle puts it closest: tyranny is the result when a monarch puts his own interest above those he governs. Likewise, aristocracy decays directly into oligarchy, and timocracy into democracy (see table 7). Given this setup, democracy is the least bad of the three bad options.

On the family side, a father's relationship to his children mirrors monarchy, in that the father looks after the well-being of his children and his children reciprocate by honoring and obeying him above all. The relationship of husband and wife mirrors aristocracy, insofar as each has something like equal footing in the relationship, albeit divided over different spheres: a husband working outside the house and a wife working inside the house. The relationship between brothers, finally, mirrors timocracy, insofar as many people look after their shared interest from positions of equal footing (see table 8).

All of these relationships within the family are, of course, ideal situations. Aristotle does not take the time to discuss fathers, wives, or children who fail at their roles. Given the widespread sexism of antiquity (to say nothing of Aristotle's own biological theories), such a discussion would have been a valuable slice of sociology. What we get instead is a normative argument: given humanity's political nature, these are the relationships people should have within a family. The family provides a context for individuals to learn the social roles that they will then bring into the state at large.[2] The state, in turn, should provide a context in which families may flourish through nurturing such relationships.

Table 7

	ONE RULER	FEW RULERS	MANY RULERS
VIRTUOUS RULERS	#1—Monarchy*	#2—Aristocracy	#3—Timocracy
NONVIRTUOUS RULERS	#6—Tyranny	#5—Oligarchy	#4—Democracy

* The numbering represents Aristotle's ranking of constitutions from the best, monarchy, to the worst, tyranny.

Table 8

	ONE RULER	FEW RULERS	MANY RULERS
FAMILY	Father	Husband and wife	Brothers

Just as *NE* 5 implicitly criticized Plato's *Republic* for seeing justice as a relationship between parts of one's soul rather than as a relationship between people, this middle section of *NE* 8–9 continues the project by looking to families, rather than character states, as the model and causal complement to different forms of political constitutions.[3]

To modern ears, the result of this new approach can sound somewhat odd. *NE* 8.2, for instance, asks, "If someone has ransomed you from pirates, should you pay him back no matter who he is? And if he does not need to be ransomed but asks to be paid back, should you pay him back or ransom your father?" If this sounds like nonsense to us, it is likely due to the emphasis on impartiality and objectivity in modern moral theory.[4] According to the main lines of Utilitarian and Kantian ethics, a person owes his father no more, morally speaking, than he owes anyone. To give relatives preferential treatment outside the home is simply nepotism. Yet, as main lines of feminist ethics point out, an attitude of impartiality is best suited to life in a society of strangers and seems ill suited to thinking about family life. For Aristotle, politics is a personal affair. When it comes to the self-sufficiency of the happy person, we must therefore take into account humanity's political/social nature and the concrete relationships in which individual human beings are positioned. Despite the Greeks' patriarchal tendencies, the relationship of father to children or husband to wife does not figure in the main arguments of the treatise's final third. It is, rather, the relationships of a mother to her children and of brothers to each other that provide the model for friendship in the truest sense. Individuals learn the skills of such relationships in the home and carry them into the city in friendships of joint activity, drinking together, working out together, and doing philosophy together.

Self-Love and Competing for the *Kalon*: *NE* 9.4–12

Everything up to this point has prepared the way for the final stage of Aristotle's discussion of friendship, which proceeds through a series of interlocking ideas. In some passages, Aristotle explicitly presents problems as puzzles (*aporiai*). In other passages, he lays out ideas that he takes as straightforward but modern readers have found puzzling. It is in the latter case that ideas drawn from the ancient gym will be of the most use.

NE 9.4–6 begins as Aristotle fleshes out what it means for one person to treat a friend as "another himself" (1166a31-32). Building on *NE*

8's discussion of families, Aristotle holds up how "mothers feel toward their children" as a paradigm case of people who relate to others as they relate to themselves (1166a1–10). When a mother wishes for what she sees as best for her children, she does so for her children's own sake, not merely as a means to her own happiness, and she acts accordingly. This is the attitude, Aristotle suggests, that a decent person (*epieikēs*; 1166a10–13; compare *NE* 5.10) has toward himself. The rest of *NE* 9.4 spells out how this can fail to happen: as we have seen in *NE* 7, weak-willed people act against their own understanding of their own self-interest. Aristotle's analysis in *NE* 9 is that such people fail to identify with their reasoning. Rather than seek their own overall good through practical wisdom, they identify with their lower appetites and thus fail to hit the mean in all they do. In modern terms, such people are their own worst enemies. A decent person, by contrast, feels goodwill (*eunoia*) toward himself. This goodwill is necessary for friendship but is not in itself sufficient. After all, one may feel goodwill toward an athletic competitor (*agonistēs*; 1166b34–1167a3), "when that person strikes one as beautiful (*kalos*), brave (*andreios*), or something like that" (1167a18–21). In such instances, the fan "will wish with him," namely, for the competitor to win, "but will not act with him." Given the individualistic nature of Greek sports, it is unclear what "acting with" could even mean. A spectator can hardly jump into the sandpit and start punching their favored competitor's opponent or lend a hand in throwing a discus. The more general point seems to be that joint action is needed for mere goodwill to turn into full friendship. *NE* 9.5 adds that friendship requires a common will (*homonoia*). This is not a matter of merely shared beliefs, but decisions (*proairesis*) in great (*megas*) questions about what course of action to pursue. Talk of decision situates common will within *NE* 3's discussion of deliberation and practical reasoning, while the greatness involved nods to *NE* 4's big spending and greatness of spirit. An individual who embodies these virtues will be a friend to himself insofar as he avoids weakness of will and the self-sabotage that comes with it. As with the individual, so with the state, which ideally will have all its citizens organizing their actions around a common will. When it comes to the relationships between individuals, the political example suggests that friends do not merely have parallel goals, but that each person is somehow integrated into the other's own particular goals.[5] With this, the stage is set for *NE* 9's final string of puzzles.

NE 9.7 asks why benefactors love their beneficiaries more than beneficiaries love their benefactors. While goodwill (*eunoia*) alone is insufficient for friendship, a benefactor (*euergetēs*) actually "does good." Aristotle presents this as a puzzle insofar as most people would take the cynical view that benefactors love their beneficiaries insofar as they relish the thought of calling in favors. This transactional thinking has a place in Greek culture, but Aristotle argues that it gets the best type of friendship wrong. People who think in terms of calling in debts are too focused on pleasure or usefulness. In terms of goal hierarchies, they are stuck in the details without seeing the whole. Proper benefactors, by contrast, are like craftsmen who love the products of their crafts or mothers who love their children. The reason is the same in each case: craft products and children are both the result of work. Aristotle goes so far as to explain that mothers love their children more than fathers do, since birthing a child is considerably "more laborious" (*epiponos*) than begetting a child. With this, Aristotle affords women a brief moment of heroic glory, as his choice of words likens the labors of childbirth to the labors (*ponoi*) of Herakles. All of this is grounded in *NE* 1's account of happiness as a life of excellent activity. For craftsmen and mothers, the fruits of their labor are intimately tied up in the goal hierarchies that ideally structure their lives. This solution, however, leads to another puzzle.

NE 9.8 asks whether a person ought to love himself or someone else most of all. Aristotle sets out this puzzle as a dilemma. On the one hand, we typically criticize people for being selfish and praise people who put the interests of others before their own. This is, in modern terms, a statement of altruism: the right thing to do is what benefits someone else. On the other hand, Aristotle has already laid out the idea that one is a friend to oneself, which suggests that an individual should put his own interests first. This is, in modern terms, a statement of egoism: the right thing to do is what benefits oneself. Since egoism and altruism make conflicting claims, we are left at an impasse. Aristotle solves this impasse by introducing *NE* 8's three-part categorization of friendship. Egoism is bad when a person's friendship with himself is based on pleasure or usefulness. Since such people do not set their sights on virtue, the pleasures they seek for themselves are physical. Physical resources, however, are limited. When confronted with a zero-sum game, such people seek what is pleasant or useful for themselves at others' expense. They are selfish in a bad sense. By contrast, a person whose friendship to himself is based on virtue will always seek the *kalon* through virtuous action. Aristotle claims that such a person is more of a self-lover insofar as he seeks the best good for himself. Meanwhile, other people would hardly complain that such an individual goes out of his way to engage in just and disciplined actions. On the contrary, this individual embodies greatness of spirit and will give up external resources in service of the common good, foregoing money, honor, pleasures, and—if need be—life itself. This turns the zero-sum game on its head, since in seeking the *kalon*, a virtuous person confers material benefits on others, his friends most of all.[6]

Aristotle goes so far as to say that people whose self-love is based on virtue will "compete (*hamillaomai*) for the *kalon* and strain after the most beautiful things for the common good" (1169a8-9). This picks up an earlier discussion in which he says that friends of virtue "compete to benefit each other," and each will "avenge himself" (*amunō*) by benefiting the other, in turn (*NE* 8.13, 1162b6-10). The verb *hamillaomai* is unusual. These are the only two times it appears in all of Aristotle's writings.[7] This suggests that he is alluding to another text. The most obvious parallel is Plato's late dialogue *Laws*, which uses the term seventeen times. The first passage, *Laws* 730e-731a, contains three of them. Here the work's mysterious Athenian Stranger explains that in an ideal state

> every citizen will strive after victory (*philonikeō*) in virtue without envy. For a man will make his state greater by himself competing (*hamillaomai*) but without slanderously cutting off others. But the jealous man, thinking that he must surpass (*hyperechō*) others through slander, exerts less effort in seeking true virtue (*aretē*) himself and obstructs those people competing against (*antihamillaomai*) him through unjust lies. Through all these things, he makes the entire city untrained (*agymnastos*) in the competition (*hamilla*) toward virtue, and he makes the city smaller insofar as he plays a part in its good reputation.

In short, just as an unenvious individual makes the city greater through truthful competition for virtue, the jealous person makes the city less through deceitful competition. *Laws*'s next thirteen uses of *hamillaomai* are explicitly connected to traditional Greek sports (running, wrestling, chariot racing), where they simply mean to compete in an event.[8] The final instance, *Laws* 968b, refers to the process of passing laws as itself a "contest." These outer passages frame what comes in between, as the various athletic competitions are set out as a means for improving the state via truthful competition for the personal excellence (*aretē*) of its citizens. Whether Aristotle is meaning to refer to *Laws* or not, this earlier text associates *hamillaomai* with athletic contests, links such contests to the good of the state, and suggests that such contests can be pursued either as zero-sum or as non-zero-sum affairs.

Scholars have found *NE* 8–9's idea of competing for the good and the beautiful to be surprisingly offensive. One author sees it as "a subtle kind of assault upon or attempt to get the better of one another," resulting in "unseemly contests" and "an infinite regress of noble self-denials."[9] Other authors have debated whether *NE* invokes a zero-sum concept of competition, though both parties to this debate admit to shortcomings in their own interpretations.[10] Translators have attempted to sidestep the whole issue by translating *hamillaomai* as "strives" rather than "competes," and *amunō* as "defends" rather than "avenges himself."[11] Rather than gloss over or explain away this aspect of *NE*, I suggest we explore more fully how athletic ideas play out through the remainder of *NE* 9.

NE 9.9 opens by raising the now familiar dispute over why a happy and therefore self-sufficient person would need friends. The ensuing discussion ties together threads stretching back to the start of *NE* 1. Aristotle starts by quickly recounting points already made: virtuous activity requires at least some external goods, and friends are the best external goods there are (compare *NE* 1.8–10 and 4.1–4). Humans are by nature political animals; thus, friends are for us a natural good (*NE* 8.7–9.3). People who think that friends are needed merely for pleasure and resources have an incomplete view of friendship (*NE* 8.1–6). Having summarized these previous passages, Aristotle presents three or four new arguments, each of which builds on *NE* 1.7's account of happiness as a life of virtuous activity.

The first two arguments present friends as a sort of mirror of the self. The first (1169b28–1170a4) builds on the fact that since virtuous activity is pleasant for an individual, observing the virtuous activity of his friend who is "another himself" is also pleasant. Aristotle introduced the idea of another himself through mothers' love for children. The second (1170a4–11) asserts that by sharing in virtuous activity, each friend makes the other's life easier, thereby making his virtuous activity more continuous and raising quality overall. Aristotle likens this to musicians who enjoy listening to each other perform.

Aristotle presents the third argument (1170a11–13) via a literary reference: "For good (*agathos*) people, living together provides a kind of practice (*askēsis*) in virtue, as Theognis says." The term *askēsis* has clear athletic overtones, though it can also be applied to craftsmen and professionals, such as doctors who practice medicine. What is noteworthy here is that in speaking of the practice of good people, Aristotle seems to have in mind people who are already virtuous. This is corroborated by the general context, which seeks to explain why happy (and therefore already virtuous) people need friends. If that is right, then *askēsis* cannot refer to the process of acquiring character virtues laid out in NE 2.[12] What, then, does it refer to?

Aristotle returns to the poet Theognis to close his discussion of friendship in NE 9.12, quoted in this chapter's epigraph. That passage in its broader context runs:

> Whatever someone holds as the goal for which he chooses to exist and be alive, that is the activity he wishes to pursue in his friend's company. Hence some friends drink together, others play dice together, while others work out at the gym together (*syngymnazō*) and go hunting together, or do philosophy together.... Hence the friendships of toxic people (*moxthēros*) turn out to be vicious, for they are unstable, and share toxic pursuits; and by becoming similar to each other, they grow vicious. But the friendship of decent people is decent (*epieikēs*) and increases the more often they meet. And they seem to become still better (*beltios*) from their activities and their mutual correction. For each molds the other in what they approve of, "learning what is noble from noble people."

The passage paraphrases Theognis, *Elegies* 1.29–38, using language and ideas drawn from NE, while the final quotation is left in Theognis's own words. What then does practice (*askēsis*) mean in NE 9.9? While Theognis does not use the term himself, Aristotle points us to Theognis to illustrate it, thereby placing questions of gym buddies squarely on the table. Given that *askēsis* can be undertaken by already virtuous people, it cannot refer exclusively to the process of acquiring virtue, which Aristotle calls training. This leaves two possibilities. First, *askēsis* might refer to the virtuous activity of people who are already virtuous. This would make practice resemble training, insofar as repetition enhances activity in both cases. In practice, though, people do not become more virtuous but better (*beltios* is the comparative form of *agathos*), which is to say that their virtuous activity is enhanced through collaboration with friends. Disciplined people who go to the gym together might not become more disciplined, but they do get stronger. Compare NE 4.3's great-spirited person, who possesses all the virtues of character and puts them to use through a life tightly structured around overarching goals. As I argued in chapter 13, greatness of spirit "makes the other virtues great" not by making a person more virtuous, but by allowing him to pursue ever greater feats of virtuous activity. Alternatively, and more plausibly I think, *askēsis* might be a general term that can refer to both acquiring virtue and using virtues that have already been formed. This has the advantage that it better accommodates the summary of Theognis, as well as the original poem, which includes virtuous people, people still developing virtue, and people who are actively vicious.

I claimed above that *NE* 9.9 presents "three or four" new arguments for why the happy person needs friends. Sandwiched between Aristotle's initial reference to Theognis and the closing summary of Theognis's poem is Aristotle's claim that we may look at the question "from a more naturalistic perspective" (*physikōteron*; 1170a13–22). The argument runs:

1. Human life is characterized by the activities of perceiving and thinking.
2. Life is especially pleasant for virtuous people.
3. This pleasure comes when a person perceives himself perceiving or thinking.
4. One's friend is another himself.
5. Therefore, virtuous friends take pleasure in perceiving each other perceive or think.

Older readings see this as simply a recasting of the mirror view of the first argument.[13] Since then, however, scholars have read this argument in terms of friends' collaborative activity, forming a "common consciousness," "refiguring separate I's into a we."[14] On this newer reading, friends in virtue treat each other neither as mere means to their respective end (the mistake of base people) nor simply as intrinsic goods in themselves (as the mirror view does). Friends, rather, constitute "integrated goods" who share common high-level goals and organize their lives around goal hierarchies that are to a fair degree intertwined.[15] From this perspective, the fourth, "more naturalistic" argument is a recasting not of the first argument but the third, which looks to Theognis to illustrate *askēsis* in virtue. Such shared goals, shared deliberation, and joint activity fit nicely with my reading of greatness of spirit, which, along with practical wisdom, structures the activities that make up one's life.[16]

Given all that, what should we make of *NE* 9's closing reference to gym buddies? First, we should note that *NE* 9's final argument lays out a stage of moral development and activity that lines up with work in developmental psychology. *NE* 2-3 lays out the beginning of a process in training whereby young people explore interests as they develop skills and talents. *NE* 4's account of greatness of spirit and *NE* 6's account of practical wisdom lay out a more developed stage in which individuals organize their lives around driving interests, creating hierarchies of high-, mid-, and low-level goals. This is a common developmental path for Angela Duckworth's gritty, elite performers to take. The point when an individual's passion for an undertaking really takes off, though, is when the individual aligns his interests with some purpose beyond himself. In psychological terms, talent is what a person is good at, and interest is what he enjoys. Purpose comes when he can align these talents and interests with a meaningful need in the world beyond himself.[17] In our world, such issues tend to come up in offices for career planning as students approach the completion of their studies. Aristotle suggests a more personal approach. Rather than viewing purpose in terms of the individual's relationship to a society of strangers, Aristotle aligns the interests of self and other through concrete relationships between individuals. While he may be wrong to suggest that those concrete relationships extend only so far as one's state, his account of drinking buddies, gym buddies, and philosophy buddies suggests that our typical career-office approach leaves out vital intermediary steps. Gym buddies help us to learn discipline more easily and to hold to our goals with greater pleasure. What is more, through such concrete relationships, we become more adept at aligning our goals with people and concerns beyond ourselves. As Aristotle first stated in *NE* 2, virtues of character strike means that are defined by reference to some *kalon* end. *NE* 8-9 finally fleshes out what that process looks like. Far from being problematic, the heroic ethos of pursuing deeds because they are awesome is what holds the account together, as concrete relationships within our families, gyms, and communities provide a context in which we may determine what awesome, *kalon* deeds would be for us.

Chapter 17

Aspiring to Immortality
NE 10

> Pleasure completes activity ... like the bloom on young men.
> —*NE* 10.4, 1174b31–33

> We must strive, so far as we can, to become immortal.
> —*NE* 10.7, 1177b33

Mihaly Csikszentmihalyi coined the term "flow" to describe the feeling elite athletes and musicians experience when everything falls into place. Time seems to slow down. It is as if you are watching yourself from afar. Everything just clicks. Research shows that this happens when the activity you are engaged in is right at the limit of what you are capable of. Csikszentmihalyi goes so far as to argue that to pursue happiness, in something like the robust sense of *eudaimonia*, we should try to maximize the amount of flow in our lives. He uses the first sentence of his seminal work, *Flow*, to credit Aristotle with first articulating the idea.[1]

Aristotle closes *NE* as he began, with happiness. *NE* 1 argued that people who think happiness is pleasure are not completely wrong; they just lack the whole picture. Aristotle thus walks a fine line, maintaining that pleasure is not the ultimate goal of life, while also maintaining that attaining one's ultimate goal will be pleasant.[2] This strategy dictates the structure of *NE* 10.1–5 as Aristotle responds to people who think pleasure is the only good (*NE* 10.2) and to people who think pleasure is not good at all (*NE* 10.3).[3] As is usually the case with Aristotle's endoxic method, the result is to preserve insights from each group, while also showing how each went wrong. This prepares the way for Aristotle's own view that pleasure is intimately bound to excellent activity (*NE* 10.4). The second half of *NE* 10 uses this discussion to present a fresh discussion of happiness.

Flow: *NE* 10.1–5

Aristotle sets out his question using nouns: What or what kind of thing is pleasure (*NE* 10.4)? He answers by switching from nouns to verbs: pleasure completes activity. The word for "completes" (*teleiō*) shares a root with "endy" (*teleion*). (The active verb form is unusual enough that standard Greek-English dictionaries cite this passage.) Aristotle seems to be struggling for words and resorts to a metaphor: "Pleasure completes activity . . . as a sort of end (*telos*) that comes to be upon something, like the bloom (*hōra*) on young men (*akmaios*)" (1174b31–33). Interpreters have struggled to make sense of this. One prominent twentieth-century philosopher accuses Aristotle of "babbling."[4] Other readers take *hōra* and *akmaios* to refer to the prime of one's life (thirty to fifty years old) but are unable to find any substance in the image.[5] Against all of this, James Warren argues that *NE* 10.4 must be understood within the context of Greek homoerotic relationships.[6] Aristotle likens pleasure to that hard-to-describe aura or vibe given off by the healthy, fit, young men that filled Greek gyms. In the realm of victory poetry, Pindar credits this bloom of youth as the attribute that made Zeus pick the Trojan prince Ganymede to be his beloved cupbearer (*Olympian* 10.104). Likewise, Pindar opens *Nemean* 8 by addressing Bloom as a goddess: "Lady Bloom, herald of Aphrodite's ambrosial tenderness / who sits on the eyelids of youthful girls and boys."

If the bloom of youth is meant to be understood in erotic terms, what does this tell us about the theory of pleasure Aristotle is trying to articulate? *NE* 10.4 presents pleasure as arising from excellent activity, strengthening and supporting it in a virtuous cycle, like a choir singing in a resonant, supportive acoustic.[7] I suggest that we have found this kind of virtuous circle in *NE*'s various depictions of ornaments (*kosmoi*) in the virtuous person's goods of fortune (*NE* 1.10), the big spender's house (*NE* 4.2), and the great-spirited person's relation to honors (*NE* 4.3). In each case, I argued for an athletic reading of *kosmos* in which inner worth is made manifest through virtuous activity, which results in outward goods, which, in turn, provide the means for further excellent activity. Greatness of spirit, likewise, is a *kosmos* of the character virtues and thus makes their work greater (*NE* 4.3). We might even add *NE* 9.9–12's practice (*askēsis*) of virtue, in which friends engage in cycles of mutual benefit in ways that blur the line between moral training through repeated action and the mature use of virtues in one's life work. In all these instances, Aristotle presents aspects of happiness as cycles of positive reinforcement, all aimed at the awesome (*kalon*). All of these fit *NE* 7.11–14's discussion of pleasure as connected to unimpeded activity, as well as *NE* 10.1–5's bloom of youth.[8] In short, elements of flow are woven throughout *NE*, first and foremost in passages presenting the athletic reading of *kosmos*.

If the parallels between the bloom of youth and the athletic *kosmos* are so strong, we may wonder why Aristotle does not simply use the term *kosmos* in *NE* 10. First, as Warren argues, there is a good chance that Aristotle is responding to a discussion in Plato's late dialogue *Philebus*. Here, Socrates attempts to explain pleasure by analogy to a homosexual couple. By invoking similar terms, Aristotle makes the connection apparent. But there are further reasons, internal to *NE*, for Aristotle to avoid *kosmos* here. Earlier, goods of fortune, honor, wealth, and a house were all listed as *kosmoi* of virtuous activity. Each of these, though, is separate from the activities that produce them, even if the virtuous actors turn around and make good use of them. Greatness of spirit fares better, insofar as it is intimately bound up with the other virtues of character and ultimately secures their unity. Even here, though, greatness of spirit comes last. As with an athletic crown, which is bestowed after an event has ended, greatness of spirit comes only when all the other virtues are in place. By contrast, where there is excellent activity, there is pleasure. The image of crowning a victor leads to yet one more potential disconnect: the crown goes only to those who compete, yet competing is no guarantee of actually winning. Even when a competitor gives his all and accomplishes wonderful feats, someone else may still outdo him. As I have argued in previous chapters, Aristotle speaks of *kosmoi* involved in virtuous cycles; he treats these as processes that happen only usually. Pleasure, it seems, is different: when the conditions are right, there is no stopping it.

Aristotle completes his account by providing criteria for ranking pleasures (*NE* 10.5). This hearkens back to *NE* 1.7's *ergon* argument, which set out animals' characteristic activities: perception for dogs, reason for humans. While we share with other animals the ability to perceive, our highest pleasure will come from our highest (and most characteristic) activity, reason. What is more, given the account of pleasure as flow, it follows that those who reason well feel more pleasure than those who reason poorly. Finally, Aristotle claims, the highest pleasure will come when we reason well about the best object of reasoning. What are the best objects of thought? As a first pass, most people can agree that thinking about lofty subjects such as the creation of the universe is more enjoyable than filing taxes. The one topic pushes our reason to its limits, the other does not. These three criteria—best faculty, best activity, best object—taken together give a scheme for ranking activities by the pleasures they bring us. On the low end of perception is a person with a head cold who can just barely smell his cough syrup, which does not smell very good to start with. At the high end of perception is a healthy person with a good palette enjoying a gourmet meal. For practical reasoning, there are people who struggle to fill out tax forms on the low end and people who thrive at politics on the high end. Theoretical reasoning takes us higher still, from struggling through a sudoku to understanding the deep truths of the universe in a glance. In all these cases, "the proper pleasure increases activity."[9] If we accept that some pleasures are more proper to rational human beings than others, then this account of pleasure has profound implications for how we live.

Expansive and Narrow Views of Happiness: *NE* 10.6–8

The takeaway from *NE* 10's discussion of pleasure, to put it in Csikszentmihalyi's terms, is that we should maximize flow in our lives, not because the pleasure of flow is our goal, but because by doing so, we live up to our full potential as human beings. To put this into practice, though, we are still left with two basic questions. First, is the best human life one that embraces a wide range of excellent activities or the one that includes one outstandingly excellent activity? Second, if we take the latter view, is that one outstandingly excellent activity going to be the same for all human beings, or will it vary from individual to individual? These two questions drive the discussion of *NE*'s six most notorious pages.

NE 10.6 begins by reiterating *NE* 1.7's two criteria for *eudaimonia*, stating that it must be self-sufficient (*autarkēs*) and endy (*teleion*). The first challenge Aristotle raises is that pleasures of "childish pastimes" seem to meet these criteria at least as well as a life of excellent activity expressing reason does. Most of us had fun being kids and just playing all day. If you were the beneficiary of a large enough trust fund, would your best life be to spend the rest of your days in one endless summer vacation? Aristotle puts it bluntly: Do we work so we can take vacations, or do we take vacations so that we can work? Work in this case can mean a lot of things. Let us focus on careers, though. According to a 2022 study conducted by the Gallup Corporation, only 33 percent of US workers are actively engaged with their jobs. The number worldwide is even lower: 21 percent. That leaves 79 percent of the world population that is not terribly engaged with what they spend a significant portion of their adult lives doing.[10] From Aristotle's perspective, this is all horribly wrong. Countries like the United States are awash in material resources, but many Americans forego careers they would find inherently valuable and settle for higher-paying jobs because they think having expensive things will make them happy. But how happy can you be if the only value you see in your work is that it pays well enough to pay for vacations to escape your life? *NE* 10's account of pleasure puts this into context. The pleasures of relaxation fail to engage our highest faculties. To see them as the goal of a mature human life aims too low.

NE 10.7–8 takes this account of pleasure to the opposite extreme. If the best pleasure is the one that employs our best faculty in the best way directed at the best object, then it seems that happiness consists in only one activity: study (*theōria*). This idea appeared in *NE* 1's poll concerning the best kind of life, only to be put off until later. Here it finally reappears as a piece of *endoxa* with roots in the vision of beauty in Plato's *Symposium* and *Republic*'s vision of the form of the good. The elements of mystery cult in *Symposium* suggest a connection to divinity.[11] Aristotle has his own version of this idea, as he presents the gods as blessed, immortal beings who engage in uninterrupted study of theoretical wisdom (*Metaphysics* 12.9). Our ability to do the same, he suggests at *NE* 10.7, 1177b26–1178a2, is an element of the divine in us. This passage is the central evidence for the narrow view of happiness. Such a life would be the most endy, in the sense that it provides a most final end for which the rest of one's life would provide the means. It is also more self-sufficient, insofar as it requires fewer resources than a life devoted to civic engagement and character virtue. What is more, the divine pleasures of study leave such a life lacking nothing.

The main problem with taking a life of study to be Aristotle's considered view on human happiness is that such a life is not attainable for a human being. Aristotle himself makes this explicit (*NE* 10.7). While understanding is a divine element in us, it is joined to a mortal, animal nature that needs resources to survive and is essentially social. While we may periodically live up to our full divine potential, we are incapable of engaging in the gods' continuous study. Aristotle concludes, "We must strive, so far as we can, to become immortal" (1177b33). The question, in practical terms, is how should we spell out this compromise: what role should the divine pleasure of study have in our lives, given that we cannot consistently engage with it across our whole lives? This is the crux of the expansive/narrow debate.

The debate has progressed as each side has stressed how its reading makes better sense of a handful of key passages. The result is what one leading scholar has called an "intellectual chess match" that has outlived its usefulness.[12] If we take a step back, though, we can see that the various options have a lot in common. Advocates of the narrow view make room in the good life for activities other than study. Richard Kraut argues that both the life of theoretical reasoning and the life of practical reasoning constitute human happiness, although practical reasoning takes second place.[13] Yet Kraut maintains that it is the act of reasoning, and not the resources used by reasoning, that constitute happiness. Gabriel Richardson Lear argues that a life of civic activity, which amounts to the account of happiness championed by the expansive reading, is a second-rate copy of the life of study, yet both types of life meet *NE* 1's criteria in that they are shaped by practical and theoretical wisdom.[14] At first glance, these views seem far removed from the expansive reading of Terence Irwin, who claims that happiness consists in a wide range of intrinsic goods, which embraces civic activity, relationships, study, external goods, and so on.[15] Nevertheless, Irwin argues that these goods must be held together in some kind of coherent whole, which requires using the same practical reasoning that Kraut identifies as partially constituting happiness and Richardson Lear makes central to the active life. Given that *NE* is a self-professedly practical work, we might well ask: What, in the end, is the difference?

On the one hand, making external goods part of what constitutes happiness, as Irwin does, threatens to place happiness outside the individual's control. In the Priam example of *NE* 1.8, Aristotle assigns some value to external goods, albeit not great enough value that their loss makes a person miserable. As I argued in chapter 11, Aristotle seems content to think that virtuous activity is usually accompanied by success in the world and the goods that come with it. External goods are a *kosmos* of virtuous activity that come about as reliably as athletic crowns do. In this, Aristotle seems to want to have it both ways, as though he were claiming that external goods and success matter to happiness, but not really.

On the other hand, the narrow and expansive readings permit different degrees of focus around overarching goals. In discussing *NE* 4,

I argued that the virtues of big spending and greatness of spirit deal with prioritizing goals. While public benefactors and elite performers make up Aristotle's central examples, I argued that the greatness of these virtues is relative to the individual. These are virtues that are available to people beyond just the rich and famous. Furthermore, given that one may not have any virtue of character in its fullest sense without having all of them, both of these virtues are necessary for happiness. Still, it is possible to be more or less great-spirited. If we recall Angela Duckworth's goal hierarchies, the grittiest of the gritty tend to arrange all their goals around a single central calling, be it athletic, artistic, or intellectual. Yet people who are still very gritty individuals, such as Duckworth herself, may arrange their lives around a handful of high-level goals such as career and family. How many high-level goals can a person pursue while still embodying great-spirited grit? Aristotle would likely say that the answer is relative to the individual, though I suspect we could count them on a single hand. If we set aside the particular goal set out in the narrow view (study), then the main difference we are left with between the two sides of the debate is the degree of grittiness or greatness of spirit. The narrow reading pushes us toward having as few high-level goals as possible, ideally just one, and arranges the rest of one's life beneath them. The expansive reading leaves open space for a greater number of high-level goals but cautions that attempting to balance too many high-level pursuits will be self-defeating.

By shifting focus away from study, I may seem to lose sight of what is at stake in the expansive/narrow debate. Questions of prioritizing goals seem pedestrian compared to the divine pleasures of study. We should note, however, that throughout *NE* Aristotle has taken elite performers as his model for the living of flourishing lives, and much of what he says about elite performers, including the ability to prioritize, lines up well with current empirical research. Those performers have included Olympic athletes, competitive kithara players, public benefactors, politicians, soldiers, and friends. *NE* 10 adds the intellectual life to the list as one more way human potential can be brought into action. I have argued that these various athletic, musical, and philanthropic examples embody an ethos exemplified by Herakles's depictions in art, myth, and poetry. The use of athletic images of crowns and *kosmoi* throughout *NE* invokes virtuous cycles in which human activity takes on a permanence that approximates the divine in something like Richardson Lear's sense. While *NE* 10's injunction to strive for immortality through study has received the lion's share of attention, it is just one more example for the list.

A focus on elite performers generally, rather than intellectuals in particular, also suggests a way to retain the core insight of the narrow view. As Duckworth notes, deliberate practice is tiring, especially compared to activities that bring about flow.[16] Since struggling through problems is an insufficiently elevated activity to ascribe to the gods, Aristotle sets it aside as, at best, a penultimate form of happiness. For us mere humans, however, even the most elite performers alternate between deliberate practice and flow. According to NE 10.4–5, the most pleasant activity is also the one that most fully engages our rationality: a flow state turned toward some lofty object. But isn't this just wrong? Sure, figuring out a math problem might be less pleasant than having already worked it out and simply seeing the solution. But surely the process of working out the answer engages our rational capacities more fully. Implicit in the question is a partitioning off of the activity of working out a solution and the activity of enjoying the solution. The question does not come up for the gods, who enjoy the continuous activity of an already actualized understanding. For actual human life, though, there is no understanding without first coming to understand. For human beings, deliberate practice and flow are two sides of a single coin. This suggests that in the search for models, the narrow/expansive debate has focused too much on Zeus and not enough on Herakles. Becoming divine and already being divine are two different things. If this is right, then the best life for a human is one that involves great rewards but also great labors as we engage in the *askēsis* of virtue.

Theory into Practice

The point of understanding happiness is to be happy (NE 10.9). But as Aristotle's account of moral development has shown, this is possible only if children are trained correctly from the start. Aristotle thus draws NE to a close by setting the task for a further work of practical philosophy: *Politics*. Here he puts NE's account of happiness to work by laying out features a state would need for its citizens to live happy, flourishing lives. Today, its account of the mean has largely passed into the realm of common sense. Greatness of spirit, by contrast, has become countercultural in the extreme. The ability to focus, prioritize, and keep one's eye on the ball is a major obstacle in the pursuit of a well-lived life, as witnessed by the dabblers and dreamers, the unengaged and the excellent sheep who fill today's schools.[17] Aristotle gives us some practical advice on how to move forward, through *NE*'s discussions of elite athletes and musicians, gym buddies and philosophy buddies, and concrete relationships in which individuals may discern *kalon* deeds in service of the common good.

Epilogue
Greek Philosophy beyond the Gym

> If you meet with any hardship or anything pleasant or reputable or disreputable, then remember that the contest is now and the Olympic Games are now and you cannot put off things anymore and that your progress is made or destroyed in a single day and a single action. Socrates became fully perfect in this way: by not paying attention to anything but his reason in everything he met with.
>
> —Epictetus, *Handbook* 51

The practice of opening philosophical schools in gyms ended with Aristotle. Yet the gym's agonistic spirit lived on in the intellectual contests between rival schools. These proceeded on a number of fronts: logic, physics, scientific method, and so on. When it comes to moral philosophy, the two main debates pick up threads we have already encountered.

The first debate centers on moral theory. In laying out his account of a life well lived, Aristotle looked to elite performers and argued that happiness consists in a life of excellent activity. Yet, to use a sports analogy, he was unclear whether excellent activity consisted in actually winning or merely how one played the game. This ambiguity is reflected in *NE*'s talk of good fortune and wealth as ornaments (*kosmoi*), which usually accompany virtuous activity. In the centuries to follow, Epicureans embraced the first option along with an idea Aristotle dismissed as fit for cows: the ultimate goal in life is pleasure. Yet rather than locating the highest pleasure in some kind of flow, Epicurus argued that pleasure reaches its limit in the absence of pain. So, while Aristotle encourages us to aim high in the pursuit of divine pleasures, Epicurus advises us to aim low so that we can avoid unnecessary stress and disappointment.[1] This is as far from the gym as Greek philosophy ever gets.[2] The Stoics embraced the second option, arguing that the only good is virtue and that human flourishing consists exclusively in how we play the hand we are dealt.[3] Pleasure, pain, life, death, wealth, family, and everything else outside of one's own virtue are, for the Stoics, a matter of indifference. Since everything else includes bodily health and athletic victory, the Stoics sever what for Plato, and to a lesser extent Aristotle, was a vital connection between the gym and moral education. Games, however, provide a useful set of analogies for Stoic living. Scholars have begun to explore Cicero on archery, Seneca on gladiators, and Epictetus on wrestling.[4] In modern terms, the Epicurean/Stoic divide provides a clear articulation of consequentialist and nonconsequentialist ethics, prefiguring the now more famous debate between Immanuel Kant and John Stuart Mill.

The second debate focuses on philosophical pedigree and practice. Apart from the Epicureans, all major schools in the centuries following Aristotle claimed Socrates as their founder one way or another. To this end, the Stoics rejected Plato's division of the human soul into rational and nonrational parts, arguing instead that all human thought, emotions included, was ultimately a matter of belief. This is in line with the idea that Socrates explores in *Laches* and elsewhere that all virtues boil down to wisdom. The central goal of Stoic philosophy, therefore, is to remove false beliefs—for instance, that pleasure is good and pain is bad—so that people may reason correctly. Medical imagery abounds.[5] At the same time as Stoicism was developing these ideas, Plato's successors at the Academy turned from the positive Platonic theories we saw in *Symposium* and *Republic* to embrace a Socratic life of inquiry. The Academic skeptics, as they are now called, developed their characteristic approach to philosophy through centuries of competition with other schools, the Stoics first and foremost. The result is a formalized version of Socratic cross-examination that shoots down all claims to knowledge yet provisionally treats some ideas as more "plausible" than others.[6]

For whatever reason, Stoicism is trending right now, from positive psychology to self-help books to online forums for misogynists and white supremacists.[7] Some of this is useful, some of it is dangerous, most of it is harmless. As I said in the preface, however, when it comes to offering frameworks for living one's life, all of this suffers from the same flaw: it speaks with a single voice. Attempts to adapt Aristotle to modern life suffer from the same problem. To provide an approach that embraces multiple voices, I will end, as I began, on a Socratic note.

Marcus Tullius Cicero is most famous as a lawyer, politician, and literary figure. During his youth, however, he studied philosophy in Athens and befriended the leading philosophers of his day. During Rome's civil war, he clashed with Julius Caesar and was briefly pushed out of the political spotlight. Under what was effectively house arrest, Cicero wrote a series of dialogues presenting Greek philosophy to Roman readers. He presents this as a service to the state as he translates ideas not only into the Latin language but also into Roman sensibilities. Like the Athenians, the Romans loved taking each other to court. Cicero thus put his legal skills to use by modeling dialogues after court cases. His works are set at country villas, where Roman senators and generals spent their leisure time (Latin, *otium*). Cicero's own villa contained two gyms, which he called the Academy and Lyceum. Each dialogue proceeds through paired speeches, which imitate lawyers arguing prosecution and defense. One character lays out a school's view of a given topic, and the next character rips it to shreds.[8] At the end, characters play judge and vote for which of the views on offer seems, if not true, at least the most plausible or truth-like. Here at the end of *Philosophy at the Gymnasium*, I invite you to do the same. My goal has not been to convince readers of any particular Socratic, Platonic, or Aristotelian theory, but to give each view a critical airing and leave readers to take what is useful to them in their own lives. As Cicero puts it: "The Academics typically do not set out their own ideas. Instead, they approve of views that seem to come nearest to the truth, to compare arguments, to draw out everything that can be said in support of any position and without claiming any authority of their own, to leave inquirers free to make up their own minds. This is the method that was handed down from Socrates" (Cicero, *On Divination* 2.150).

Notes

Preface

1. For an introduction to ancient Greek education, H. I. Marrou, *A History of Education in Antiquity*, trans. George Lamb (Madison: University of Wisconsin Press, 1956) is still the standard. Stephen Miller, "Training: The World of the *Gymnasion* and the *Palaistra*," in *Ancient Greek Athletics* (New Haven: Yale University Press, 2004), 176–195, uses archaeological and literary sources to survey the educational aspects of ancient gyms in particular. For an in-depth look at the relation of public speaking and the gym, see Debra Hawhee, *Bodily Arts: Rhetoric and Athletics in Ancient Greece* (Austin: University of Texas Press, 2004).

2. I will focus on the United States as the education system I work in and know best. While I think Greek moral philosophy is particularly useful for the bind US education is currently in, I do not mean to limit its usefulness to the United States alone.

3. The older curriculum sought out authors, such as Xenophon and Caesar, who helped solidify the value system of elite US culture. Classicists today more commonly seek out ancient texts to challenge cultural norms and help us think beyond our own horizons. This has led to a much more expansive approach to the ancient literary canon, paying more attention, for instance, to the experiences of ancient women and the impact figures in North Africa and other regions beyond Greece and Italy had on classical culture.

4. This process was complex. For a solid introduction, see Fareed Zakaria, "A Brief History of Liberal Education," in *In Defense of a Liberal Education* (New York: W. W. Norton & Company, 2015), 40–71. For more in-depth analysis, see James Davison Hunter, *Culture Wars: The Struggle to Control the Family, Art, Education, Law, and Politics in America* (New York: Basic Books, 1991), and *The Death of Character: Moral Education in an Age without Good or Evil* (New York: Basic Books, 2000). Alasdair MacIntyre, *After Virtue* (Notre Dame: University of Notre Dame Press, 1984), offers an even earlier critique of the status quo, focusing on academic ethicists who, according to MacIntyre, got buried in the details and lost sight of the big picture.

5. William Deresiewicz was an early and vocal critic of this problem. In *Excellent Sheep: The Miseducation of the American Elite & the Way to a Meaningful Life* (New York: Free Press, 2014), he narrates how he left his position as an English professor at Yale University because he was so fed up with his students who could "do school" but not think for themselves.

6. Richard Arum, *Academically Adrift: Limited Learning on College Campuses* (Chicago: University of Chicago Press, 2011).

7. Martin Seligman, the founder of the field, offers a great introduction in *Flourish: A Visionary New Understanding of Happiness and Well-Being* (New York: Atria Paperback, 2011). His student Angela Duckworth builds on his work in *Grit: The Power of Passion and Perseverance* (New York: Scribner, 2016). We will return to Duckworth in part 3. For application of positive psychology to education, the classic discussion is William Damon, *The Path to Purpose: How Young People Find Their Calling in Life* (New York: Free Press, 2008).

8. Daniel Kahneman and Angus Deaton, "High Income Improves Evaluation of Life but Not Emotional Well-Being," *Proceedings of the National Academy of Sciences* 107, no. 38 (September 2010): 16489–16493, https://doi.org/10.1073/pnas.1011492107. $75k is a rough figure, which varies depending on cost of living in one's particular context.

9. For discussion of such a course at Yale University, see Molly Oswaks, "Over 3 Million People Took This Course on Happiness; Here's What Some Learned," *New York Times*, March 13, 2021.

10. "Network for Vocation in Undergraduate Education (NetVUE)," Council of Independent Colleges, accessed March 17, 2021, https://www.cic.edu/programs/netvue. Colleges within this group draw from their own faith traditions with everything from spiritual classics such as Augustine's *Confessions* to popular films. James Martin, *The Jesuit Guide to (Almost) Everything: A Spirituality for Real Life* (New York: Harper One, 2010), is a fun addition for Roman Catholic readers.

11. For an outside assessment of the program, see Tim Clydesdale, *The Purposeful Graduate: Why Colleges Must Talk to Students about Vocation* (Chicago: University of Chicago Press, 2015).

12. NetVUE's publication, David Cunningham, ed., *Hearing Vocation Differently: Meaning, Purpose, and Identity in the Multi-Faith Academy* (Oxford: Oxford University Press, 2019), pushes beyond Christianity to explore concepts of vocation in other faith traditions. This is a step toward greater inclusion, yet it is still tied up in theological language, which will present barriers for many students today.

13. Edith Hall, *Aristotle's Way: How Ancient Wisdom Can Change your Life* (London: Penguin Press, 2019); Massimo Pigliucci, *How to Be a Stoic: Using Ancient Philosophy to Live a Modern Life* (New York: Basic Books, 2017).

14. Jonathan Haidt, *The Happiness Hypothesis: Finding Modern Truth in Ancient Wisdom* (New York: Basic Books, 2006).

15. Heather Reid, *Athletics and Philosophy in the Ancient World* (London: Routledge, 2011), sets out much of the groundwork I build on here. Where Reid's work and mine differ most is in their respective purposes. Reid is working against centuries of cultural drift to argue that philosophy and athletics were once connected in meaningful ways and can be again. I continue the project by using the gym lens to present existing scholarly debates from fresh perspectives. What is more, Reid writes for readers with prior background in Greek philosophy. This book is written for those coming to Greek philosophy for the first time.

Reid has also organized and published conferences on athleticism in Plato. See Heather Reid, Mark Ralkowski, and Coleen Zoller, eds., *Athletics, Gymnastics, and* Agon *in Plato* (Sioux City, IA: Parnassos Press, 2020). Similar work on Aristotle is still lacking.

Part I

1. Socrates's distrust of written philosophy is set out at Plato, *Phaedrus* 274c-278b. Throughout, citations of Plato's works are given in "Stephanus numbers." These refer to page numbers and column letters in the first printed, rather than handwritten, edition of Plato's works, published in the sixteenth century. They refer to the Greek text and are used as a common frame of reference for translations into modern languages.

1. Bravery

1. For translation and overview, see Rosamond Kent Sprague, trans., *Plato: Laches and Charmides* (Indianapolis: Hackett, 1992).
2. Because this book is aimed primarily at students with no background in the Greek language, all Greek words will be given in Latin letters. I have adapted spellings to draw out parallels with English words—for example, *psyche* rather than *psukhē* for "soul." Unless there is compelling reason to do otherwise, such as with plural forms, words will be given in their "dictionary form" (present, singular, nominative, etc.). For readers wanting to dive deeper into original texts, detailed citations are provided throughout.
3. Matthew Sears, "The Hoplite Phalanx: The Rise of the Polis," in *Understanding Greek Warfare* (New York: Routledge, 2019), 31-59.
4. Stephen Miller, *Ancient Greek Athletics* (New Haven: Yale University Press, 2004), 176-195. Plato argues for the philosophical uses of this curriculum at *Republic* 376c-412c (see chapter 8 of this book). The comic playwright Aristophanes sets out a detailed, if somewhat silly, account of this same approach to education at *Clouds* 961-1023.
5. While this phrase today is often associated with small, elite colleges, the liberal-arts tradition manifests itself in the breadth of knowledge sought by general-education courses that are characteristic of American undergraduate education across the board.
6. Angela Hobbs, "Arms and the Man: *Andreia* in the *Laches*," in *Plato and the Hero: Courage, Manliness, and the Impersonal Good* (Cambridge: Cambridge University Press, 2000), 76-112, reads *Laches*, in part, as an attempt to distinguish between courage and manliness. For a review of older scholarship on this question, see Walter Schmid, *On Manly Courage: A Study of Plato's "Laches"* (Carbondale: Southern Illinois University Press, 1992).
7. Gareth Matthews, "Getting Perplexed about the Virtues," in *Socratic Perplexity and the Nature of Philosophy* (Oxford: Oxford University Press, 1999), 19-30, describes this passage as Socrates capturing Nicias in a "conceptual vise" that he cannot escape.
8. This idea will recur in Plato's *Charmides* (see chapter 2). Plato's dialogue *Protagoras* is the other main source. For discussion, see Terry Penner, "The Unity of Virtue," *Philosophical Review* 82, no. 1 (January 1973): 35-68. The Stoic school looked to Socrates as the origin of this idea, which the Stoics made central to their ethical theory (see the epilogue).
9. I will return to this point at length in the introduction to part 3.

10. For an introduction to cognitive behavioral therapy (CBT), see Martin Seligman, "How You Think, How You Feel," in *Flourish: A Visionary New Understanding of Happiness and Well-Being* (New York: Atria Paperback, 2011), 71-91. Greg Lukianoff and Jonathan Haidt, *The Coddling of the American Mind: How Good Intentions and Bad Ideas Are Setting Up a Generation for Failure* (New York: Penguin Press, 2018), argue that current parenting and educational practices, from a culture of safety and trigger warnings to trophies for participation, are doing the opposite of what CBT advises. Lukianoff and Haidt offer a detailed analysis of trends in US culture and education. They advocate teaching something like CBT in schools and end with a quick overview of CBT techniques (275-274).

11. Carol Dweck, *Mindset: Changing the Way You Think to Fulfil Your Potential* (Boston: Little, Brown Book Group, 2017).

12. I defend this reading in "Socrates at the Wrestling School: Plato's *Laches, Lysis,* and *Charmides,*" in *Athletics, Gymnastics, and* Agon *in Plato*, ed. Heather Reid, Mark Ralkowski, and Coleen Zoller (Sioux City, IA: Parnassos Press, 2020), 51-66. "Care for virtue" (*epimeleomai aretēs*) recurs in Plato's *Apology*. See chapter 5.

13. For a more in-depth discussion of *Laches*, see Francisco Gonzales, *Dialectic and Dialogue: Plato's Practice of Philosophical Inquiry* (Evanston, IL: Northwestern University Press, 1998), 19-61.

2. Discipline

1. For an overview of the ancient gym and descriptions of the various rooms in figure 3, see Stephen Miller, *Ancient Greek Athletics* (New Haven: Yale University Press, 2004), 176-195. For a selection of primary sources, see Stephen Miller, ed., "*Gymnasion,* Athletics, and Education," in *Arete: Greek Sports from Ancient Sources* (Berkeley: University of California Press, 2012), 126-152. Matthew Evans, "Architectural and Spatial Features of Plato's *Gymnasia* and *Palaistra,*" in *Athletics, Gymnastics, and* Agon *in Plato*, ed. Heather Reid, Mark Ralkowski, and Coleen Zoller (Sioux City, IA: Parnassos Press, 2020), 31-50, discusses gyms from Plato's dialogues in detail.

2. For ancient sources, see Steven Miller, ed., "Nudity and Equipment," in Miller, *Arete*, 16-22.

3. Pausanias 1.44.1.

4. For the connection of nude sports and democracy, see Heather Reid, "Boxing with Tyrants," in *Athletics and Philosophy in the Ancient World* (London: Routledge, 2011), 32-42, and Paul Christensen, "Sports and Democratization in Sixth- and Fifth-Century BCE Greece," in *Sports and Democracy* (Cambridge: Cambridge University Press, 2012), 164-183.

5. Christopher Moore and Christopher Raymond have provided an excellent new translation and commentary, *Plato: Charmides* (Indianapolis: Hackett, 2019).

6. See N. B. Crowther, "Male 'Beauty' Contests in Greece: The Euandria and Euexia," *L'antiquité classique* 54 (1985): 285-291.

7. *Charmides* 155c-d. The Greek uses *ēporoun*, a verb form of *aporia*, i.e., "was perplexed."

8. Moore and Raymond, trans., *Charmides*, xxvii-xxxvii.

9. Cf. *Laches* 188d-e.

10. For extended discussion, see Christopher Moore, "Charmides: On Impossibility and Uselessness," in *Socrates and Self-Knowledge* (Cambridge: Cambridge University Press, 2015), 54-100.

11. The Greek term *epistēmē* refers to any structured body of knowledge such as geometry or medicine. Its Latin equivalent is *scientia*, which is the root of our term *science*. Rosamond Kent Sprague, trans., *Plato: Laches and Charmides* (Indianapolis: Hackett, 1992), therefore translates Critias's final definition of discipline as the science of science. This is confusing insofar as people today use "science" as shorthand for "empirical science," which is as much a process as it is a body of knowledge. I thus follow Moore and Raymond with "knowledge of knowledge."

12. CNN anchor Fareed Zakaria writes eloquently about this in *In Defense of a Liberal Education* (New York: W. W. Norton, 2015). In his chapter "Coming to America," 15-39, he recounts growing up in India and coming to the United States to pursue an undergraduate degree at Yale. Through this bit of autobiography, he provides a compelling view of the US educational system from the outside.

13. Erik Kenyon, "Philosophy for Children and Community-based Pedagogy," in *Intentional Disruptions: New Directions in Pre-college Philosophy*, ed. Stephen Miller (Wilmington, DE: Vernon Press, 2021), 35-48.

14. Susan Ambrose et al., "How Do Students Become Self-Directed Learners?," in *How Learning Works: 7 Research-Based Principles for Smart Teaching* (San Francisco: Jossey-Bass, 2010), 188-216.

15. American Association of Colleges and Universities, "Value," https://www.aacu.org/value, accessed March 20, 2021.

3. Friendship

1. For detailed discussions, see Kenneth Dover, *Greek Homosexuality* (Cambridge, MA: Harvard University Press, 1989), and Thomas Scanlon, *Eros and Greek Athletics* (Oxford: Oxford University Press, 2002).

2. See chapter 9 for discussion of marriage age for young women.

3. Working with limited data and a very high infant mortality rate, scholars calculate life expectancies in Socrates's Athens as ranging from twenty-five to forty-five years. Ben Akrigg, "Demography and Classical Athens," in *Demography and the Greco-Roman World: New Insights and Approaches*, ed. Claire Holleran and April Pudsey (Cambridge: Cambridge University Press, 2011), 37-59.

4. For a translation and brief introduction, see C. D. C. Reeve, *Plato on Love: Lysis, Symposium, Phaedrus, and Alcibiades with Selections from Republic and Laws* (Indianapolis: Hackett, 2006). For a detailed analysis, see Terry Penner and Christopher Rowe, *Plato's Lysis* (Cambridge: Cambridge University Press, 2005).

5. For an introduction see Nigel Spivey, "Sweet Victory," in *The Ancient Olympics* (Oxford: Oxford University Press, 2012), 129-173. See also the introduction to part 3 of this book.

6. Andrea Nightingale, "The Folly of Praise: Plato's Critique of Encomiastic Discourse in the *Lysis* and *Symposium*," *Classical Quarterly* 43, no. 1 (1993): 112-130, argues that *Lysis* offers Plato a vehicle for contrasting Hippothales's speech writing with Socrates's approach to flirting through discussion.

7. David Wolfsdorf, "Φιλία in Plato's *Lysis*," *Harvard Studies in Classical Philology* 103 (2007): 235-259, takes the hidden-message approach, arguing that *Lysis* presents a positive, philosophical account of friendship and that the text's *aporia* is meant merely to uproot everyday conceptions. Gary Alan Scott, "Setting Free the Boys: Limits and Liberation in Plato's *Lysis*," *disClosure: A Journal of Social Theory* 4 (1995): 24-43, and Benjamin Rider, "A Socratic Seduction: Philosophical Protreptic in Plato's *Lysis*," *Aperion* 44 (2011): 40-66, argue that it is the act of seduction rather than a "right answer" about the nature of friendship that ultimately drives *Lysis*. This seduction, however, forms part of a broader philosophical project in line with what I argue for below.

4. Justice

1. For the political implications of sports in Egypt and early Greece, see Heather Reid, "Athletic Heroes," in *Athletics and Philosophy in the Ancient World* (London: Routledge, 2011), 11-21.

2. For an influential but controversial account of modern, race-based slavery, see Ibram X. Kendi, *Stamped from the Beginning: The Definitive History of Racist Ideas in America* (New York: Bold Type Books, 2017). Kendi's basic thesis is that in the fifteenth century, white, Christian Europeans justified enslaving black, Muslim Africans as a way of saving them from false religion. Over time, skin color replaced religion as the main marker of difference.

3. A "book" in this context is what would fit on an ancient scroll.

4. See Charles Kahn, "Proleptic Composition in the *Republic*, or Why Book 1 Was Never a Separate Dialogue," *Classical Quarterly* 43 (1993): 131-142, and Christopher Rowe, "The Literary and Philosophical Style of the *Republic*," in *The Blackwell Guide to Plato's "Republic*,*"* ed. Gerasimos Santas (Oxford: Blackwell, 2006), 7-24.

5. For an elaboration of the "trailer" view, see Rachel Barney, "Socrates' Refutation of Thrasymachus," in Santas, *Blackwell Guide to Plato's "Republic*,*"* 44-62.

6. United States Census Bureau, "Quick Facts," https://www.census.gov/quickfacts, accessed March 22, 2021; Federal Bureau of Prisons, "Inmate Race," https://www.bop.gov/about/statistics/statistics_inmate_race.jsp, accessed March 22, 2021.

7. Amanda Dick, "The Immature State of Our Union: Lack of Legal Entitlement to Prison Programming in the United States as Compared to European Countries," *Arizona Journal of International and Comparative Law* 35, no. 2 (2018): 287-324.

8. Death Penalty Information Center, https://deathpenaltyinfo.org/policy-issues/costs, accessed December 20, 2022.

9. David G. Myers, "A Satisfied Mind," in *The Pursuit of Happiness* (New York: Harper Collins, 1992), 47–67.

10. For discussion based on evidence from around the world, see Martin Seligman, "The Politics and Economics of Well-Being," in *Flourish: A Visionary New Understanding of Happiness and Well-Being* (New York: Atria Paperback, 2011), 221–241.

11. This is what Gregory Vlastos, "The Socratic Elenchus," in *Plato*, vol. 1, ed. Gail Fine (Oxford: Oxford University Press, 1999), 36–63, has dubbed "the problem of the elenchus." Hugh Benson, *Socratic Wisdom: The Model of Knowledge in Plato's Early Dialogues* (Oxford: Oxford University Press, 2000), responds that the goal of the *elenchos* is not to arrive at knowledge but to test individuals' overall set of beliefs. Harold Tarrant, "Socratic Method and Socratic Truth," in *A Companion to Socrates*, ed. Sara Ahbel-Rappe and Rachana Kamtekar (Oxford: Oxford University Press, 2006), 254–272, argues that the *elenchos* is meant primarily to test people, not establish beliefs. Gareth Matthews, *Socratic Perplexity and the Nature of Philosophy* (Oxford: Oxford University Press, 1999), carefully analyzes different forms of perplexity and argues that they have value in themselves; see especially "Shared Perplexity: The Self-Stinging Stingray," 43–54, for his response to Vlastos.

12. For "logic of domination," see Coleen Zoller, "Plato's Rejection of the Logic of Domination," in *Athletics, Gymnastics, and* Agon *in Plato*, ed. Heather Reid, Mark Ralkowski, and Coleen Zoller (Sioux City, IA: Parnassos Press, 2020), 223–238. See also Roslyn Weiss, "Wise Guys and Smart Alecks in *Republic* 1 and 2," in *Cambridge Companion to Plato's "Republic,"* ed. G. Ferrari (Cambridge: Cambridge University Press, 2007), 90–115. For "cooperative inquiry," see Lee Coulson, "The *Agones* of Platonic Philosophy: Seeking Victory without Triumph," in Reid, Ralkowski, and Zoller, *Athletics, Gymnastics, and* Agon *in Plato*, 211–222, esp. 215.

13. Zoller, "Plato's Rejection," 228.

14. Kevin Crotty, "Why Is Thrasymachus So Angry?," in *The City-State of the Soul* (Lanham, MD: Lexington Books, 2016), 1–26, praises Thrasymachus's account of justice for its philosophical generality and insight into the values of the democratic culture he represents. To show the shortcomings of these values, Crotty argues, Socrates must become a "culture-critic," laying out a theoretical framework within which to view democracy, which Socrates finally returns to in book 8 of *Republic*.

5. Wisdom

1. For a translation and discussion of Plato's *Apology* and other ancient depictions of Socrates's trial, see Thomas Brickhouse and Nicholas Smith, *The Trial and Execution of Socrates* (Oxford: Oxford University Press, 2002).

2. Stephen Miller, "Delphi," in *Ancient Greek Athletics* (New Haven: Yale University Press, 2004), 95–101.

3. For an overview, see Angela Duckworth, "Interest," "Practice," and "Purpose," in *Grit: The Power of Passion and Perseverance* (New York: Scribner, 2016), 93–168.

4. For a more detailed discussion, see my "Socrates at the Wrestling School: Plato's *Laches, Lysis*, and *Charmides*," in *Athletics, Gymnastics, and Agon in Plato*, ed. Heather Reid, Mark Ralkowski, and Coleen Zoller (Sioux City, IA: Parnassos Press, 2020), 51–66.

5. Miles Burnyeat, "The Impiety of Socrates," in Brickhouse and Smith, *Trial and Execution of Socrates*, 133–144.

6. William Damon, *The Path to Purpose: How Young People Find Their Calling in Life* (New York: Free Press, 2008), presents a classic discussion.

7. It is possible that the wealth necessary to pay for a chariot team may itself have been seen by the public as an expression of *aretē*. If that is right, Socrates here seems to take a potshot at this public perception. See the introduction to part 3 for discussion.

8. These ideas return in the Hellenistic period, as both the Stoics and the Academic skeptics look to Socrates as their moral role model, albeit in very different ways. See the epilogue for a brief discussion.

Part II

1. For detailed discussion of the *halma*, see Stephen Miller, *Ancient Greek Athletics* (New Haven: Yale University Press, 2004), 63–68.

2. We might note that the English word *invention* comes from the Latin *inventio*, literally "a coming into," which can mean either "a discovery" or "a creation." According to the *Oxford English Dictionary*, the English word *invent* once had both meanings, but the "discovery" sense has become obsolete.

3. Modern psychologists describe such experiences in terms of flow. This is the feeling of time slowing down when people throw themselves into an athletic or musical performance in ways that fully engage their capabilities without overtaxing them. The classic discussion is Mihaly Csikszentmihalyi, *Flow: The Psychology of Optimal Experience* (New York: Harper Perennial Modern Classics, 2008).

4. A probably apocryphal story recounts that Pythagoras discovered musical intervals by noticing that anvils struck by certain hammers produce harmonies. Upon examination, he discovered that it was the size of the hammers that made the difference. He was able to describe this in terms of whole-number ratios and translate it into different media such as strings. See Christopher Riedweg, *Pythagoras: His Life, Teaching, and Influence* (Ithaca, NY: Cornell University Press, 2002), 27–30.

5. Miller, *Ancient Greek Athletics*, 83–84.

6. Heather Reid, "Plato's Gymnasium," in *Athletics and Philosophy in the Ancient World* (London: Routledge, 2011), 55–68, breaks this trend by exploring ways in which Plato reimagined traditional aspects of the Greek gymnasium for the cultivation of virtue. Her chapter serves as a synoptic introduction to themes explored in part 2 of this book. See also the collection of essays in

Heather Reid, Mark Ralkowski, and Coleen Zoller, eds., *Athletics, Gymnastics, and Agon in Plato* (Sioux City, IA: Parnassos Press, 2020).

7. Stephen Miller, *The Berkeley Plato: From Neglected Relic to Ancient Treasure* (Berkeley: University of California Press, 2009).

8. Richard Kraut, "Introduction to the Study of Plato," in *The Cambridge Companion to Plato*, ed. Richard Kraut (Cambridge: Cambridge University Press, 1992), 1-50.

9. *Republic* 617e. See Miller, *Berkeley Plato*, 12-16.

10. See David Sedley, "Divinization," in *Plato's "Symposium": A Critical Guide*, edited by Pierre Destrée and Zina Giannopoulou (Cambridge: Cambridge University Press, 2017), 88-107.

11. This text, along with Polykleitos's original bronze sculptures, has been lost. Scholars have reconstructed Polykleitos's mathematical schemes based on Roman copies of his work. For discussion, see Warren G. Moon, *Polykleitos, the Doryphoros, and Tradition* (Madison: University of Wisconsin Press, 1995).

12. Laurence Totelin, "Therapeutics," in *The Cambridge Companion to Hippocrates*, ed. Peter Portmann (Cambridge: Cambridge University Press, 2018), 200-216, argues that Hippocratic doctors of the time borrowed many of their prescriptions and practices from existing folk traditions and midwives. Where they differed was in the explanations doctors gave for why these prescriptions and practices worked.

13. Plato uses a similar image at *Republic* 611a-612b where he likens the sea god, Glaucus, who is encrusted with shells, seaweed, and rocks, to the human soul as we experience it in everyday life. To see Glaucus's divinity and the soul's immortality, Plato argues, we must chip away the outer crust to reveal what is within.

14. These are presented as true arts. Plato extends the analogy in another dimension by laying out the "knacks" that resemble these arts: cosmetics and pastry baking for the body; sophistry and oratory for the soul. Among other things, this elaborate design presents the very Greek advice "If you want to seem beautiful, wear makeup; if you want to be beautiful, get to the gym."

15. For detailed discussion, see T. A. Cavanaugh, *Hippocrates' Oath and Asclepius' Snake: The Birth of the Medical Profession* (Oxford: Oxford University Press, 2018).

16. Elizabeth Craik, "The 'Hippocratic Question' and the Nature of the Hippocratic Corpus," in Portmann, *Cambridge Companion to Hippocrates*, 25-37.

17. Totelin, "Therapeutics," 211.

18. The Roman physician Galen, for instance, was particularly fond of the treatise "Nature of Man." Craik, "Hippocratic Question," 25-37.

19. For a clear and engaging introduction to the history of medicine, East and West, see Gary B. Ferngren, *Medicine and Religion: A Historical Introduction* (Baltimore: Johns Hopkins University Press, 2014).

20. For a detailed discussion of ancient Greek and Roman medicine, see Vivian Nutton, *Ancient Medicine* (New York: Routledge, 2004).

21. Elizabeth Craik, "Plato and Medical Texts: *Symposium* 185c-193d," *Classical Quarterly* 51, no. 5 (2001): 109-114, argues that "Nature of Man" and

"Regimen for Health" were likely in wide circulation in the early fourth century BCE. In "Hippocrates and Early Greek Medicine," in *The Oxford Handbook of Science and Medicine in the Classical World*, ed. Paul Keyser (Oxford: Oxford University Press, 2018), 215–232, Craik argues that "Airs, Waters, Places" has some claim to be written by Hippocrates himself. J. Chadwick and W. N. Mann, *Hippocratic Writings* (New York: Penguin Books, 1978), provide translations for "Nature of Man" (260–271), "Regimen for Health" (272–276), and "Airs, Waters, Places" (148–169).

22. See Totelin, "Therapeutics," 207–211, for discussion.

23. Brooke Holmes, "Body," in Portmann, *Cambridge Companion to Hippocrates*, 63–88.

24. See Totelin, "Therapeutics," for extended discussion.

25. Jim Hankinson, "Aetiology," in Portmann, *Cambridge Companion to Hippocrates*, 89–118, discusses "Regimen for Health," which is closely connected to "Nature of Man" in the manuscript tradition (116), yet contradicts theories laid out in the treatise "On Ancient Medicine," which also dates to the earliest stage of the Hippocratic corpus.

26. The new movement in value-based care seeks to integrate typical medical treatment with human service agencies, referring patients to agencies that can help remove causes of illness, such as substandard housing. Given the complexity of our medical industry, funding such measures is challenging. See Arvin Garg, Charles J. Homer, and Paul H. Dworkin, "Addressing Social Determinants of Health: Challenges and Opportunities in a Value-Based Model" *Pediatrics* 143, no. 4 (2019).

27. T. A. LaVeist et al., "Environmental and Socio-Economic Factors as Contributors to Racial Disparities in Diabetes Prevalence." *Journal of General Internal Medicine* 24, no. 1144 (2009).

28. Merlin Chowkwanyun and Adolph L. Reed Jr., "Racial Health Disparities and Covid-19—Caution and Context." *New England Journal of Medicine* 383 (2020): 201–203.

29. David Cantor, "Western Medicine since the Renaissance," in Portmann, *Cambridge Companion to Hippocrates*, 362–383.

30. Deanna Anderlini, "The United States Health Care System Is Sick: From Adam Smith to Overspecialization," *Cureus* 10, no. 5 (2018): e2720, discusses our current situation as "Fordism applied to health care."

31. This emphasis on holistic, preventative medicine is well established in current discussions. See Sharon K. Hull, "A Larger Role for Preventive Medicine," *AMA Journal of Ethics* 10, no. 11 (2008): 724–729. The health-care (and insurance) industry, however, is so cumbersome that bringing about such reforms is, as they say, like trying to repair an engine while it is running. Jennifer Trilk et al., "Including Lifestyle Medicine in Medical Education: Rationale for American College of Preventive Medicine/American Medical Association Resolution 959," *American Journal of Preventive Medicine* 56, no. 5 (2019): e169–e175, argue that reforms of the medical school curricula are coming much too slowly. Charles Preston et al., "Role of Preventive Medicine Residencies in Medical Education: A National Survey," *American Journal of Preventive*

Medicine 41, no. 4, Supplement 3 (2011): S290-S295, point out that existing resources are underused.

32. Special thanks to Jacob Riegler for his help relating Hippocratic medicine to current challenges and discussions in health care.

6. Drinking Games

1. Heran Mamo, "Rihanna's 2023 Super Bowl Halftime Show Is Now the Most-Watched of All Time," *Billboard*, May 22, 2023, https://www.foxsports.com/presspass/blog/2023/02/13/fox-sports-presentation-of-super-bowl-lvii-scores-six-year-high-with-113-million-viewers/.

2. This is likely an exaggeration, yet the relative sums are close enough for scholars to debate the claim. David Pritchard, "Costing Festivals and War: Spending Priorities of the Athenian Democracy," *Historia: Zeitschrift für Alte Geschichte* 61 (2012): 18-65, argues that during wartime, Athens actually spent five to fifteen times more on the military than on religious festivals. To put that into perspective, in 2019, the US federal government spent 16 percent of its annual budget on defense (https://www.cbpp.org/research/federal-budget/where-do-our-federal-tax-dollars-go), while .003 percent went to the National Endowment for the Arts (https://www.arts.gov/about/appropriations-history).

3. For a critical discussion of tragedy and Dionysiac religion in Plato's *Symposium*, see Marie-Élise Zovko, "*Agōn* and *Erōs* in Plato's *Symposium*," in *Athletics, Gymnastics, and* Agon *in Plato*, ed. Heather Reid, Mark Ralkowski, and Coleen Zoller (Sioux City, IA, Parnassos Press, 2020), 143-156.

4. We find a similar idea in today's fraternities with the system of big and little brothers. While the hazing and other abuses of today's system tend to make the news, a fair amount of mentoring goes on as well. For a critical but sympathetic look at the modern fraternity system, see Alexandra Robbins, *Fraternity: An Inside Look at a Year of College Boys Becoming Men* (Boston: Dutton, 2019). It is the educational aspect of the symposium that survives in the English word, which almost always refers to a gathering of "academics" to discuss big ideas.

5. Less relevant here is *agapē* (Latin, *caritas*), which centuries later becomes a central Christian virtue: the love of God and neighbor, which is expressly nonsexual.

6. Richard Seaford, "Dionysiac Drama and the Dionysiac Mysteries," *Classical Quarterly* 31, no. 2 (1981): 252-275.

7. Luc Brisson, "Agathon, Pausanias, and Diotima in Plato's *Symposium*: *Paiderastia* and *Philosophia*," in *Plato's Symposium: Issues in Interpretation and Reception*, ed. James Lesher, Debra Nails, and Frisbee Sheffield (Washington, DC: Center for Hellenic Studies, 2006), 229-251, presents what we know about the relationships of the actual people on whom these characters are based, and uses that to interpret Plato's stance on homoerotic relationships as a social institution.

8. "Gays in the military" has been a point of controversy in the late twentieth and twenty-first centuries. Phaedrus's idea, however, was actually put into

place by the Thebans, whose "Sacred Band" was a special force made up entirely of homosexual couples. They remained undefeated for forty years.

9. The story is best known today through Euripides's play *Alcestis*.

10. The story culminates in a burial with funeral games including boxing, wrestling, discus, archery, and a chariot race (*Iliad* 23). Among other things, this is one of the earliest pieces of textual evidence for the development of Greek sports. See Heather Reid, "Athletic Heroes," in *Athletics and Philosophy in the Ancient World* (London: Routledge, 2011), 11–21.

11. Playing hard to get was a key feature in heterosexual courtship as well, as was ritualized in various footraces for young women of marriageable age. See chapter 9.

12. There may be innuendo at play with this talk of hiccups. Coleen Zoller, *Plato and the Body* (Albany: SUNY Press, 2018), 88–90, sees Eryximachus's three cures as symbolizing different strategies for dealing with sexual desire.

13. See the introduction to part 2 for discussion of Hippocratic theory.

14. A number of scholars have dismissed Eryximachus's speech as merely comic relief, which does nothing to advance the work's central exploration of *erōs*. Against this thinking, Franco Trivigno, "A Doctor's Folly: Diagnosing the Speech of Eryximachus," in *Plato's "Symposium": A Critical Guide*, ed. Pierre Destrée and Zina Giannopoulou (Cambridge: Cambridge University Press, 2017), 48–69, sets Eryximachus's speech against the context of Hippocratic medicine, and argues for taking its philosophical contribution to the dialogue seriously.

15. The exact meaning of the "wrinkles" left in the stomach is unclear. For a different interpretation, see Elizabeth Craik, "Plato and Medical Texts: *Symposium* 185c-193d," *Classical Quarterly* 51, no. 5 (2001): 109–114.

16. In many readings of this speech, Zeus tends to come across as somewhere between bumbling and wicked. For a compelling pessimistic reading of Aristophanes's speech, see Suzanne Obdrzalek, "Aristophanic Tragedy," in Lesher, Nails, and Sheffield, *Plato's Symposium*, 70–87. For a more optimistic reading of Aristophanes's speech as a Platonic myth, see Gábor Betegh, "Tale, Theology, and Teleology in the *Phaedo*," in *Plato's Myths*, ed. Catalin Partenie (Cambridge: Cambridge University Press, 2009), 77–100.

17. In other sources, Agathon is presented as somewhat effeminate. In the comedy *Thesmophoriazeusai*, Aristophanes presents Agathon dressing in women's clothes to get himself into the right mood for writing female characters.

18. As with Eryximachus, scholars tend to dismiss Agathon's contribution to *Symposium*'s philosophical project. Against this, Francisco Gonzales, "Why Agathon's Beauty Matters," in Destrée and Giannopoulou, *Plato's "Symposium,"* 108–124, argues that Agathon represents a model philosophical student and that the aspects of his speech that scholars like to dismiss, for example, his playful use of poetry (115), are the sort of things that Plato's Socrates does all the time without being dismissed by scholars.

19. This is a driving question in scholarship on *Symposium*, including those studies cited so far. Jeremy Reid, "Unfamiliar Voices: Harmonizing the Non-Socratic Speeches and Plato's Psychology," in Destrée and Giannopoulou, *Plato's "Symposium,"* 28–47, offers an ingenious scheme in which the main points of the first four speeches line up with the main objectives of the educational

program laid out in Plato's *Republic*: instilling a sense of shame (Phaedrus), lawfulness (Pausanias), and balance (Eryximachus), while curbing desires that manifest themselves in the original humans' attempt to overtake Olympus (Aristophanes). Within *Symposium*, in turn, Agathon ends up embodying these qualities, making him the prime example of a philosophical beloved, while Alcibiades, whom we will meet shortly, does not. As with any great work of literature, there is more than one way to see the connections between the parts of *Symposium*. While Reid finds an order through parallels with *Republic*, the reading I present seeks to make sense of *Symposium* as a self-contained whole. The two readings need not be mutually exclusive.

20. Mark McPherran, "Medicine, Magic, and Religion in Plato's *Symposium*," in Lesher, Nails, and Sheffield, *Plato's Symposium*, 71-95, undertakes a similar project, by situating the speeches of Eryximachus, Aristophanes, and Agathon within the context of the whole. The three threads he traces (medicine, magic, and religion) partly overlap with my analysis here, making our two readings mutually compatible.

21. Brooke Holmes, "Body," in *The Cambridge Companion to Hippocrates*, ed. Peter Portmann (Cambridge: Cambridge University Press, 2018), 87, discusses "the presentation of the [Hippocratic] physician as a knower whose knowledge or thought bears no explicit relationship to the state of his body."

22. The original phrase, by the poet Juvenal, is *mens sana in corpore sano*.

23. Andrew Gregory, "Pythagoras and Plato," in *The Oxford Handbook of Science and Medicine in the Classical World*, ed. Paul Keyser (Oxford: Oxford University Press, 2018), 147-170, situates Plato's cosmological ideas about harmonies of opposites against the background of the earlier theories of Pythagoras, Philolaus, and Archytas, who see similar continuities between physics, music, and mathematics.

24. The definitive study is Hugh Benson, *Clitophon's Challenge: Dialectic in Plato's "Meno," "Phaedo," and "Republic"* (Oxford: Oxford University Press, 2015). In this study, Benson limits himself to dialogues in which the method of hypothesis is explicitly reflected on and discussed. I go beyond that project by applying Benson's model to *Symposium*, which, I argue, uses this method but does not call it by its name. See chapter 7 of this book for further discussion.

25. In Plato's *Meno*, for instance, Socrates explains a slave's ability to solve a geometry problem without ever having been taught geometry by way of the hypothesis that we have all lived multiple lives, and thus the slave is making use of ideas he learned in a former life.

26. For a helpful discussion of this particular strategy, see Frisbee Sheffield, "The Role of the Earlier Speeches in the *Symposium*: Plato's Endoxic Method," in Lesher, Nails, and Sheffield, *Plato's Symposium*, 23-46. Like Sheffield, I explore the relation of Socrates's speech to the first five in what follows. Unlike Sheffield, I take the intermediate step of looking at how Agathon's speech functions similarly to Socrates's, and I set both within the context of the method of hypothesis. Sheffield is right, I think, in seeing parallels between Socrates's method in *Symposium* and the "endoxic" method later developed by Aristotle (see chapter 11).

7. Mysteries of Love

1. The Latin root for *cult* (*colo*) means "to care for or nurture"; it is the root of *agriculture* (care of fields), *cultured* (describing someone whose artistic manners and attitudes have been nurtured), and by extension *culture* itself. In the ancient context, cult was simply caring for the gods.

2. For discussion, see Helene Foley, *The Homeric Hymn to Demeter: Translation, Commentary, and Interpretive Essays* (Princeton: Princeton University Press, 1994), esp. 65–76.

3. The Greek for "plenty" is *poros*. Its negative form provides *aporia* (perplexity).

4. Gabriel Richardson Lear, "Permanent Beauty and Becoming Happy in Plato's *Symposium*," in *Plato's Symposium: Issues in Interpretation and Reception*, ed. James Lesher, Debra Nails, and Frisbee Sheffield (Washington, DC: Center for Hellenic Studies, 2006), 96–123, at 98, 120.

5. Frisbee Sheffield, "*Erōs* and the Pursuit of Form," in *Plato's "Symposium": A Critical Guide*, ed. Pierre Destrée and Zina Giannopoulou (Cambridge: Cambridge University Press, 2017), 125–141, reads Diotima's account of spiritual pregnancy within the educational context of ancient homoerotic relationships. Andrea Nightingale, "The Mortal Soul and Immortal Happiness," in Destrée and Giannopoulou, *Plato's "Symposium,"* 142–159, argues for the ongoing nature of the philosophical undertaking.

6. Aristotle, perhaps in responding to this problem from *Symposium*, presents a similar train of thought at *NE* 1.10–11. See chapter 11.

7. Mihaly Csikszentmihalyi, *Flow: The Psychology of Optimal Experience* (New York: Harper Perennial Modern Classics, 2008), 1, credits Aristotle with articulating the experience now referred to as "flow." I suspect that passages in Plato such as *Symposium*'s account of beauty provide the background to Aristotle's thinking.

8. Heather Reid, "Athletic Beauty as *Mimēsis* of Virtue: The Case of the Beautiful Boxer," in *Looking at Beauty:* To Kalon *in Western Greece*, ed. Heather Reid and Tony Leyh (Sioux City, IA: Parnassos Press), 77–91, identifies this middle stage of Diotima's ascent at play in later ancient reflections on the famous Terme Boxer statue. While the statue of a brawny, bruised, and bleeding boxer does not fit classical ideals of physical beauty, it provides spectators a visual means of understanding the virtues of endurance and self-control.

9. David Sedley, "Divinization," in Destrée and Giannopoulou, *Plato's "Symposium,"* 88–107, defends this reading in terms of human beings striving for divine understanding, setting Aristophanes's account of our original wheeled nature against another philosophical myth in Plato's *Timaeus* that likens the spherical motions of the heavens to the spherical motions of thinking within the human head.

10. Later reprinted as Gregory Vlastos, "The Individual as an Object of Love in Plato," in *Plato*, ed. Gail Fine (Oxford: Oxford University Press, 1999), 2:137–163.

11. See, for instance, Frisbee Sheffield, *Plato's Symposium: The Ethics of Desire* (Oxford: Oxford University Press, 2006), 204.

12. For a reading along these lines, see Guilherme Domingues de Motta, "What Beauty Is Socrates Seeking by Chasing Handsome Youths?," in Reid and Leyh, *Looking at Beauty*, 149-159.

13. Radcliffe Edmunds, "Alcibiades the Profane: Images of the Mysteries," in Destrée and Giannopoulou, *Plato's "Symposium,"* 194-215.

14. Mateo Duque, "Two Passions in Plato's *Symposium*: Diotima's *To Kalon* as a Reorientation of Imperialistic *Erōs*," in Reid and Leyh, *Looking at Beauty*, 95-110, makes a compelling case for dispensing with talk of a "ladder" and, instead, referring to steps in an ascent.

15. *Symposium* 210b. The Greek *kataphroneō* is sometimes translated as "disdain," though it can also be the weaker "look down on" or "think slightly of" something. This is an instance when details of translation matter for how we understand the passage as a whole. See Coleen Zoller, *Plato and the Body* (Albany: SUNY Press, 2018), 83-86.

16. So argues Frisbee Sheffield, "The *Symposium* and Platonic Ethics: Plato, Vlastos, and a Misguided Debate," *Phronesis* 57 (2012): 117-141.

17. Sheffield, "*Symposium* and Platonic Ethics," 127.

18. Richard Kraut, "Eudaimonism and Platonic *Erōs*," in Destrée and Giannopoulou, *Plato's "Symposium,"* 235-252.

19. See esp. Zoller, "Beauty, Education, and Erotic Ascent in the *Symposium* and *Phaedrus*," in *Plato and the Body*, 59-104.

20. Kraut, "Eudaimonism," 252. The reference is to *Republic* 2. See chapter 8.

21. Kraut, "Eudaimonism," 243 and 248.

22. Duque, "Two Passions."

23. Edmunds, "Alcibiades the Profane," argues that in performing the mysteries outside of Eleusis, Alcibiades attempted to take something that belonged to the city as a whole and make it his own. According to Edmunds, Alcibiades makes a similar mistake in *Symposium*, when he sees Socrates's wisdom as a possession to be acquired by swapping sexual favors.

24. Nicola Stafano Galgano, "Logoi Kaloi: The Method of Philosophy at *Symposium* 210a-212b," in Reid and Leyh, *Looking at Beauty*, 111-121, extends this thinking about proportionality to Diotima's "beautiful speeches," which are "truthful, non-contradictory and harmonic argument[s]" (120).

25. By the medieval period, the liberal arts were sorted into a canonic list of seven: the so-called trivium, or "three roads," of grammar, rhetoric, and dialectic, and the quadrivium, or "four roads," of arithmetic, geometry, music, and astronomy. In earlier centuries, though, these lists were more fluid. Some sources list nine liberal arts (one for each Muse), including medicine and architecture. See Danuta Shanzer, "Augustine's Disciplines: *Silent diuitius Musae Varronis?*," in *Augustine and the Disciplines*, ed. Karla Pollmann and Mark Vessey (Oxford: Oxford University Press, 2005), 69-112. Plato, and the speech he writes for Eryximachus, sit at the early stages of all of this. Eryximachus presents medicine as a sort of umbrella for the whole quadrivium.

26. Brooke Holmes, "Body," in *The Cambridge Companion to Hippocrates*, ed. Peter Portmann (Cambridge: Cambridge University Press, 2018), 63-88.

27. Konstantinos Gkaleas, "Ἔρως and Γυμναστική in the Platonic Corpus: The Quest for the Form of Καλόν," in Reid and Leyh, *Looking at Beauty*, 123–131, offers a reading in line with my own. He assumes, however, that the first five speeches do not represent Platonic thought (124), and thus looks to other Platonic works for thinking about *gymnastikē* rather than going to Eryximachus's discussion of it in *Symposium* itself.

28. Undergraduates often find this the most impressive part of the work. Given that Alcibiades also stresses Socrates's endurance on the battlefield, such details presumably serve some philosophical purpose beyond merely recounting anecdotes about Socrates.

29. Ruby Blondell, "Where Is Socrates on the 'Ladder of Love'?," in Lesher, Nails, and Sheffield, *Plato's Symposium*, 147–178.

30. Sheffield, "*Symposium* and Platonic Ethics," 127–128.

8. Music, Gymnastics, and Moral Development

1. We might be tempted to distinguish eating cookies from the pleasure eating them brings, and to see this pleasure as a consequence of the eating. Glaucon's point seems to be, rather, that we do not need to bring other factors into play in order to explain the value of cookies. It is not necessary, for instance, for someone else to see me eating cookies for me to enjoy the pleasure of eating them. While cookie envy may bring additional pleasure, this pleasure would be different from the one Glaucon refers to here.

2. It may seem odd that Glaucon places exercise (*gymnazō*) in the final category. The consequences of gym exercise are clearly valuable: health, strength, people to talk with about philosophy, etc. But why does Glaucon say that exercise is not also good in itself? Granted, gym exercise is not always pleasant. Still, is it not possible to come to enjoy not only having strong quads but leg day itself? Judging by other dialogues, the historical Socrates seems to have been fond of gym work. Perhaps this just reflects Glaucon's own views. The issue does not come up again in the text, so we are left without much to go on.

3. This is likely the inspiration for Tolkien.

4. For detailed discussion of *Republic* 2's setup, see Terence Irwin, "*Republic* 2: Questions about Justice," in *Plato*, ed. Gail Fine (Oxford: Oxford University Press, 1999), 2:164–185, and Christopher Shields, "Plato's Challenge: The Case against Justice in *Republic* II," in *The Blackwell Guide to Plato's "Republic*," ed. Gerasimos Santas (Oxford: Blackwell Publishing, 2006), 63–83.

5. Malcolm Schofield, "Music all pow'rful," in *Plato's "Republic": A Critical Guide*, ed. Mark McPherran (Cambridge: Cambridge University Press, 2010), 229–248, analyzes the relations between *musikē* (rhythm and harmonies) and *grammata* (reading, writing, and literature) within *Republic*, and those between *Republic* and educational practices of the time.

6. My former student Halie Jo Fuller was inspired by this passage of Plato and used it to create an audition tape for American Ninja Warrior, which alternates between scenes of her in an evening gown playing a flute concerto and kickboxing to rap music and other athletic pursuits (https://youtu.be/

a86qXhgxTaA). Stamatia Dova, "On *Philogymnastia* and Its Cognates in Plato," in *Athletics, Gymnastics, and* Agon *in Plato*, ed. Heather Reid, Mark Ralkowski, and Coleen Zoller (Sioux City, IA: Parnassos Press, 2020), 107-126, explores the dangers of overdevotion to either the gym or music throughout Plato's writings.

7. For this two-part division of athletic training, see James Wilberding, "Curbing One's Appetites in Plato's *Republic*," in *Plato and the Divided Self*, ed. Rachel Barney, Tad Brennan, and Charles Brittain (Cambridge: Cambridge University Press, 2012), 128-149. While this division is not given much attention in *Republic* 2-3, its significance will become clear when we move to discussing the soul's virtues later in the work.

8. See Fareed Zakaria, "The Natural Aristocracy," in *In Defense of a Liberal Education* (New York: W. W. Norton, 2015), 106-134.

9. Tad Brennan, "The Nature of the Spirited Part of the Soul and Its Object," in Barney, Brennan, Brittain, *Plato and the Divided Self*, 102-127, argues that, at a psychological level, spirit's most basic role is to negotiate concepts of honor and shame within social interactions. This vocabulary of honor and shame, however, can also be turned onto one's own soul as a way of controlling one's own appetites. In sociological terms, spirit starts out with other-directed shame, which is then turned to self-directed guilt.

10. Scholars have differing responses to *Republic* 4's division of the soul into three. John Cooper, "Plato's Theory of Human Motivation," in Fine, *Plato*, 2:186-206, sees the three-part soul as psychologically insightful from an empirical standpoint. Brennan, "Nature of the Spirited Part," 121-125, argues that spirit is a necessary middle term, binding together reason and appetite in an embodied soul. Because of this, the soul must have three parts. On other readings, the human soul only sometimes has three parts. Christopher Shields, "Plato's Divided Soul," in McPherran, *Plato's "Republic,"* 147-170, and Jennifer Whitting, "Psychic Contingency in the *Republic*," in Barney, Brennan, and Brittain, *Plato and the Divided Self*, 174-208, argue that having three parts is a mark of the soul's unjust status, and that a just soul has only one part: the rational one. Because of this, Shields takes the soul to be essentially only one part. Kevin Crotty, *City-State of the Soul* (Lanham, MD: Lexington Books, 2016), agrees that the soul does not have a fixed number of parts, yet he argues that its attaining three parts is a great accomplishment and a mark of its justice.

9. Women at the Gym

1. International Olympic Committee, "Gender Equality through Time," https://olympics.com/ioc/gender-equality/gender-equality-through-time/at-the-olympic-games, accessed June 23, 2023.

2. What follows is drawn from Stephen Miller, "Women and Athletics," in *Ancient Greek Athletics* (New Haven: Yale University Press, 2004), 150-159. See also Nigel Spivey, *The Ancient Olympics* (Oxford: Oxford University Press, 2012), 120-128. For more in-depth discussion, see Thomas Scanlon, "Racing for Hera—A Girls' Contest at Olympia," "'Only We Produce Men'—Spartan Female

Athletics and Eugenics," and "Race or Chase of 'the Bears' at Brauron?," in *Eros and Greek Athletics* (Oxford: Oxford University Press, 2002), 98-174.

3. The Spartan princess Kyniska famously entered and won the chariot race at the main Olympic festival. Yet this merely means that she owned the horses, chariot, and driver; she herself was not present during the competition.

4. Heather Reid, "Heroic *Parthenoi* and the Virtues of Independence: A Feminine Philosophical Perspective on the Origin of Women's Sports," *Sports, Ethics and Philosophy* 14, no. 4 (2020): 511-524.

5. See Miller, *Ancient Greek Athletics*, 11-14, for the origins of nude athletics.

6. See the introduction to part 2 for discussion of Hippocrates and social determinants of health.

7. "Nature" (*physis*) in this argument can be taken in a few ways. The default might be to talk about "human nature," which does not vary between men and women apart from questions of reproduction. Kevin Crotty, *The City-State of the Soul* (Lanham, MD: Lexington Books, 2016), 37-43, argues for taking nature to mean an individual's "native ability" or "distinctive talent," which can be developed into a professional skill.

8. Julia Annas, "Plato's *Republic* and Feminism," in *Plato*, ed. Gail Fine (Oxford: Oxford University Press, 1999), 2:265-279, argues against the common view that Plato was the "first feminist" on the grounds that in making women into guardians Plato has the good of the state, not women's individual freedom and happiness, in mind. Furthermore, since his reforms are directed only at the guardian class, Annas takes Plato as content to leave "potters' wives" in their traditional household roles, rather than allowing them to pursue careers as potters themselves. Annas is right to point out Plato's silence on women in the productive class, as well as the casual misogyny of the culture around him that Plato echoes in passing, e.g., women being weaker than men on the whole. Still, her view of Plato's city as an "authoritarian state," which treats its citizens as nothing more than resources, misses *Republic*'s overarching approach to what people today call purpose exploration, that is, the process of aligning individuals' skills and interests with needs of the broader community. Granted, Plato focuses more on skills than interests, so it is possible that guardians could try to shoehorn women into roles they are good at but do not enjoy. But given the goal of making the city as happy as possible (its individual citizens included), an ideal ruler, as laid out by Socrates, would look for more creative approaches to helping all citizens find a purpose around which to build their own meaningful lives. Heather Reid, "Plato on Women in Sport," *Journal of the Philosophy of Sport* 47, no. 3 (2020): 344-361, offers a more positive view on Plato's account of women in *Republic* and *Laws*. Rather than see the works' casual misogyny as indicative of Plato's view, she sets it within the dialogical context of figures easing their discussion partners into radical new ideas, as "the sugar of apparently sexist statements helps the medicine of logic to go down" (348).

9. This term is applied to Lysis at *Lysis* 206c.

10. Reid, "Heroic *Parthenoi*," 511.

11. Reid, "*Heroic Parthenoi*," builds a case for Plato's *Republic* as influencing these shifts in Hellenistic athletics.

12. Coleen Zoller, given her focus in *Plato and the Body* (Albany: SUNY Press, 2018), devotes considerable attention to analyzing the apparent paradoxes in "the rare, quirky sort of people" that become philosophers (122–130), and applying *Republic*'s account of the philosopher to Socrates himself (130–147).

13. See the discussion of "finding a rhythm" in the introduction to part 2.

14. See William Damon, *The Path to Purpose: How Young People Find Their Calling in Life* (New York: Free Press, 2008), and Angela Duckworth, *Grit: The Power of Passion and Perseverance* (New York: Scribner, 2016), esp. chapters 6 and 7.

15. The reading I set out is in line with Gail Fine, "Knowledge and Belief in *Republic* 5–7," in Fine, *Plato*, 1:215–246, who argues that understanding the form of the good amounts to holistic, synoptic understanding of how all basic ideas fit together in an organic whole.

16. For an overview of play in Greek culture, see Armand D'Angour, "Plato and Play: Taking Education Seriously in Ancient Greece," *American Journal of Play* 5, no. 3 (2013): 293–307.

17. For a discussion of this history, see Eric Chaline, *The Temple of Perfection: A History of the Gym* (London: Reaktion Books, 2015).

18. In chapter 7, I argued for reading the first five speeches in *Symposium* as creating a progression in line with Plato's use of the mathematical sciences in *Republic* 7. Ideas of numerical proportion were limited to Eryximachus's talk of balance in medicine, gym training, music, and related arts, but did not get into details of the math. One way to defend my reading of *Symposium* is to see it as focused on the initial "play" stages of *Republic*'s more expansive ascent to the good. While the role of harmonies is made explicit in *Symposium*, the rationale for them is left for a more in-depth analysis. Whatever the relation between *Symposium* and *Republic* in terms of theory building and order of composition, both reflect a common constellation of ideas drawn from Hippocratic medicine, gym training, and music theory. Heather Reid, "Sport and Moral Education in Plato's *Republic*," *Journal of the Philosophy of Sport* 34 (2007): 160–175, corroborates this view. On her reading, the rhythmic motions involved in sports and dance provide instances of the soul's control over the body. In children, who are prone to follow appetites over reason, this is especially important as external rules provide a way for children to practice keeping their appetites in check.

19. For discussion of the "ruler's choice," see Richard Kraut, "Return to the Cave: *Republic* 519–521," in Fine, *Plato*, 2:235–254, and Nicholas Smith, "Return to the Cave," in *Plato and the Divided Self*, ed. Rachel Barney, Tad Brennan, and Charles Brittain (Cambridge: Cambridge University Press, 2012), 83–102.

20. My reading of Plato's curriculum, particularly the role of mathematical studies within it, is in line with Mitchell Miller, "Beginning the 'Longer Way,'" in *The Cambridge Companion to Plato's "Republic,"* ed. G. Ferrari (Cambridge: Cambridge University Press, 2007), 310–344.

21. Unlike *Symposium*, *Republic* explicitly engages in the language of hypothesis. For analysis, see Hugh Benson, "Plato's Philosophical Method in the *Republic*: The Divided Line (510b-511b)," in *Plato's "Republic": A Critical Guide*, ed. Mark McPherran (Cambridge: Cambridge University Press, 2010), 188–208.

22. C. D. C. Reeve, "Blindness and Reorientation: Education and the Acquisition of Knowledge in the *Republic*," in McPherran, *Plato's "Republic,"* 209-228, walks through *Republic*'s education program largely along the same lines as I do. Given that *Republic* does not complete the inquiry to arrive at a nonhypothetical first principle, Reeve concludes, "*Republic* itself is best seen as a raft only—a splendid prototype to use in thinking about education" (227).

23. Benson, "Plato's Philosophical Method," 200, points out that the confirmation portion of the method is "notoriously obscure." He suggests that Socrates, by disclaiming knowledge at this point in *Republic*, shows himself to be someone engaged in the true, albeit incomplete, pursuit of understanding, as opposed to people who have mistaken their hypothetical "knowledge" for nonhypothetical "understanding." In this respect, the gaping hole in the middle of *Republic*'s argument ends up being a strength akin to "human wisdom" in *Apology*—i.e., Socrates does not take himself to know (or, in *Republic* 6's terms, "understand") things that he does not.

10. Justice as Civic and Mental Health

1. David Sachs, in an influential article, "A Fallacy in Plato's Republic," *Philosophical Review* 72, no. 2 (1963): 141-158, argues that Socrates has actually failed to do this. Sachs distinguishes the common conception of justice as set out by Glaucon (not robbing temples, not murdering people, etc.) from the Platonic conception of justice (each part of the soul doing its own task). For Socrates's response to Glaucon to work, Sachs argues, Socrates would have to show that all people who perform actions commonly thought of as just embody Platonic justice in their souls, and vice versa. Since he finds no such arguments, Sachs suggests Plato is motivated by the idea that rules of conduct (i.e., common justice) always have exceptions, which is why Socrates shifts his focus onto states of the soul. Rachana Kamtekar, "Ethics and Politics in Socrates' Defense of Justice in Plato's *Republic*," in *Plato and the Divided Self*, ed. Rachel Barney, Tad Brennan, and Charles Brittain (Cambridge: Cambridge University Press, 2012), 65-82, responds that there are aspects of common justice in *Republic* that do *not* have exceptions, e.g., do not harm friends. On her reading, Socrates's shift into psychology brings questions of motivation into the discussion, since the Platonically just person who performs commonly just actions is in fact happier than someone with a disordered soul who performs commonly just actions out of coercion, e.g., out of fear of enraging a vicious ruler. Kamtekar argues that *Republic* is not providing the kind of demonstrative proof Sachs seems to want but rather setting out an account of justice as the most plausible hypothesis.

2. James Wilberding, "Curbing One's Appetites in Plato's *Republic*," in Barney, Brennan, and Brittain, *Plato and the Divided Self*, 128-149.

3. Compare Pausanias's concern for customs (*nomoi*) in *Symposium*.

4. These competing constitutions were in use during Plato's lifetime. Zena Hitz, "Degenerate Regimes in Plato's *Republic*," in Barney, Brennan, and Brittain, *Plato and the Divided Self*, 103-131, sees *Republic* 8 and 9 as Plato's

attempt to make sense of the political chaos of his youth by presenting each constitution in terms of the ultimate standard it uses in making political choices.

5. In the political sphere this comes about as the impoverished masses overthrow the wealthy elite. Coleen Zoller, *Plato and the Body* (Albany: SUNY Press, 2018), 148–153, relates *Republic*'s discussion of poverty to wealth disparity today.

6. We noted above that scholars disagree about how best to read *Republic* 4's three-part division of the soul. At least part of that disagreement stems from trying to make book 4's account fit with what Socrates lays out in books 8 and 9. Jennifer Whitting, "Psychic Contingency in the *Republic*," in Barney, Brennan, and Brittain, *Plato and the Divided Self*, 174–208, takes a hybrid approach. She argues that in book 4 Socrates relies on musical and Hippocratic medical language to describe the relationships between parts of the soul. In an ideal state, bodily humors are mixed in proper proportions; when illness occurs, individual elements are separated out in ways that they are not meant to be (e.g., the phlegm noticeable in winter). This separation, she argues, transitions into political language of rival parties, which gets picked up in books 8 and 9. Thus, according to Whitting, the soul has one part when healthy and multiple parts when ill.

7. Karl Popper, *The Open Society and Its Enemies* (Princeton: Princeton University Press, 1963).

8. This contrast between Plato's thinking and people such as Popper is mirrored in Plato's thinking about astronomy. As Andrew Gregory puts it in "Pythagoras and Plato," in *The Oxford Handbook of Science and Medicine in the Classical World*, ed. Paul Keyser (Oxford: Oxford University Press, 2018), 147–170, "For Plato, regular and orderly motion was characteristic of intelligence, while irregularity was characteristic of matter on its own. In contrast, we take mechanism, in particular clockwork, to be a paradigm of regularity and contrast that with human frailty." This parallel in astronomical and moral thinking matters, given that Plato's guardians are trained through a rigorous course of astronomy and other mathematical sciences so as to condition them to thinking in certain ways.

9. Kevin Crotty, "Freedom," in *The City-State of the Soul* (Lanham, MD: Lexington Books, 2016), 227–253, presents the same general reading, though he points out that the philosopher also enjoys freedom from opinion.

10. Richard Perry, "The Unhappy Tyrant and the Craft of Inner Rule," in *The Cambridge Companion to Plato's "Republic,"* ed. G. Ferrari (Cambridge: Cambridge University Press, 2007), 386–414, presents *Republic* 9's critique of the tyrannical soul and sets it within the context of *Republic* as a whole.

11. Crotty, *City-State of the Soul*, 124–126; cf. *Republic* 596–597.

12. Granted, carpenters do not go beyond *knowledge* of the form of the couch to understanding of goodness. Because of this, they are not qualified to rule the city as a whole. Yet, on Crotty's reading at least, this does not stop them from obtaining a degree of personal virtue. This is all the more likely to happen when they live by the rules set for them by wise rulers. For a less optimistic

account of the nonphilosopher's virtue, see Rachana Kamtekar, "Imperfect Virtue," *Ancient Philosophy* 18 (1998): 315–339.

13. Scholars disagree on what keeping parts of the soul "in check" amounts to. Zoller, *Plato and the Body*, 115–122, contrasts "austere dualism," which recognizes rational goods as the only goods with "normative dualism," which recognizes spirited and appetitive goods as goods, albeit of less worth than rational ones. Scholars who read Plato in terms of austere dualism tend to see reason ruling in a tyrannical manner. Against this, Zoller rightly points out that reason's role in *Republic* is to care for the goods of each part of the soul in a way that keeps the whole in balance.

14. This passage looks to poetic content and music theory to argue that poets must be banished from the ideal city. Malcolm Schofield, "Music all pow'rful," in *Plato's "Republic": A Critical Guide*, ed. Mark McPherran (Cambridge: Cambridge University Press, 2010), 229–248, argues that Socrates's account of music's power to harmonize the soul through rhythms and harmonies is more central to *Republic*'s argument than the critique of poetic content we find in books 2, 3, and 10, even if the critique of poetic content takes up considerably more space. Schofield buttresses this reading by looking to Plato's later work, *Laws*, which presents *Republic* 3's account of music but sets the critique of poetry aside. Gabriel Richardson Lear, "Plato on Learning to Love Beauty," in *The Blackwell Guide to Plato's "Republic,"* ed. Gerasimos Santas (Oxford: Blackwell Publishing, 2006), 104–124, connects both categories. On her reading, appearing beautiful provides a forum for spirit's love of winning. In a context where people see material wealth as beautiful, a child will strive to appear beautiful by being wealthy, likewise in a context that presents military prowess, cunning, or virtue as beautiful. The content of beautiful poems may thus help harmonize the soul by presenting virtuous and good people as beautiful, thus giving the spirited part of the soul role models that will help direct the whole soul to virtue and the good, which are the ultimate objects of the rational part.

15. For discussion, see G. R. F. Ferrari, "Glaucon's Reward, Philosophy's Debt: The Myth of Er," in *Plato's Myths*, ed. Catalin Partenie (Cambridge: Cambridge University Press, 2009), 116–133.

16. Crotty, *City-State of the Soul*, is the major exception to this. His central message is that the kind of thinking that goes into Socrates's founding of an ideal city provides a model, inviting talented young people to think about themselves as "founders" of their own souls.

17. According to Richard Kraut, "Eudaimonism and Platonic *Erōs*," in *Plato's "Symposium": A Critical Guide*, ed. Pierre Destrée and Zina Giannopoulou (Cambridge: Cambridge University Press, 2017), 235–252, one of Plato's main ethical insights is that "one should live one's life in response to something superior to oneself."

18. See the introduction to part 2.

19. For a current discussion of sustainability and Greek theories of happiness, see Bruce Stephenson, *Portland's Good Life: Sustainability and Hope in an American City* (Lanham, MD: Lexington Books, 2021).

Part III

1. Citation schemes for *NE* abound. For general passages, I will use the format *NE* book.chapter (e.g., *NE* 1.8). For specific passages, I will use Bekker numbers, which refer to the first print edition of the Greek; I will use the following format: page number/column letter/line number (e.g., 1099a3).

2. We first encountered this term in chapter 3, as Socrates's first question about a new gym was about attractive (*kalos*) men there. *Kalos* is the masculine form of the word. In what follows, I will use the neuter form, *kalon*, which is Aristotle's default for talking about actions, virtues, and other attributes.

3. The traditional start date for the Olympic Games is 776 BCE. This marked the first Olympiad, i.e., the four-year period until the next set of games. Each Olympiad was subsequently referred to by the winner of the games' founding competition, a 200-meter sprint known as the *stadion*.

4. For a detailed account of ancient sources for the myth, see Emma Stafford, "Monsters and the Hero I: The Twelve Labors," in *Herakles* (New York: Routledge, 2012), 23–50. For visual sources, see Jenifer Neils, "Myth and Greek Art: Creating a Visual Language," in *The Cambridge Companion to Greek Mythology*, ed. Roger Woodard (Cambridge: Cambridge University Press, 2007), 286–304, esp. 296–297.

5. For a detailed discussion of the connection between ancient virtue theory, Herakles, and the Olympic Games, see Heather Reid and Georgios Mouratidis, "Naked Virtue: Ancient Athletic Nudity and the Olympic Ethos of *Aretē*," *Olympika* 29 (2020): 29–55.

6. This meaning shows up often in Homer. Given the formulaic nature of Homer's poetry, phrases such as "in good order" and "not in order" are repeated several times. See, for instance, *Iliad* 10.472 and 2.214. Homer typically uses the verb form in military contexts, e.g., "to set in order the horses and the shield-bearing men" (*Iliad* 2.554).

7. This sense appears at *NE* 3.3, 6.7, and 10.3. Translation of these passages is not controversial.

8. At *Olympian* 11.13, Pindar addresses the champion in a boys' wrestling contest, saying, "I will add a sweet-voiced *kosmos* to your crown (*stephanos*) of golden olive."

9. The gender charge here is unfortunate. While women did compete in various games (e.g., the Heraian Games, which were also held at Olympia in honor of Hera), neither Pindar nor any other poet wrote victory poetry for them that has survived. The main exception is Kyniska, princess of Sparta, who won the Olympic chariot race in 396 BCE. The few surviving sources, however, seem to contradict one another on the value of this victory. In this particular event, it was the owner of the team, rather than the driver, who was considered victor. According to one source, Kyniska's brother Agesilaos talked her into entering the race "to show the Greeks that an equestrian victory was the result of wealth and expenditure, not in any way the result of *aretē*" (Plutarch, *Agesilaos* 20.1, in *Arete: Greek Sports from Ancient Sources*, trans. Stephen Miller (Berkeley: University of California Press, 2012), no. 151c). Nevertheless, Kyniska herself took the

opportunity to erect a statue at Olympia, on whose base she inscribed, "Kings of Sparta were my fathers and brothers. Kyniska, victorious at the chariot race with her swift-footed horses, erected this statue. I assert that I am the only woman in all Greece who won this crown" (IvO 160, in Miller, *Arete*, no. 151b). While neither source uses the term *kosmos*, Kyniska's own reflection on the event seems more in keeping with the term's athletic sense, while her brother's seems closer to the cosmetic.

10. Gianna Stergiou, "*Ponos* and *Aretē* in Pindar's Poetry," in *Ageless Aretē*, ed. Heather Reid and John Serrati (Sioux City, IA: Parnassos Press, 2022), 91–108. Given that Pindar was writing for tyrants such as Theron, it is perhaps unsurprising that he blurs the line between inherited wealth and personal excellence. Socrates, in Plato's *Apology*, seems somewhat more skeptical (see chapter 5). Aristotle finds one way around this ambiguity in his account of the virtue of magnificence (*megaloprepeia*) or big spending, as I will call it. See chapter 13.

11. Anthony Verity, *Pindar: The Complete Odes* (Oxford: Oxford World Classics, 2007), 143. In what follows, I use Verity's translation with alterations.

12. Amphitryon was Herakles's mortal father in the same way Joseph was Jesus's.

13. It is possible to contest this translation. Yet our end goal at present is to understand *NE*, which explicitly says that the crown goes not to the fastest or the strongest, but to the one who competes. Whether Pindar meant virtues or deeds of virtue, Aristotle clearly meant the latter.

14. Heather Reid, "Aristotle's Pentathlete," in *Athletics and Philosophy in the Ancient World* (London: Routledge, 2011), 69–80, gives a brief survey of some of the main ideas I will discuss.

11. A Sketch of the Good Life

1. Pew Research Center, "What Makes Life Meaningful? Views from 17 Advanced Economies," November 18, 2021, https://www.pewresearch.org/global/2021/11/18/what-makes-life-meaningful-views-from-17-advanced-economies/.

2. There is some controversy as to whether Aristotle is in fact following the endoxic method in *NE*. Terence Irwin, trans., *Aristotle: Nicomachean Ethics* (Indianapolis: Hackett, 1999), 326–327, and Richard Kraut, "How to Justify Ethical Propositions: Aristotle's Method," in *The Blackwell Guide to Aristotle's "Nicomachean Ethics,"* ed. Richard Kraut (Oxford: Wiley-Blackwell, 2006), 76–95, take Aristotle at his word. As does C. D. C. Reeve, "Aristotle's Philosophical Method," in *The Oxford Handbook of Aristotle*, ed. Christopher Shields (Oxford: Oxford University Press, 2012), 150–170, who lays out how the endoxic method fits into Aristotle's larger methodology and theory of knowledge. Against this interpretation, Gregory Salmieri, "Aristotle's Non-'Dialectical' Methodology in the *Nicomachean Ethics*," *Ancient Philosophy* 29 (2009): 311–335, argues that since *NE* is explicitly written for readers who were brought up "the right way," the work does not rely on the preexisting opinions (*endoxa*) of Aristotle's predecessors or contemporaries but on the current observations of his select readers. Siding with Salmieri, Dorothea Frede, "The

Endoxon Mystique: What *Endoxa* Are and What They Are Not," in *Oxford Studies in Ancient Philosophy*, vol. 43, ed. Brad Inwood (Oxford: Oxford University Press, 2012), 185–215, argues that in practice *NE* rarely "starts from" the *endoxa* but merely uses others' opinions to "confirm" Aristotle's own views. On her reading, the endoxic method is a fairly formal matter, while what *NE* demonstrates is merely careful thinking of the sort any rational person should aspire to. This debate has practical implications for how we approach *NE*. If, as Aristotle claims, *NE* follows the endoxic method, beginning inquiry into happiness from commonly held beliefs, then people today who are looking for guidance in life, e.g., undergraduates taking an Intro to Ethics course, may simply start at the beginning and puzzle their way through it. If *NE* is not following the endoxic method but, say, working out the implications of theories of human nature defended in other Aristotelian texts, then *NE*'s use in ethics curricula around the world is misguided. I, for one, take Aristotle at his word and structure my discussion accordingly.

3. D. S. Hutchinson and Monte Ransome Johnson, "Protreptic Aspects of Aristotle's *Nicomachean Ethics*," in *The Cambridge Companion to Aristotle's "Nicomachean Ethics,"* ed. Ronald Polansky (Cambridge: Cambridge University Press, 2014), 383–409, esp. 389–393. The basic setup appears to go back to Pythagoras, who is quoted centuries later by Cicero at *Tusculan Disputations* 5.8–9. John Hare, *God and Morality: A Philosophical History* (Oxford: Oxford University Press, 2007), 11, presents Pythagoras's version but then draws what seems to be the wrong conclusion: "The most honorable (the noblest most *kalon*) form of life is to contemplate with the mind alone, in the middle is the life of business and 'affairs,' and the least honorable is the man whose life is devoted to the body." While Hare does not cite his source for this, to dismiss Olympic athletes as simply devoted to the body and therefore less honorable than businessmen seriously misunderstands what goes into being an elite athlete, and the high regard in which Olympic athletes were held in Greek society. Cicero's report that athletes compete "for the sake of glory and the nobility of a crown" seems more accurate in both regards. (It also lines up with how Hutchinson and Johnson, 389, read the passage.) Hare's study makes valuable contributions to bringing Aristotle's thinking about divinity back into scholarly discussions. Yet his downplaying of athletics, as seen here and elsewhere, leaves out an important aspect of how pre-Christian Greeks approached the divine.

4. The psychological toll of social media on girls has been well documented. Alex Hawgood, "What Is 'Bigorexia'?," *New York Times*, March 5, 2022, discusses media's impact on boys, focusing on fitness models who associate self-worth and follower counts in ways that encourage body dysmorphia.

5. Andrea Nightingale, *Spectacles of Truth in Classical Greek Philosophy: Theoria in Its Cultural Context* (Cambridge: Cambridge University Press, 2004), explores this athletic/religious/philosophical connection at length.

6. Given current pressures to see higher education as career preparation, critics within the world of Catholic colleges, who tend to sympathize with Aristotle, have gone so far as to praise education aimed at "useless" pursuits. John E. Jalbert, "Leisure and Liberal Education: A Plea for Uselessness," *Philosophical Studies in Education* 40 (2009): 222–233.

7. This is sometimes referred to as a "monolithic" understanding of happiness, which is advocated by C. D. C. Reeve, "Beginning and Ending with *Eudaimonia*," in *The Cambridge Companion to Aristotle's "Nicomachean Ethics,"* ed. Ronald Polansky (Cambridge: Cambridge University Press, 2014), 14–33, and Richard Kraut, *Aristotle on the Human Good* (Princeton: Princeton University Press, 1989).

8. This is sometimes referred to as an "inclusive" or "compound" understanding of happiness. William Francis Ross Hardie, "The Final Good in Aristotle's Ethics," *Philosophy* 40 (1965): 277–295, initiated this line of thought, and John Ackrill, "Aristotle on *Eudaimonia*," in *Essays on Aristotle's Ethics*, ed. Amélie Oksenberg Rorty (Berkeley: University of California Press, 1980), 15–33, made it popular. For a useful discussion of how the debate emerged from the preoccupations of twentieth-century ethics, see Nicholas White, "Conflicting Parts of Happiness in Aristotle's Ethics," *Ethics* 105 (January 1995): 258–283. Terence Irwin, "Conceptions of Happiness in the *Nicomachean Ethics*," in Shields, *Oxford Handbook of Aristotle*, 495–528, reviews more recent developments.

9. Angela Duckworth, *Grit: The Power of Passion and Perseverance* (New York: Scribner, 2016). I look to Duckworth not because she presents a particularly insightful analysis of Aristotle. Indeed, her two mentions of Aristotle (146 and 271–272) are brief to the point of being misleading. Nevertheless, she has arrived at many of the same conclusions about the well-lived life and how to pursue it.

10. Duckworth, "How Gritty are You?" in *Grit*, 53–78.

11. Duckworth, *Grit*, 61.

12. Richard Arum, *Academically Adrift: Limited Learning on College Campuses* (Chicago: University of Chicago Press, 2011).

13. These students are the target of William Deresiewicz, *Excellent Sheep: The Miseducation of the American Elite & the Way to a Meaningful Life* (New York: Free Press, 2014).

14. In terms of methodology, it is at this point that Aristotle seems to stray the furthest from his endoxic method as he draws on ideas that he has established in his own previous works. Frede, "*Endoxon* Mystique," 191–192, criticizes Aristotle for importing such views without treating them as *endoxa* in need of scrutiny. That said, the larger argument in this passage can be spelled out in terms that are fairly intuitive, even if his talk of plant souls strikes modern ears as odd. For more detailed discussion, see Terence Irwin, "The Metaphysical and Psychological Basis of Aristotle's Ethics," in Rorty, *Essays on Aristotle's Ethics*, 35–54.

15. Samuel Baker, "The Concepts of *Ergon*: Towards an Achievement Interpretation of Aristotle's 'Function Argument'," in Inwood, *Oxford Studies in Ancient Philosophy*, 227–266, argues that we should read *ergon* in *NE* 1.7 as meaning "work," which may apply to actions *and* products. In this he pushes against the scholarly consensus that reads *ergon* as "function" or "characteristic activity" and thus focuses on activities alone. In the end, Baker admits that the conclusion to Aristotle's argument is that happiness is an activity not a product. Yet Baker's careful reading helps us understand how Aristotle arrives

at this conclusion. See also Baker, "A Monistic Conclusion to Aristotle's *Ergon* Argument: The Human Good as the Best Achievement of a Human," *Archiv für Geschichte der Philosophie* 103, no. 3 (2021): 373–403.

16. The Latin root *excello* literally means "to rise up above another." For the cultural antecedents of this idea, see Gregory Nagy, *The Best of the Achaeans: Concepts of the Hero in Archaic Greek Poetry* (Baltimore: Johns Hopkins University Press, 1999).

17. Debra Hawhee, *Bodily Arts: Rhetoric and Athletics in Ancient Greece* (Austin: University of Texas Press, 2004), 17.

18. Duckworth, *Grit*, 119–120.

19. Plato sets out the term in *Republic* 8, though his account of this person's character is the main subject of *Republic* 5–7. See chapter 10 for discussion. Aristotle explicitly embraces aristocratic thinking in his discussion of justice in *NE* 5. See chapter 14 for discussion.

20. Thanks to my former student Gavin Clark for pointing me to this line of questioning. I started pairing readings from *NE* and *Grit* in courses shortly after *Grit* was published. It was only after several terms of this that Clark questioned the usefulness of professional athletes and billionaire tech moguls as role models for people in general. While his critique was aimed at Duckworth, it applies to Aristotle as well, as I have spelled out here.

21. On its cosmetic reading, *kosmos* could easily have been used here. Given that Aristotle chooses to use charm bracelet (*periaptos*) instead provides at least some evidence that he is reserving *kosmos* for a noncosmetic sense when it appears a few pages later at *NE* 1.10.

22. Heather Reid and Georgios Mouratitidis, "Naked Virtue: Ancient Athletic Nudity and the Olympic Ethos of *Aretē*," *Olympika* 29 (2020): 29–55, trace the socioeconomic factors at play in the Olympics over the millennia, pointing out that ancient victors tended to come from wealthy families, while modern victors tend to come from wealthy countries (35).

23. Aristotle lays this idea out more fully at *NE* 10.1–5, where he sets out forerunners to contemporary thinking about flow. See chapter 17.

24. The last of these is not recorded by Homer but appears in various vase paintings. See, e.g., Attic black-figure amphora, ca. 520–510 BCE, from Vulci, Louvre, Department of Greek, Etruscan and Roman Antiquities, Sully, room 39, case 6.

25. *NE* 1.3, 1094b19–27 claims that ideas in political science "usually" hold good. Later, in discussing the kind of thinking that goes into planning and executing activities, *NE* 3.3, 1112b3–4 claims, "We deliberate about what comes about through our agency but in different ways on different occasions."

26. Pindar, *Olympians* 1.23 and 8.83. Richard Kraut, "An Aesthetic Reading of Aristotle's Ethics," in Politeia *in Greek and Roman Philosophy* (Cambridge: Cambridge University Press, 2011), 231–250, cites *NE* 1.10 to connect *kosmos* with *kalon* as he builds a case against overly moral readings of *kalon*. He even points out that a virtuous person "sparkles" (*lampei*). Yet he does not set these notions of beauty within the athletic context that Pindar helps bring into focus.

27. In calling this person great-spirited (*megalopsychos*), Aristotle invokes a virtue that was not part of the Socratic or Platonic canon. He will turn to defining it in *NE* 4, where it is closely connected with *NE*'s other three controversial instances of *kosmos*. See chapter 13.

28. In more formal terms, Aristotle seems to waffle between the strict consequentialism adopted by the later Epicurean school and the strict nonconsequentialism adopted by the Stoics. See the epilogue.

29. There are two notable exceptions. Anthony Long, "Aristotle on *Eudaimonia, Nous,* and Divinity," in *Aristotle's "Nicomachean Ethics": A Critical Guide*, ed. Jon Miller (Cambridge: Cambridge University Press, 2011), 92–113, reads *NE* 1.9 in light of *NE* 1.6's passing mention of divinity and intellect (*nous*) to suggest that this divine thing within us might just be our intellect, which fits with *NE* 1.7's account of happiness in terms of rational activity. Hare, *God and Morality*, 19–20, points out that the word "divine" appears nearly twice as often in *NE* as "happy" does. He also helpfully talks about the god within us as that which is "human but not merely human" (25–27). This nicely captures what I refer to as *NE*'s aspirational account of happiness.

30. Reid and Mouratidis, "Naked Virtue," 36, point out the explicit connection between athletic *agōn* and Herakles's labors in Pindar, *Isthmian* 4.47.

31. Martin West, "Heracles," in *East Face of Helicon* (Oxford: Oxford University Press, 1997), 458–472, esp. 470–472.

12. Training

1. Pausanias 6.14.5–8, in *Arete: Greek Sports from Ancient Sources*, trans. Stephen Miller (Berkeley: University of California Press, 2012), 111.

2. *Anthologia Graeca* 11.36, in Miller, *Arete*, 29.

3. Athenaeus, *The Gastronomers* 10.412F, in Miller, *Arete*, 112.

4. Quintilian, *Institutio Oratoria* 1.9.5.

5. Bodybuilders will also appreciate Milo's fame for vascularity. According to Pausanias 6.14.5–8, Milo could tie a ribbon around his forehead, hold his breath, and break the ribbon merely by the strength of his veins. (See Miller, *Arete*, no. 163a).

6. Most translations render *ethos* and the related term *ethismos* as "habit" and "habituation." *NE* 2, however, is full of examples drawn from the gym. I thus follow Heather Reid, "Athletic Virtue and Aesthetic Values in Aristotle's Ethics," *Journal of the Philosophy of Sport* 47, no. 1 (2020): 63–74, esp. 67, by translating both as "training," which covers both the process (*ethismos*) and the state to which it leads (*ethos*). While this comes at the price of making Aristotle's language somewhat less precise, context should make it clear which is being referred to, and the payoff is to make Aristotle's account much more concrete and readily understood by modern readers.

7. *Hexis* derives from the verb "to hold" (*echō*), so we might think of it as how a person holds herself. This is sometimes translated as "habit," which follows conventions of Latin philosophy. I follow Heather Reid's suggestion in calling this a condition (pers. comm., November 20, 2022).

8. Lesley Brown, "Why Is Aristotle's Virtue of Character a Mean? Taking Aristotle at His Word (*NE* ii 6)," in *The Cambridge Companion to Aristotle's "Nicomachean Ethics,"* ed. Ronald Polansky (Cambridge: Cambridge University Press, 2014), 64–80, argues that *NE*'s talk of deficiency, mean, and excess indicates that all have both descriptive and normative senses, and that in likening ethical virtues to crafts, Aristotle means to invoke the normative sense. Such things are not merely middling but appropriate or just right.

9. Lesley Brown, "What Is 'the Mean Relative to Us' in Aristotle's *Ethics*?," *Phronesis* 42, no. 1 (1997): 77–93. The distinction matters insofar as some modern virtue theorists have read Aristotle as seeing the virtues themselves, rather than the individual choices that result from them, as varying from individual to individual. Brown rightly argues that this goes too far.

10. The function of *NE* 3.1–5 in the work's overall argument is controversial. I build on the reading of Michael Pakaluk, "Actions as Signs of Character (*Nicomachean Ethics* 3.1–5)," in *Aristotle's "Nicomachean Ethics": An Introduction* (Oxford: Oxford University Press, 2005), 118–150. For a critical overview of such readings and a detailed reconstruction of the passage's argument, see Suzanne Bobzien, "Choice and Moral Responsibility (*NE* iii 1–5)," in Polansky, *Cambridge Companion to Aristotle's "Nicomachean Ethics,"* 81–109.

11. This is a catchphrase of the American Association of Colleges and Universities for communicating the value of a general education. The goal is not to prepare students to perform tasks with existing scripts (e.g., long division) but to perform tasks for which no scripts (yet) exist. See, for instance, Carol Schneider, "Carol Geary Schneider on Educating Students for Unscripted Problems," https://youtu.be/WVQdVVFyLA4.

12. Pakaluk, "Actions as Signs," 139.

13. Many readers, myself included, may find this conclusion problematic. As we saw in part 2, Hippocrates and Plato took social determinants of health seriously. It is well within Aristotle's intellectual horizons to reply that some people are born into situations that force them into bad habits before they are old enough to think rationally about what they are doing. Are these people responsible for their vices? Such questions are outside of Aristotle's current focus. Rather than ask whether it is ever fitting to hold people accountable, he simply assumes that it is and then sets out criteria to determine when we should do so. As Pakaluk, "Actions as Signs," 144n16, argues, Aristotle is not here raising the questions of free will and determinism that will be central to debates between the Epicureans, Stoics, and Academic skeptics.

14. Hendrik Lorenz, "Virtues of Character in Aristotle's *Nicomachean Ethics*," in *Oxford Studies in Ancient Philosophy*, vol. 37, ed. Brad Inwood (Oxford: Oxford University Press, Summer 2009), 177–212, cites various scholars who have defended this reading and responds to them in detail, setting *NE* 3.1–5 within *NE*'s broader account of reason's role in virtues of character.

15. This could be problematic for those of us not involved in literal combat, as it would make bravery irrelevant for our lives. Alternatively, we might follow Pakaluk, *Aristotle's "Nicomachean Ethics,"* 152–153, in seeing Aristotle as looking at "central-cases" of a virtue as a way of illustrating that virtue's

structure. If this is right, then bravery might be at play in noncombat scenarios as well.

16. There is some confusion about whether confidence and fear are meant to be two distinct axes or continua or the two ends of a single axis or continuum. I take the former view. For discussion and defense of this position, see J. O. Urmson, "Aristotle's Doctrine of the Mean," and David Pears, "Courage as a Mean," in *Essays on Aristotle's Ethics*, ed. Amélie Oksenberg Rorty (Berkeley: University of California Press, 1980), 157-170 and 171-187, respectively. Charles Young, "Courage," in *A Companion to Aristotle*, ed. George Anagnostopoulos (Oxford: Wiley-Blackwell, 2009), 442-456, translates the pair as "fear" and "cheer," and argues that Aristotle treats them as a single continuum in *Eudemian Ethics* and as two continua in *NE*.

17. Aristotle does not spell out the exact content of confidence. I follow Lawrence Hinman, *Ethics: A Pluralistic Approach to Moral Theory* (Belmont, CA: Thomson-Wadsworth, 2008), 272-273, in taking it to be confidence "in our own ability." Young, "Courage," 447-452, lays out several options as the object of "cheer" (confidence): the prospect of danger, the prospect of safety, the prospect of success at whatever one is trying to accomplish. Young cites J. L. Stocks, a philosopher whose experience fighting in World War I changed his reading of *NE*, as he learned of the possibility of cheerfulness in the face of imminent evil (Young's first option).

18. Pears, "Courage as a Mean," 176, calls this hypothetical virtue "darage" and claims, "It is dysfunctional and might well extinguish the species."

19. Anna Lännström, *Loving the Fine: Virtue and Happiness in Aristotle's "Ethics"* (Notre Dame, IN: University of Notre Dame Press, 2006), and Terence Irwin, "Beauty and Morality in Aristotle," in *Aristotle's "Nicomachean Ethics": A Critical Guide*, ed. Jon Miller (Cambridge: Cambridge University Press, 2011), 239-253, place *kalon* toward the morality end of the spectrum and default to translating it as "fine." Richard Kraut, "An Aesthetic Reading of Aristotle's *Ethics*," in *Politeia in Greek and Roman Philosophy*, ed. Verity Harte and Melissa Lane (Cambridge: Cambridge University Press, 2013), 231-250, responds to Irwin, arguing that ideas of beautiful shape, order, and size are at work in many more passages of *NE* than Irwin allows. Gabriel Richardson Lear, "Aristotle on Moral Virtue and the Fine," in *The Blackwell Guide to Aristotle's "Nicomachean Ethics,"* ed. Richard Kraut (Oxford: Wiley-Blackwell, 2006), 116-136, takes a similar approach but stresses that in Aristotle beautiful order is always directed at some purpose or end (*telos*) and that, unlike mere goodness, the *kalon* is necessarily visible. There is a related question around the phrase *kalokagathia*. Literally, this means "beautiful and good," but as a technical phrase it may be translated as "nobility" or "gentlemanliness" (on the moral side of the spectrum) or "beautiful goodness." Reid, "Athletic Virtue and Aesthetic Values," 63-74, and Nigel Spivey, "In Training for 'Beautiful Goodness',", in *The Ancient Olympics* (Oxford: Oxford University Press, 2012), 31-70, place it on the beauty side of the spectrum. Reid's focus is the final chapter of Aristotle's less well-known work, *Eudemian Ethics*, yet she suggests ways of approaching *NE* as well.

20. Pindar, *Olympian* 1.23 and 8.83.

21. Acting for the sake of reputation itself, either to earn a good reputation or to avoid a bad one, is sometimes referred to as "civic courage." Zena Hitz, "Aristotle on Law and Moral Education," in *Oxford Studies in Ancient Philosophy*, vol. 42, ed. Brad Inwood (Oxford: Oxford University Press, 2012), 263-306, reviews the scholarly literature on the subject. She contrasts Miles Burnyeat, who argues that civic courage is a "pre-philosophical virtue, grounded in good habits and proper pleasures," with Gabriel Richardson Lear, who holds it to be a "waystation in the process of correct habituation" (270). To put it in athletic terms, an entry-level bike vs. training wheels. Against both, Hitz argues that civic courage is a "defective virtue" (i.e., a broken bike), which she uses to draw out implications for the educational system laid out in Aristotle's *Politics*.

22. Kraut, "Aesthetic Reading," 243, makes the same general point: "It is a beautiful thing to master fear by combining it with practical wisdom . . . because it is the occasion for his exercise of that skill."

23. On this reading, *NE* comes closer to Plato's *Symposium* than is normally acknowledged. While Plato focused on the immortal nature of beauty, which for him is tied up in questions of mathematics, Aristotle's athletic example invokes a set of associations that sidestep mathematics and draw on aspects of hero culture. Aristotle concludes his discussion by returning to states that resemble bravery (3.9). From a current perspective, the most provocative claim is that hopeful people (*euelpis*) are not brave. He compares them to drunks who appear brave in emergencies but crumble when things get tough. Given that hope is both a central Christian virtue and a major theme of positive psychology, it would be nice if Aristotle had said more about hope. From the paragraph we have to go on, his critique seems to be that hopeful people are confident in a groundless and therefore excessive way. On the basis of his comment about drunks, he seems to think hope lacks the depth of character that bravery has.

24. Older translations render this "temperance," and its opposite "intemperance." For the sake of contemporary English and the connection to athletics, I will use "discipline" and "lack of discipline" throughout.

25. Gavin Lawrence, "Human Excellence in Character and Intellect," in Anagnostopoulos, *Companion to Aristotle*, 419-441, suggests combining each of these categories to form a star to guide our deliberations.

26. Angela Duckworth, *Grit: The Power of Passion and Perseverance* (New York: Scribner, 2016), 63.

27. Kraut, "Aesthetic Reading," 244-246, argues that this may go beyond mere limiting conditions: deliberations over how to achieve ends can be seen as analogous to craftsmen constructing houses or furniture, making every piece just right.

28. Brown, "Mean Relative to Us," 83-84, argues against older interpretations that take this passage to state that the mean for an individual depends on that individual's temperament. Rather, she argues, this passage shows that there is one correct mean for all human beings in relatively comparable circumstances, but that some people struggle more than others to hold to that mean.

29. Aristotle's second discussion of *sōphrosunē* has to do with the process by which we get there. See chapter 15.

13. Greatness of Spirit

1. The Latin word *magnanimitas* means the same thing as the Greek, though it is not clear that the English *magnanimity* does. That said, Terence Irwin, "Magnanimity as Generosity," in *The Measure of Greatness*, ed. Sophia Vasalou (Oxford: Oxford University Press, 2019), 21–48, defends this translation as not totally off point insofar as magnanimity, like *megalopsychia*, involves letting go of slights.

2. Dirk Held, "Μεγαλοψῡχία in *Nicomachean Ethics* iv," *Ancient Philosophy* 13 (1993): 95–110, draws from anthropology to contrast modern "guilt culture" with ancient "shame culture" and argues that greatness of spirit, as Aristotle presents it, makes better sense in the latter. Since Held published this piece, social media has changed everyday life, bringing the world more closely in line with one where "moral integrity and social worth are closely bound to honor" (103) and people are "figuratively speaking always on stage" (104). Susanna McGrew, "Carving Out Space for Aristotle's *Megalopsychos*," *Episteme* 31 (2021): 44–56, attempts to approach greatness of spirit via the social sciences, in this case drawing on political ideals of equality, to defend *NE* against older critiques.

3. Howard Curzer, "Aristotle's Much Maligned *Megalopsychos*," *Australasian Journal of Philosophy* 69, no. 2 (1991): 131–151, systematically reviews these complaints, stretching back to David Ross in the 1920s, and responds to each. He concludes by "speculating" that widespread dislike for greatness of spirit springs from the fact that it is a virtue for cultures unlike our own, and, as a result, people who try to understand it draw the wrong models from their lived experience and misunderstand what Aristotle is talking about. Terence Irwin, "Disunity in the Aristotelian Virtues," in *Oxford Studies in Ancient Philosophy, Supplementary Volume,* ed. Julia Annas (Oxford: Oxford University Press, 1988), 61–78, sets standing critiques aside and instead argues that Aristotle contradicts himself by claiming, first, that the only way to have one virtue of character is to have all of them and, second, that it is possible for a person to have a virtue concerned with small-scale honors without being great-spirited. Irwin uses greatness of spirit to raise fundamental questions about *NE*'s account of happiness, virtue, and external goods. There has been a lively if somewhat diffuse body of newer work (discussed below) as scholars have responded point for point to Irwin and to older scholarship but less often to each other.

4. Mark Newman, "1947: A Time for Change," MLB.com, April 13, 2007, archived 2009, http://mlb.mlb.com/news/article.jsp?ymd=20070412&content_id=1895445&vkey=perspectives&fext=.jsp&c_id=mlb.

5. Eunshil Bae, "'An Ornament of the Virtues'," *Ancient Philosophy* 23 (2003): 337–349.

6. The Greek literally means "freedom," which in Aristotle's context refers to people who are not enslaved. Given that Aristotle thinks that slaves are generally incapable of virtue and happiness, this does not really set generosity apart from other virtues. As the Latin equivalent, *liberalitas*, also means freedom, some translators render *eleutheria* as "liberality." This translation,

however, has political connotations that are at best confusing for this discussion.

7. Irwin, "Disunity in the Aristotelian Virtues," 62–64.

8. Michael Pakaluk, "On an Alleged Contradiction in Aristotle's *Nicomachean Ethics*," in *Oxford Studies in Ancient Philosophy*, Summer 2002, ed. Brad Inwood (Oxford: Oxford University Press, Summer 2002), 201–219.

9. This foreshadows *NE* 5.3, where Aristotle presents "justice in distribution," which assigns resources to individuals based on individuals' relative worth.

10. On this point, I part ways with Pakaluk, "Alleged Contradiction," who argues that not all acts of big spending need aim at the public good.

11. It is in this sense that Hesiod uses *kosmos* to speak of "adorning Pandora." See the introduction to part 3 for discussion.

12. Bae, "'Ornament of the Virtues'," argues that greatness of spirit may manifest itself through greatness in any virtue. James Stover and Ronald Polansky, "Moral Virtue and *Megalopsychia*," *Ancient Philosophy* 23 (2003): 351–359, argue in an accompanying article that greatness of spirit is possible only with greatness in every virtue. Roger Crisp, "Aristotle on Greatness of Soul," in *The Blackwell Guide to Aristotle's "Nicomachean Ethics*," ed. Richard Kraut (Oxford: Wiley-Blackwell, 2006), 158–178, sides with Bae, arguing that greatness of spirit helps one engage in deeds of any particular virtue and thus develop that virtue further (167).

13. Recall Plato's *Republic* 347e–352d, where Socrates ridicules nonmusicians who think they can outdo musicians in tuning instruments, since an instrument is either in tune or not.

14. Daniel Russell, "Aristotle's Virtues of Greatness," in *Oxford Studies in Ancient Philosophy Supplementary Volume*, ed. Rachana Kamtekar (Oxford: Oxford University Press, 2012), 115–147, critiques this line of thought, arguing instead that greatness here involves high social rank. This limits the possibility for developing greatness of spirit to the few, just as Irwin's requirement of great wealth limits big spending. Rather than disarm Irwin's critique as Pakaluk does, Russell argues that certain forms of elitism are necessary and therefore unproblematic, given that we live in a world of social distinctions. Insofar as Aristotle thinks that one cannot have any virtue without having all of them, Russell concludes that this works one way for people with common virtues and another way for people in positions of social prominence, which seems problematic at best. Shane Drefcinski, "A Different Solution to an Alleged Contradiction in Aristotle's *Nicomachean Ethics*," in *Oxford Studies in Ancient Philosophy*, vol. 30, ed. Brad Inwood (Oxford: Oxford University Press, 2006), 201–210, offers a possible way out. On his reading, both healthy pride and greatness of spirit are species of a more general, unnamed virtue concerned with honor. Generosity and big spending, likewise, are species of an unnamed virtue dealing with spending. This would allow Aristotle to claim that to have any virtue one must have every general virtue but not every specific form of it. For a related discussion of different forms of elitism and equality, see McGrew, "Carving Out Space."

15. Irwin, "Disunity in the Aristotelian Virtues," 64–66, stresses the centrality of success to Aristotle's account of the mean and contrasts this to the Stoics, who require merely the right effort (77). Drawing on *NE* 1.10, however, Irwin admits that one may be virtuous and unsuccessful in situations when external factors interfere.

16. See the introduction to part 3 for discussion.

17. Our passage ends by connecting greatness of spirit with "beautiful goodness" (*kalokagathia*). This term, which also appears at *NE* 1.8 in connection with crowning Olympic victors, is not much discussed in *NE*. Aristotle's *Eudemian Ethics*, however, treats it as an architectonic virtue. Heather Reid, "Athletic Virtue and Aesthetic Values in Aristotle's Ethics," *Journal of the Philosophy of Sport* 47, no. 1 (2020): 63–74, places the term in historical context, which was split between older ideas of inherited goodness and newer ideas of athletic, earned goodness.

18. Bae, "'Ornament of the Virtues'," 344–345; Crisp, "Greatness of Soul," 167; Hellen Cullyer, "The Social Virtues (*NE* iv)," in *The Cambridge Companion to Aristotle's "Nicomachean Ethics*," ed. Ronald Polansky, 135–150, esp. 143–144; Michael Pakaluk, "The Meaning of Aristotelian Magnanimity," in *Oxford Studies in Ancient Philosophy*, vol. 26, ed. David Sedley (Oxford: Oxford University Press, 2004), 241–275, esp. 247 and 270–272.

19. Neil Cooper, "Aristotle's Crowning Virtue," *Apeiron* 22 (1989): 191–205, attempts to rescue Aristotle by seeing greatness of spirit as concerned with friendship rather than honor, though it is unclear to me what this accomplishes. Howard Curzer, "Megalopsychia and Appropriate Ambition (*NE* IV.3-4)," in *Aristotle and the Virtues* (Oxford: Oxford University Press, 2012), 121–142, concludes that greatness of spirit is not a virtue at all but a propensity to stay at the high end of the mean and perform great and heroic acts.

20. Pakaluk, "Alleged Contradiction," 215–218, distinguishes between proper pride and greatness of spirit in terms of occasions: proper pride is for everyday affairs, e.g., performance reviews, while greatness of spirit is for eulogies and awards banquets. My reading, while similar, looks not to the frequency of such thinking but how it figures in one's continual structuring of goals.

21. My reading differs slightly from that of Bae, Crisp, Cullyer, and Pakaluk (cited earlier). I agree with them that greatness of spirit is ultimately inward looking, yet they see it as a matter of self-worth, while I see it as a matter of striving after goals that a good person, whether oneself or others, should appreciate.

22. Pakaluk, "Meaning of Aristotelian Magnanimity," presents Aristotle's great-spirited person in terms of a Socratic protreptic to philosophy. This is a compelling picture of a way to structure one's life around a high-level goal. On my reading, though, it need not be the only one.

23. I side with Stover and Polansky, who see greatness of spirit as an ornament of all character virtues, rather than with Bae, who sees it as an ornament of any character virtue. My reason for drawing this conclusion, however, differs from theirs.

24. Cullyer, "Social Virtues," 148.

14. Sportsmanship and Thinking on One's Feet

1. Richard Kraut, *Aristotle: Political Philosophy* (Oxford: Oxford University Press, 2002), 118, calls general justice "the exercise of the other ethical virtues in accordance with the law for the good of the state." Hallvard Fossheim, "Justice in the *Nicomachean Ethics* Book V," in *Aristotle's "Nicomachean Ethics": A Critical Guide*, ed. Jon Miller (Cambridge: Cambridge University Press, 2011), 254–275, argues that general justice is not a virtue of character at all but a strong tendency to obey laws. Kraut, "Justice in the *Nicomachean Ethics*," in *Political Philosophy*, 98–177, discusses the difference between general and particular justice. Michael Pakaluk, "Justice as a Character-Related Virtue," in *Aristotle's "Nicomachean Ethics": An Introduction* (Oxford: Oxford University Press, 2005), 181–205, lays out the relationship between Plato and Aristotle on justice, arguing that Aristotle's distinction between general and particular justice seeks to correct a basic mistake in *Republic*'s account of justice.

2. Some readers take Aristotle to present three types of particular justice. Here I follow Ronald Polansky, "Giving Justice Its Due," in *The Cambridge Companion to Aristotle's "Nicomachean Ethics*," ed. Ronald Polansky (Cambridge: Cambridge University Press, 2014), 151–179, in seeing only one virtue, particular justice, which is put to work in different contexts.

3. While the example sounds a bit silly, Aristotle suggests at the start of *NE* 5.5 that some people understand justice in such literal terms. Lindsay Judson, "Aristotle on Fair Exchange," *Oxford Studies in Ancient Philosophy*, vol. 15, ed. C. C. W. Taylor (Oxford: Oxford University Press, 1997), 147–206, esp. 150–151, stresses that Aristotle intends an "equal return," i.e., giving things of equal value, rather than an "identical return," i.e., giving the exact thing that was taken beyond one's fair share.

4. Older translations have rendered *chreia* as "demand," which is ultimately an individual's subjective sense of what he desires, as opposed to need, which is an objective fact based on the individual's biology and circumstances (compare moral relativism versus the mean relative to the individual). This older translation has led various readers to see an early version of the market economy at play in *NE* 5.5. Scott Meikle, *Aristotle's Economic Thought* (Oxford: Oxford University Press, 1995), provides a critical survey of economic interpretations of *NE* 5.5 stretching back to Adam Smith and Karl Marx. According to Meikle, economic and ethical ideas were more intimately connected in Aristotle's time, and pinning down how exactly is critical to interpreting *NE* 5.5's argument. Judson, "Fair Exchange," by contrast, argues that *NE* 5.5 is a discussion carried on via exclusively ethical terms, and the plethora of interpretations offered by economists results from the fact that they are looking for economic thinking where there is none.

5. Kraut, "Justice in the *Nicomachean Ethics*," 145–156.

6. The structure of *NE* 5's argument is a matter of dispute. I follow Polansky, "Giving Justice Its Due," in seeing *NE* 5.6–11 as defending the account of particular justice set out in *NE* 5.3–5.

7. Kraut, "Justice in the *Nicomachean Ethics*," 107. In the same work (132–136), Kraut contrasts Aristotle, who sees justice in terms of active civic

engagement, and Plato, who presents it in *Republic* as each person minding his own business.

8. *NE* 6's list of virtues of thought can come across as answers in need of a question or distinctions in need of a purpose. J. O. Urmson, *Aristotle's Ethics* (Oxford: Basil Blackwell, 1988), 79, argues that the task of *NE* 6 is to provide practical guidance to fill out *NE* 2-5's very schematic account of virtues of character, though he concludes that *NE* 6 fails to deliver. Pakaluk, *Aristotle's "Nicomachean Ethics,"* 209-216, responds that Urmson has misrepresented the task Aristotle sets for *NE* 6. My reading sides with Pakaluk. Carlo Natali, "The Book of Wisdom," in Polansky, *Cambridge Companion to Aristotle's "Nicomachean Ethics,"* 180-202, takes the same basic position as Pakaluk on the task pursued in *NE* while giving a more extensive literature review on various controversies along the way. He and Pakaluk, however, take opposite views on whether *NE* 6 advances an expansive (Natali, 192) or narrow (Pakaluk, 214-216, 226-228) conception of happiness.

9. Archery is perhaps the most obvious image at play here. Alternatively, the ancient javelin was thrown using a leather strap (*ankylē*) that was wrapped around the javelin's shaft to act as a kind of slingshot and to help give spin. Wrapping was a delicate process, as throwers found the middle point between too tight to give a good release and too loose to hold together leading up to the throw. Stephen Miller, *Ancient Greek Athletics* (New Haven: Yale University Press, 2004), 68-74. The goal, however, was not accuracy (hitting a target) but distance. Archery, therefore, seems the most plausible candidate for Aristotle's image.

10. Pakaluk, *Aristotle's "Nicomachean Ethics,"* 207. Jessica Moss, "Aristotle's Ethical Psychology," in *The Cambridge Companion to Ancient Ethics*, ed. Christopher Bobonich (Cambridge: Cambridge University Press, 2017), 124-142, situates *NE* 6's account of virtues of thought against Aristotle's broader theory of human nature as set out in *NE* 1, *Eudemian Ethics*, and other psychological works.

11. Moss, "Aristotle's Ethical Psychology," 138-140, argues that the activity of practical wisdom itself constitutes part of the end.

12. Daniel Russell, "*Phronesis* and the Virtues," in Polansky, *Cambridge Companion to Aristotle's "Nicomachean Ethics,"* 203-220.

13. *NE* 4.3 presents greatness of spirit as a *kosmos* of the other virtues. Here perhaps we find a hint of the strategic sense of *kosmos*, as greatness of spirit attends to the high-level goal around which mid- and low-level goals are to be "arrayed."

14. The image of a medieval crown sitting on a monarch's head seems to be the default in the scholarship. Sarah Broadie, *Ethics with Aristotle* (Oxford: Oxford University Press, 1991), 412-419, for instance, suggests that study crowns the active life, but she then adjusts the metaphor to say that it is more like a coping stone, which holds things together, than a cupola, which merely sits on top. The original Greek sense of *stephanos*, which means "wreath" as much as anything, implies encircling. This presents the image Brodie is looking for without the need for adjustment. Likewise, in "Practical Truth in Aristotle," *American*

Catholic Philosophical Quarterly 90, no. 2 (2006): 281–298, Broadie claims, "Perhaps *sophia* [wisdom] is a virtue only for the gods, and for us just an occasional beautiful contingent ornament, not a flowering of fundamental human nature" (269). Here she spells out the cosmetic sense of *kosmos* but contrasts it to something else, which I suggest is a rather nice statement of the athletic sense of *kosmos*. I call attention to these passages not to challenge Broadie's interpretation but to suggest that existing interpretations such as hers may find additional textual support by reading *kosmos* against an athletic context.

15. Angela Duckworth, *Grit: The Power of Passion and Perseverance* (New York: Scribner, 2016), 65.

16. David Brooks, *Road to Character* (New York: Random House, 2016), xi, and Brooks, "Moral Bucket List," *New York Times*, April 11, 2015.

15. Enjoying Discipline

1. Aristotle explicitly lists one's relationships to victory, honor, wealth (1174b30), children, and parents (1148a31).

2. My presentation follows the reconstruction of Paula Gottlieb, "The Practical Syllogism," in *The Blackwell Guide to Aristotle's "Nicomachean Ethics,"* ed. Richard Kraut (Oxford: Wiley-Blackwell, 2006), 218–233.

3. Gottlieb, "Practical Syllogism," argues that particular roles are often central to how Aristotle deploys practical syllogisms. General premises often spell out who should commit or refrain from an action not insofar as someone is human but insofar as he is a doctor, temperate person, parent, soldier, etc.

4. A. W. Price, "Acrasia and Self-Control," in Kraut, *Blackwell Guide to Aristotle's "Nicomachean Ethics,"* 243–254, refers to this as "hard" as opposed to "soft" weakness of will.

5. Price, "Acrasia and Self-Control," 237.

6. Rachel Barney, "Becoming Bad: Aristotle on Vice and Moral Habituation," in *Oxford Studies in Ancient Philosophy*, vol. 57, ed. Victor Caston (Oxford: Oxford University Press, 2019), 273–307.

7. Above, I claimed that children are undisciplined insofar as they do not know what amounts to the mean in a sphere of activity. On this reading, undiscipline is merely the absence of discipline. Barney, by contrast, sees undiscipline as the presence of discipline's opposite, a vicious state brought about through repeated immoderate actions. If she is right, then typical people do not move through all four stages of Aristotle's scheme. Rather than starting at undiscipline, children may occupy another category, e.g., the natural virtue discussed in *NE* 6.

8. Miles Burnyeat champions this reading in his influential article "Aristotle on Learning to Be Good," in *Essays on Aristotle's Ethics*, ed. Amélie Oksenberg Rorty (Berkeley: University of California Press, 1980), 69–92.

9. Mihaly Csikszentmihalyi, *Flow: The Psychology of Optimal Experience* (New York: Harper Perennial Modern Classics, 2008), 1, coins the term to refer to the euphoric feeling of floating or effortlessness elite performers experience when everything about a performance falls into place.

10. Burnyeat, "Learning to Be Good," 78.

11. Howard Curzer, "Aristotle's Painful Path to Virtue," and "Shame and Moral Development," in *Aristotle and the Virtues* (Oxford: Oxford University Press, 2012), 318–366.

12. Curzer, "Painful Path," 327; italics in the original.

13. Curzer, "Painful Path," 327.

14. Curzer, "Painful Path," 323.

15. Curzer, "Painful Path," 330.

16. Burnyeat, "Learning to Be Good," 73.

17. This is the main argument of Curzer, "Practical Wisdom and Reciprocity of Virtue," in *Aristotle and the Virtues*, 293–317.

18. Curzer, "Practical Wisdom and Reciprocity of Virtue," 299–300, 312, 314. Curzer ends his reconstruction of Aristotle's theory of moral development (*Aristotle and the Virtues*, 363–366) by criticizing its emphasis on internalized shame and other negative emotions. Given that these features, by Curzer's own admission, do not present the most obvious reading in the text, I have trouble seeing how his rather dark reading of Aristotle on moral development is "charitable."

19. William Damon, *The Path to Purpose: How Young People Find Their Calling in Life* (New York: Free Press, 2008). For an overview of Damon's work, see Angela Duckworth, "Interest," in *Grit: The Power of Passion and Perseverance* (New York: Scribner, 2016), 95–116.

20. K. Anders Ericsson, R. T. Krampe, and C. Tesch-Römer, "The Role of Deliberate Practice in the Acquisition of Expert Performance," *Psychological Review* 100, no. 3 (1993): 363–406, https://doi.org/10.1037/0033-295X.100.3.363, discussed by Duckworth, "Practice," in Grit, 117–142.

16. Gym Buddies

1. What I present here is perhaps the most obvious reading of the text, as laid out by Terence Irwin, trans., *Aristotle: Nicomachean Ethics* (Indianapolis: Hackett, 1999), 277. Against this, John Cooper, "Aristotle on Forms of Friendship," in *Reason and Emotion: Essays on Ancient Moral Psychology and Ethical Theory* (Princeton: Princeton University Press, 1999), 312–335, argues that in a friendship based on pleasure or usefulness, one person may still value the other for himself and wish him well. This well-wishing (*eunoia*), however, is contingent on that person getting pleasure or use out of the relationship. Alexander Nehemas, "Aristotle's *Philia*, Modern Friendship," in *Oxford Studies in Ancient Philosophy*, vol. 32, ed. Brad Inwood (Oxford: Oxford University Press, 2010), 213–247, esp. 222–225, agrees with Cooper but stipulates that a friend in each sort of relationship will wish for the other what he himself gets out of that relationship. Thus, friends of pleasure will wish pleasure for each other, and friends of usefulness will wish usefulness for each other. Corrine Gartner, "Aristotle on Love and Friendship," in *The Cambridge Companion to Ancient Ethics*, ed. Christopher Bobonich (Cambridge: Cambridge University Press, 2017), 143–163, approaches Nehemas's reading from the slightly different angle that a person

within any given class of friendship will wish for his friends whatever appears to him to be good.

2. Michael Pakaluk, "Friendship," in *Aristotle's "Nicomachean Ethics": An Introduction* (Oxford: Oxford University Press, 2005), 271–276.

3. Aristotle's understanding of human nature, which focuses here on reproductive roles, leads him to see the family as involving a man, woman, and children. Plato's understanding of human nature, which focuses on rationality, leads him in *Republic* to deny any difference between the sexes, at least as regards ruling the state, and to dissolve the nuclear family in the interests of the state. Plato's *Symposium*, meanwhile, presents heterosexual relationships as decidedly second-rate. In modern terms, Aristotle embraces the heteronormative, while Plato rejects it.

4. Nehemas, "Aristotle's *Philia*, Modern Friendship."

5. Zena Hitz, "Aristotle on Self-Knowledge and Friendship," *Philosophers' Imprint* 11, no. 12 (2011): 1–28, defends this general thesis against rival views. The current passage lays the groundwork for this dispute, which I will turn to shortly.

6. In terms of the egoism debate we explored in conjunction with *NE* 8, Nehemas, "Aristotle's *Philia*, Modern Friendship," 229 and 236, takes this passage to show that self-sacrifice is not possible in a friendship based on virtue, insofar as the person sacrificing external goods comes away with a greater good for himself.

7. He uses its noun form, *hamilla*, once to say, "Where there is competition, there is also victory" (*Rhetoric* 1371a6-7).

8. Plato, *Laws* 765a, 829e-384e, and 905e-906e.

9. Lorraine Smith Pangle, "Friendship and Self-Love in Aristotle's *Nicomachean Ethics*," in *Action and Contemplation: Studies in the Moral and Political Thought of Aristotle*, ed. Robert Bartlett and Susan Collins (New York: State University of New York Press, 1999), 171–201, esp. 181.

10. Julia Annas, "Self-Love in Aristotle," and Richard Kraut, "Comments on Julia Annas' 'Self-Love in Aristotle'," in "Aristotle's Ethics," Spindel Supplement, *Southern Journal of Philosophy* 27 (1988): 1–18 and 19–23, respectively. The two pieces are presented as Kraut responding to Annas, though Annas is in fact responding to a draft of Kraut's book *Aristotle on the Human Good* (Princeton: Princeton University Press, 1989), which was not published until the following year, in particular the chapter "Self and Others," 78–154. Put briefly, Kraut sees a zero-sum competition in Aristotle, in particular a competition for public office that provides opportunities for virtuous activity. Drawing from a discussion in Aristotle's *Politics*, Kraut suggests that this competition is tempered through term limits in office. While this solution is clever, it is unclear that it applies to interpersonal relationships outside of public offices. Annas, by contrast, argues that *NE* presents a non-zero-sum competition. Yet, by her own admission, this merely delays the problem, since it takes the virtuous person's acts of self-sacrifice to be self-serving in the end. At worst, she argues, this betrays itself as a remnant of a Homeric ethos in which heroes aim to be "superior" (*hypeirochos*) to others. What Annas sees as the worst-case scenario,

I take to be Aristotle's considered position, and an attractive one at that. For a precursor to Kraut's and Annas's discussion, see Marcia Homiak, "Virtue and Self-Love in Aristotle's Ethics," *Canadian Journal of Philosophy* 11, no. 4 (1981): 633–651.

11. Terence Irwin and Joe Sachs, respectively.

12. The only other use of *askēsis* in *NE* comes at 1.9, 1099b9–10. Here, Aristotle poses the question of whether "happiness is acquired by learning (*mathēsis*) or training (*ethiston*) or by practice (*askēsis*) in some other way." At *NE* 2.1, 1103a14–18, Aristotle presents learning and training as the means of acquiring theoretical and practical virtues, respectively. *NE* 1.9 at least suggests that *askēsis* refers to something other than the acquisition of virtue. The passage proceeds without ever stating what *askēsis* would look like in this scenario.

13. R. A. Gauthier and J. Y. Jolif, *L'Éthique à Nicomaque* (Louvain: Publications Universitaires, 1970), ad loc, claim this passage "pretends to be more profound, but is only more laborious." Cf. Nehemas, "Aristotle's *Philia*, Modern Friendship," 239.

14. Aryeh Kosman, "Aristotle on the Desirability of Friends," *Ancient Philosophy* 24 (2004): 135–154, esp. 148–149.

15. Hitz, "Aristotle on Self-Knowledge," esp. 18–23.

16. Patrick Lee Miller, "Finding Oneself with Friends," in *The Cambridge Companion to Aristotle's "Nicomachean Ethics,"* ed. Ronald Polansky (Cambridge: Cambridge University Press, 2014), 319–349, presents a different refinement of the collaborative reading by focusing on study, in which friends strongly identify with their theoretical intellect. Given that theoretical intellect is the same for everyone, friends simply become each other by becoming one and the same intellect. This combines the mirror and collaborative views, albeit in a way that erases human individuality in some kind of mystical union.

17. Angela Duckworth, "Purpose," in *Grit: The Power of Passion and Perseverance* (New York: Scribner, 2016), 143–168.

17. Aspiring to Immortality

1. Mihaly Csikszentmihalyi, *Flow: The Psychology of Optimal Experience* (New York: Harper Perennial Modern Classics, 2008), 1.

2. Verity Harte, "The *Nicomachean Ethics* on Pleasure," in *The Cambridge Companion to Aristotle's "Nicomachean Ethics,"* ed. Ronald Polansky (Cambridge: Cambridge University Press, 2014), 288–318, esp. 289.

3. The role of pleasure in the good life was hotly debated within Plato's Academy. Some of the competing opinions, however, have been preserved only in *NE*. James Warren, "Aristotle on Speusippus on Eudoxus on Pleasure," in *Oxford Studies in Ancient Philosophy*, vol. 36, ed. Brad Inwood (Oxford: Oxford University Press, 2009), 249–281, helpfully reconstructs these discussions and situates *NE* 10.1–5 within them. Aristotle's response to those who think pleasure is not a good at all is unusually technical. For analysis, see Christopher Shields, "Perfecting Pleasures: The Metaphysics of Pleasure in *Nicomachean*

Ethics X," in *Aristotle's "Nicomachean Ethics": A Critical Guide*, ed. Jon Miller (Cambridge: Cambridge University Press, 2011), 191-210.

4. G. E. M. Anscombe, *Intention* (Oxford: Basil Blackwell, 1976), 76. Shields, "Perfecting Pleasures," responds to Anscombe at length.

5. David Bostock, *Aristotle's Ethics* (Oxford: Oxford University Press, 2000), 156. Peter Hadreas, "Aristotle's Simile of Pleasures at *NE* 1174b33," *Ancient Philosophy* 17 (1997): 371-374, cites the frequent uses of *akmaios* in Aristotle's zoological works to refer not to the young but to animals who have reached reproductive maturity. He likewise cites *Rhetoric* 1390b13-15 where Aristotle uses the term to refer to men in their physical and intellectual primes.

6. James Warren, "The Bloom of Youth," *Apeiron* 48, no. 3 (2015): 327-345, catalogues talk of blooms in Plato, Xenophon, and *NE* itself, which speaks of a lover losing interest in his beloved as his bloom (*hōra*) fades with age (8.4).

7. Shields, "Perfecting Pleasure," 208-209.

8. There is a standing debate on whether *NE* 7 and *NE* 10 give contradictory views of pleasure. I side with G. E. L. Owen, "Aristotelian Pleasures," *Proceedings of the Aristotelian Society* 72 (1971/2): 135-152, who sees the two books as addressing different questions but giving complementary answers. Not all readers agree. For a review of the debate, see A. W. Price, "Varieties of Pleasure in Plato and Aristotle," in *Oxford Studies in Ancient Philosophy*, vol. 52, ed. Victor Caston (Oxford: Oxford University Press, 2017), 177-208.

9. In the same spirit, Angela Duckworth, *Grit: The Power of Passion and Perseverance* (New York: Scribner, 2016), 177, presents psychological data on how an individual's happiness will cause him to do better work.

10. Gallup, "State of the Global Workplace 2022 Report: The Voice of the World's Employees," Gallup, Inc. 2022, https://www.gallup.com/workplace/349484/state-of-the-global-workplace.aspx?utm_source=google&utm_medium=cpc&utm_campaign=gallup_access_branded&utm_term=&gclid=CjwKCAjw9suYBhBIEiwA7iMhNFmFkFHSeBKz0diOkjaOaYwb0ye_vCJMtTy0RiT5vF9txUN79x8f-RoCQ3UQAvD_BwE, accessed September 5, 2022.

11. Plato's *Phaedrus*, which we have not discussed, makes the connection even more explicit.

12. Anthony Long, "Aristotle on *Eudaimonia, Nous*, and Divinity," in Miller, *Aristotle's "Nicomachean Ethics,"* 92-113.

13. Richard Kraut, "Two Lives," in *Aristotle on the Human Good* (Princeton: Princeton University Press, 1989), 15-77.

14. Gabriel Richardson Lear, "Acting for the Sake of an Object of Love," in *Happy Lives: An Essay on Aristotle's "Nicomachean Ethics"* (Princeton: Princeton University Press, 2004), 72-92, argues that the life of study provides a "final cause" or model for the lives humans actually live.

15. Terence Irwin, "Conceptions of Happiness in the *Nicomachean Ethics*," in *The Oxford Handbook of Aristotle*, ed. Christopher Shields (Oxford: Oxford University Press, 2012), 495-528.

16. Duckworth, *Grit*, chapter 11.

17. See chapter 11 for discussion of Richard Arum, *Academically Adrift: Limited Learning on College Campuses* (Chicago: University of Chicago Press, 2011).

Epilogue

1. This reflects what is known in current psychology as an adaptive theory of happiness. For discussion, see James Warren, "Removing Fear," and Voula Tsouna, "Epicurean Therapeutic Strategies," in *The Cambridge Companion to Epicureanism*, ed. James Warren (Cambridge: Cambridge University Press, 2009), 234–248 and 249–265, respectively.

2. Heather Reid makes the most anyone is likely to make of Epicurean thinking about sports in "The Epicurean Spectator," in *Athletics and Philosophy in the Ancient World* (London: Routledge, 2011), 81–89.

3. Terence Irwin, "Virtue, Praise, and Success: Stoic Responses to Aristotle," *The Monist* 73, no. 1 (1990): 59–79.

4. Jacob Klein, "Of Archery and Virtue: Ancient and Modern Concepts of Value," *Philosophers' Imprint* 14, no. 19 (2014): 1–16; Heather Reid, "Seneca's Gladiators," in *Athletics and Philosophy in the Ancient World*, 90–98. For application of Stoic thinking to contemporary sports, see Michael Tremblay, "MMA as a Path to Stoic Virtue," in *The Philosophy of Mixed Martial Arts*, ed. Jason Holt and Marc Ramsay (London: Routledge, 2021), 122–133. For a focus on ancient images, see Michael Tremblay, "Digestion and Moral Progress in Epictetus," *Journal of Ancient Philosophy* 13, no. 1 (2019): 100–119, and "Athletic Imagery as an Educational Tool in Epictetus," *Journal of the Philosophy of Sport* 49, no. 1 (2022): 68–82.

5. Martha Nussbaum, *The Therapy of Desire: Theory and Practice in Hellenistic Ethics* (Princeton: Princeton University Press, 1994), and Margaret Graver, *Stoicism and Emotion* (Chicago: University of Chicago Press, 2007), present two classic discussions.

6. The writings of the original Greek Academic skeptics survive mostly through later works, Cicero's first and foremost. Given the state of the sources, and the fact that Academic and Stoic philosophy developed in a centuries-long ping-pong match, sorting out the various layers of theory and practice quickly gets complicated. See the introduction to Charles Brittain's translation, *Cicero: On Academic Skepticism* (Indianapolis: Hackett, 2006).

7. The most useful introduction is Tad Brennan, *The Stoic Life: Emotions, Duties, and Fate* (Oxford: Oxford University Press, 2005). Donna Zuckerberg, *Not All Dead White Men: Classics and Misogyny in the Digital Age* (Cambridge, MA: Harvard University Press, 2018), explores abuses of Stoicism by the Far Right.

8. Subjects include the possibility of knowledge (*On Academic Skepticism*), ethics (*On Moral Ends*), and topics in religion (*On Fate, On Divination, On the Nature of the Gods*).

Bibliography

Ackrill, John. "Aristotle on *Eudaimonia*." In Rorty, *Essays on Aristotle's Ethics*, 15-33.
Akrigg, Ben. "Demography and Classical Athens." In *Demography and the Greco-Roman World: New Insights and Approaches*, edited by Claire Holleran and April Pudsey, 37-59. Cambridge: Cambridge University Press, 2011.
Ambrose, Susan, et al. *How Learning Works: 7 Research-Based Principles for Smart Teaching*. San Francisco: Jossey-Bass, 2010.
Anagnostopoulos, Georgios, ed. *A Companion to Aristotle*. Oxford: Wiley-Blackwell, 2009.
Anderlini, Deanna. "The United States Health Care System Is Sick: From Adam Smith to Overspecialization." *Cureus* 10, no. 5 (2018): e2720. doi:10.7759/cureus.2720.
Annas, Julia. "Plato's *Republic* and Feminism." In Fine, *Plato*, 2:265-279.
Annas, Julia. "Self-Love in Aristotle." In "Aristotle's Ethics," Spindel Supplement, *Southern Journal of Philosophy* 27 (1988): 1-18.
Anscombe, G. E. M. *Intention*. Oxford: Basil Blackwell, 1976.
Arum, Richard. *Academically Adrift: Limited Learning on College Campuses*. Chicago: University of Chicago Press, 2011.
American Association of Colleges and Universities. "Value." https://www.aacu.org/value. Accessed March 20, 2021.
Bae, Eunshil. "'An Ornament of the Virtues'." *Ancient Philosophy* 23 (2003): 337-349.
Baker, Samuel. "The Concepts of *Ergon*: Towards an Achievement Interpretation of Aristotle's 'Function Argument'." In *Oxford Studies in Ancient Philosophy*, vol. 43, edited by Brad Inwood, 227-266. Oxford: Oxford University Press, 2012.
Baker, Samuel. "A Monistic Conclusion to Aristotle's *Ergon* Argument: The Human Good as the Best Achievement of a Human." *Archiv für Geschichte der Philosophie* 103, no. 3 (2021): 373-403.
Barney, Rachel. "Becoming Bad: Aristotle on Vice and Moral Habituation." In *Oxford Studies in Ancient Philosophy*, vol. 57, edited by Victor Caston, 273-307. Oxford: Oxford University Press, 2019.
Barney, Rachel. "Socrates' Refutation of Thrasymachus." In Santas, *Blackwell Guide to Plato's "Republic,"* 44-62.
Barney, Rachel, Tad Brennan, and Charles Brittain, eds. *Plato and the Divided Self*. Cambridge: Cambridge University Press, 2012.
Benson, Hugh. *Clitophon's Challenge: Dialectic in Plato's "Meno," "Phaedo," and "Republic."* Oxford: Oxford University Press, 2015.

Benson, Hugh. "Plato's Philosophical Method in the *Republic*: The Divided Line (510b-511b)." In McPherran, *Plato's "Republic,"* 188-208.

Benson, Hugh. *Socratic Wisdom: The Model of Knowledge in Plato's Early Dialogues*. Oxford: Oxford University Press, 2000.

Betegh, Gábor. "Tale, Theology, and Teleology in the *Phaedo*." In Partenie, *Plato's Myths*, 77-100.

Blondell, Ruby. "Where Is Socrates on the 'Ladder of Love'?" In Lesher, Nails, and Sheffield, *Plato's Symposium*, 147-178.

Bobonich, Christopher, ed. *The Cambridge Companion to Ancient Ethics*. Cambridge: Cambridge University Press, 2017.

Bobzien, Suzanne. "Choice and Moral Responsibility (*NE* iii 1-5)." In Polansky, *Cambridge Companion to Aristotle's "Nicomachean Ethics,"* 81-109.

Bostock, David. *Aristotle's Ethics*. Oxford: Oxford University Press, 2000.

Brennan, Tad. "The Nature of the Spirited Part of the Soul and Its Object." In Barney, Brennan, and Brittain, *Plato and the Divided Self*, 102-127.

Brennan, Tad. *The Stoic Life: Emotions, Duties, and Fate*. Oxford: Oxford University Press, 2005.

Brickhouse, Thomas, and Nicholas Smith, trans. *The Trial and Execution of Socrates*. Oxford: Oxford University Press, 2002.

Brisson, Luc. "Agathon, Pausanias, and Diotima in Plato's *Symposium*: *Paiderastia* and *Philosophia*." In Lesher, Nails, and Sheffield, *Plato's Symposium*, 229-251.

Brittain, Charles. *Cicero: On Academic Skepticism*. Indianapolis: Hackett, 2006.

Broadie, Sarah. *Ethics with Aristotle*. Oxford: Oxford University Press, 1991.

Broadie, Sarah. "Practical Truth in Aristotle." *American Catholic Philosophical Quarterly* 90, no. 2 (2006): 281-298.

Brooks, David. "Moral Bucket List." *New York Times*, April 11, 2015.

Brooks, David. *Road to Character*. New York: Random House, 2016.

Brown, Lesley. "What Is "the Mean Relative to Us" in Aristotle's *Ethics*?" *Phronesis* 42, no. 1 (1997): 77-93.

Brown, Lesley. "Why Is Aristotle's Virtue of Character a Mean? Taking Aristotle at His Word (*NE* ii 6)." In Polansky, *Cambridge Companion to Aristotle's "Nicomachean Ethics,"* 64-80.

Burnyeat, Miles. "Aristotle on Learning to Be Good." In Rorty, *Essays on Aristotle's Ethics*, 69-92.

Cantor, David. "Western Medicine since the Renaissance." In Portmann, *Cambridge Companion to Hippocrates*, 362-383.

Cavanaugh, T. A. *Hippocrates' Oath and Asclepius' Snake: The Birth of the Medical Profession*. Oxford: Oxford University Press, 2018.

Chaline, Eric. *The Temple of Perfection: A History of the Gym*. London: Reaktion Books, 2015.

Chowkwanyun, Merlin, and Adolph L. Reed Jr. "Racial Health Disparities and Covid-19—Caution and Context." *New England Journal of Medicine* 383 (2020): 201-203. https://doi.org/10.1056/NEJMp2012910.

Christensen, Paul. *Sports and Democracy in the Ancient and Modern Worlds*. Cambridge: Cambridge University Press, 2012.

Clydesdale, Tim. *The Purposeful Graduate: Why Colleges Must Talk to Students about Vocation*. Chicago: University of Chicago Press, 2015.
Cooper, John. "Aristotle on Forms of Friendship." In *Reason and Emotion: Essays on Ancient Moral Psychology and Ethical Theory*, 312-335. Princeton: Princeton University Press, 1999.
Cooper, John. "Plato's Theory of Human Motivation." In Fine, *Plato*, 2:186-206.
Cooper, Neil. "Aristotle's Crowning Virtue." *Apeiron* 22 (1989): 191-205.
Coulson, Lee. "The *Agones* of Platonic Philosophy: Seeking Victory without Triumph." In Reid, Ralkowski, and Zoller, *Athletics, Gymnastics, and* Agon, 211-222.
Council of Independent Colleges. "Network for Vocation in Undergraduate Education (NetVUE)." https://www.cic.edu/programs/netvue. Accessed March 17, 2021.
Craik, Elizabeth. "Hippocrates and Early Greek Medicine." In Keyser, *Oxford Handbook of Science and Medicine*, 215-232.
Craik, Elizabeth. "The 'Hippocratic Question' and the Nature of the Hippocratic Corpus." In Portmann, *Cambridge Companion to Hippocrates*, 25-37.
Craik, Elizabeth. "Plato and Medical Texts: *Symposium* 185c-193d." *Classical Quarterly* 51, no. 5 (2001): 109-114.
Crisp, Roger. "Aristotle on Greatness of Soul." In Kraut, *Blackwell Guide to Aristotle's "Nicomachean Ethics,"* 158-178.
Crotty, Kevin. *The City-State of the Soul*. Lanham, MD: Lexington Books, 2016.
Crowther, N. B. "Male 'Beauty' Contests in Greece: The Euandria and Euexia." *L'antiquité classique* 54 (1985): 285-291.
Csikszentmihalyi, Mihaly. *Flow: The Psychology of Optimal Experience*. New York: Harper Perennial Modern Classics, 2008.
Cullyer, Hellen. "The Social Virtues (*NE* iv)." In Polansky, *Cambridge Companion to Aristotle's "Nicomachean Ethics,"* 135-150.
Cunningham, David, ed. *Hearing Vocation Differently: Meaning, Purpose, and Identity in the Multi-Faith Academy*. Oxford: Oxford University Press, 2019.
Curzer, Howard. "Aristotle's Much Maligned *Megalopsychos*." *Australasian Journal of Philosophy* 69, no. 2 (1991): 131-151.
Curzer, Howard. *Aristotle and the Virtues*. Oxford: Oxford University Press, 2012.
Damon, William. *The Path to Purpose: How Young People Find Their Calling in Life*. New York: Free Press, 2008.
D'Angour, Armand. "Plato and Play: Taking Education Seriously in Ancient Greece." *American Journal of Play* 5, no. 3 (2013): 293-307.
Death Penalty Information Center. https://deathpenaltyinfo.org/policy-issues/costs. Accessed December 20, 2022.
de Motta, Guilherme Domingues. "What Beauty Is Socrates Seeking by Chasing Handsome Youths?" In Reid and Leyh, *Looking at Beauty*, 149-159.
Deresiewicz, William. *Excellent Sheep: The Miseducation of the American Elite and the Way to a Meaningful Life*. New York: Free Press, 2014.
Destrée, Pierre, and Zina Giannopoulou, eds. *Plato's "Symposium": A Critical Guide*. Cambridge: Cambridge University Press, 2017.

Dick, Amanda. "The Immature State of Our Union: Lack of Legal Entitlement to Prison Programming in the United States as Compared to European Countries." *Arizona Journal of International and Comparative Law* 35, no. 2 (2018): 287–324.

Dova, Stamatia. "On *Philogymnastia* and Its Cognates in Plato." In Reid, Ralkowski, and Zoller, *Athletics, Gymnastics, and* Agon, 107–126.

Dover, Kenneth. *Greek Homosexuality*. Cambridge, MA: Harvard University Press, 1989.

Drefcinski, Shane. "A Different Solution to an Alleged Contradiction in Aristotle's *Nicomachean Ethics*." In *Oxford Studies in Ancient Philosophy*, vol. 30, edited by Brad Inwood, 201–210. Oxford: Oxford University Press, 2006.

Duckworth, Angela. *Grit: The Power of Passion and Perseverance*. New York: Scribner, 2016.

Duque, Mateo. "Two Passions in Plato's *Symposium*: Diotima's *To Kalon* as a Reorientation of Imperialistic *Erōs*." In Reid and Leyh, *Looking at Beauty*, 95–110.

Dweck, Carol. *Mindset: Changing the Way You Think to Fulfil Your Potential*. Boston: Little, Brown Book Group, 2017.

Edmunds, Radcliffe. "Alcibiades the Profane: Images of the Mysteries." In Destrée and Giannopoulou, *Plato's "Symposium,"* 194–215.

Engberg-Pedersen, Troels. *Aristotle's Theory of Moral Insight*. Oxford: Clarendon Press, 1983.

Ericsson, K. Anders, R. T. Krampe, and C. Tesch-Römer. "The Role of Deliberate Practice in the Acquisition of Expert Performance." *Psychological Review* 100, no. 3 (1993): 363–406. https://doi.org/10.1037/0033-295X.100.3.363.

Evans, Matthew. "Architectural and Spatial Features of Plato's *Gymnasia* and *Palaistra*." In Reid, Ralkowski, and Zoller, *Athletics, Gymnastics, and* Agon, 31–50.

Federal Bureau of Prisons. "Inmate Race." https://www.bop.gov/about/statistics/statistics_inmate_race.jsp. Accessed March 22, 2021.

Ferngren, Gary B. *Medicine and Religion: A Historical Introduction*. Baltimore: Johns Hopkins University Press, 2014.

Ferrari, G. R. F., ed. *The Cambridge Companion to Plato's "Republic."* Cambridge: Cambridge University Press, 2007.

Ferrari, G. R. F. "Glaucon's Reward, Philosophy's Debt: The Myth of Er." In Partenie, *Plato's Myths*, 116–133.

Fine, Gail. "Knowledge and Belief in *Republic* 5–7." In Fine, *Plato*, 1:215–246.

Fine, Gail, ed. *Plato*. Oxford: Oxford University Press, 1999.

Foley, Helene. *The Homeric Hymn to Demeter: Translation, Commentary, and Interpretive Essays*. Princeton: Princeton University Press, 1994.

Fossheim, Hallvard. "Justice in the *Nicomachean Ethics* Book V." In Miller, *Aristotle's "Nicomachean Ethics,"* 245–275.

Frede, Dorothea. "The *Endoxon* Mystique: What *Endoxa* Are and What They Are Not." In *Oxford Studies in Ancient Philosophy*, vol. 43, edited by Brad Inwood, 185–215. Oxford: Oxford University Press, 2012.

Fuller, Halie Jo. "Audition Video: American Ninja Warrior." https://youtu.be/a86qXhgxTaA. Accessed February 21, 2023.

Galgano, Nicola Stafano. "Logoi Kaloi: The Method of Philosophy at *Symposium* 210a-212b." In Reid and Leyh, *Looking at Beauty*, 111-112.
Gallup. "State of the Global Workplace 2022 Report: The Voice of the World's Employees." Gallup, Inc. 2022. https://www.gallup.com/workplace/349484/state-of-the-global-workplace.aspx?utm_source=google&utm_medium=cpc&utm_campaign=gallup_access_branded&utm_term=&gclid=CjwKCAjw9suYBhBIEiwA7iMhNFmFkFHSeBKz0diOkjaOaYwb0ye_vCJMtTy0RiT5vF9txUN79x8f-RoCQ3UQAvD_BwE.
Garg, Arvin, Charles J. Homer, and Paul H. Dworkin. "Addressing Social Determinants of Health: Challenges and Opportunities in a Value-Based Model." *Pediatrics* 143, no. 4 (2019). https://doi.org/10.1542/peds.2018-2355.
Gartner, Corinne. "Aristotle on Love and Friendship." In Bobonich, *Cambridge Companion to Ancient Ethics*, 143-163.
Gauthier, R. A., and J. Y. Jolif. *L'Éthique à Nicomaque*. Louvain: Publications Universitaires, 1970.
Gkaleas, Konstantinos. "Ἔρως and Γυμναστική in the Platonic Corpus: The Quest for the Form of Καλόν." In Reid and Leyh, *Looking at Beauty*, 123-131.
Gonzales, Francisco. *Dialectic and Dialogue: Plato's Practice of Philosophical Inquiry*. Evanston, IL: Northwestern University Press, 1998.
Gonzales, Francisco. "Why Agathon's Beauty Matters." In Destrée and Giannopoulou, *Plato's "Symposium,"* 108-124.
Gottlieb, Paula. "The Practical Syllogism." In Kraut, *Blackwell Guide to Aristotle's "Nicomachean Ethics,"* 218-233.
Graver, Margaret. *Stoicism and Emotion*. Chicago: University of Chicago Press, 2007.
Gregory, Andrew. "Pythagoras and Plato." In Keyser, *Oxford Handbook of Science and Medicine*, 147-170.
Hadreas, Peter. "Aristotle's Simile of Pleasures at *NE* 1174b33." *Ancient Philosophy* 17 (1997): 371-374.
Haidt, Jonathan. *The Happiness Hypothesis: Finding Modern Truth in Ancient Wisdom*. New York: Basic Books, 2006.
Hall, Edith. *Aristotle's Way: How Ancient Wisdom Can Change your Life*. London: Penguin Press, 2019.
Hankinson, Jim. "Aetiology." In Portmann, *Cambridge Companion to Hippocrates*, 89-118.
Hardie, William Francis Ross. "The Final Good in Aristotle's Ethics." *Philosophy* 40 (1965): 277-295.
Hare, John. *God and Morality: A Philosophical History*. Oxford: Oxford University Press, 2007.
Harte, Verity. "The *Nicomachean Ethics* on Pleasure." In Polansky, *Cambridge Companion to Aristotle's "Nicomachean Ethics,"* 288-318.
Hawgood, Alex. "What Is 'Bigorexia'?" *New York Times*, March 5, 2022.
Hawhee, Debra. *Bodily Arts: Rhetoric and Athletics in Ancient Greece*. Austin: University of Texas Press, 2004.
Held, Dirk. "Μεγαλοψῡχία in *Nicomachean Ethics* iv." *Ancient Philosophy* 13 (1993): 95-110.

Hinman, Lawrence. *Ethics: A Pluralistic Approach to Moral Theory*. Belmont, CA: Thomson-Wadsworth, 2008.

Hitz, Zena. "Aristotle on Law and Moral Education." In *Oxford Studies in Ancient Philosophy*, vol. 42, edited by Brad Inwood, 263–306. Oxford: Oxford University Press, 2012.

Hitz, Zena. "Aristotle on Self-Knowledge and Friendship." *Philosophers' Imprint* 11, no. 12 (2011): 1–28.

Hitz, Zena. "Degenerate Regimes in Plato's *Republic*." In Barney, Brennan, and Brittain, *Plato and the Divided Self*, 103–131.

Hobbs, Angela. *Plato and the Hero: Courage, Manliness, and the Impersonal Good*. Cambridge: Cambridge University Press, 2000.

Holmes, Brooke. "Body." In Portmann, *Cambridge Companion to Hippocrates*, 63–88.

Homiak, Marcia. "Feminism and Aristotle's Rational Ideal." In *A Mind of One's Own: Feminist Essays on Reason and Objectivity*, edited by Louise Antony and Charlotte Witt, 1–18. Boulder, CO: Westview Press, 1993.

Homiak, Marcia. "Virtue and Self-Love in Aristotle's Ethics." *Canadian Journal of Philosophy* 11, no. 4 (1981): 633–651.

Hull, Sharon K. "A Larger Role for Preventive Medicine." *AMA Journal of Ethics* 10, no. 11 (2008): 724–729. https://doi.org/10.1001/virtualmentor.2008.10.11.medu1-0811.

Hunter, James Davison. *Culture Wars: The Struggle to Control the Family, Art, Education, Law, and Politics in America*. New York: Basic Books, 1991.

Hunter, James Davison. *The Death of Character: Moral Education in an Age without Good or Evil*. New York: Basic Books, 2000.

Hutchinson, D. S., and Monte Ransome Johnson. "Protreptic Aspects of Aristotle's *Nicomachean Ethics*." In Polansky, *Cambridge Companion to Aristotle's "Nicomachean Ethics,"* 383–409.

International Olympic Committee, "Gender Equality through Time," https://olympics.com/ioc/gender-equality/gender-equality-through-time/at-the-olympic-games. Accessed June 23, 2023.

Irwin, Terence, trans. *Aristotle: Nicomachean Ethics*. Indianapolis: Hackett, 1999.

Irwin, Terence. "Beauty and Morality in Aristotle." In Miller, *Aristotle's "Nicomachean Ethics,"* 239–253.

Irwin, Terence. "Conceptions of Happiness in the *Nicomachean Ethics*." In Shields, *Oxford Handbook of Aristotle*, 495–528.

Irwin, Terence. "Disunity in the Aristotelian Virtues." In *Oxford Studies in Ancient Philosophy, Supplementary Volume*, edited by Julia Annas, 61–78. Oxford: Oxford University Press, 1988.

Irwin, Terence. "Magnanimity as Generosity." In *The Measure of Greatness*, edited by Sophia Vasalou, 21–48. Oxford: Oxford University Press, 2019.

Irwin, Terence. "The Metaphysical and Psychological Basis of Aristotle's Ethics." In Rorty, *Essays on Aristotle's Ethics*, 35–54.

Irwin, Terence. "*Republic* 2: Questions about Justice." In Fine, *Plato*, 2:164–185.

Irwin, Terence. "Virtue, Praise, and Success: Stoic Responses to Aristotle." *The Monist* 73, no. 1 (1990): 59–79.

Jalbert, John E. "Leisure and Liberal Education: A Plea for Uselessness." *Philosophical Studies in Education* 40 (2009): 222–233.
Jaschik, Scott. "Use of Test-Optional and Test-Free Admissions Keeps Rising." *Inside Higher Ed*, November 14, 2022.
Judson, Lindsay. "Aristotle on Fair Exchange." *Oxford Studies in Ancient Philosophy*, vol. 15, edited by C. C. W. Taylor, 147–206. Oxford: Oxford University Press, 1997.
Kahn, Charles. "Proleptic Composition in the *Republic*, or Why Book 1 Was Never a Separate Dialogue." *Classical Quarterly* 43 (1993): 131–142.
Kahneman, Daniel, and Angus Deaton. "High Income Improves Evaluation of Life but Not Emotional Well-Being." *Proceedings of the National Academy of Sciences* 107, no. 38 (September 2010): 16489–16493. https://doi.org/10.1073/pnas.1011492107.
Kamtekar, Rachana. "Ethics and Politics in Socrates' Defense of Justice in Plato's *Republic*." In Barney, Brennan, and Brittain, *Plato and the Divided Self*, 65–82.
Kamtekar, Rachana. "Imperfect Virtue." *Ancient Philosophy* 18 (1998): 315–339.
Kendi, Ibram X. *Stamped from the Beginning: The Definitive History of Racist Ideas in America*. New York: Bold Type Books, 2017.
Kenyon, Erik. "Philosophy for Children and Community-Based Pedagogy." In *Intentional Disruptions: New Directions in Pre-college Philosophy*, edited by Stephen Miller, 35–48. Wilmington, DE: Vernon Press, 2021.
Kenyon, Erik. "Socrates at the Wrestling School: Plato's *Laches, Lysis*, and *Charmides*." In Reid, Ralkowski, and Zoller, *Athletics, Gymnastics, and Agon*, 51–66.
Kenyon, Erik, Diane Terorde-Doyle, and Sharon Carnahan. *Ethics for the Very Young: A Philosophy Curriculum for Early Childhood Education*. Lanham, MD: Rowman and Littlefield, 2019.
Keyser, Paul. *The Oxford Handbook of Science and Medicine in the Classical World*. Oxford: Oxford University Press, 2018.
Klein, Jacob. "Of Archery and Virtue: Ancient and Modern Concepts of Value." *Philosophers' Imprint* 14, no. 19 (2014): 1–16.
Kosman, Aryeh. "Aristotle on the Desirability of Friends." *Ancient Philosophy* 24 (2004): 135–154.
Kraut, Richard. "An Aesthetic Reading of Aristotle's *Ethics*." In *Politeia in Greek and Roman Philosophy*, edited by Verity Harte and Melissa Lane, 231–250. Cambridge: Cambridge University Press, 2013.
Kraut, Richard. *Aristotle: Political Philosophy*. Oxford: Oxford University Press, 2002.
Kraut, Richard. *Aristotle on the Human Good*. Princeton: Princeton University Press, 1989.
Kraut, Richard, ed. *The Blackwell Guide to Aristotle's "Nicomachean Ethics."* Oxford: Wiley-Blackwell, 2006.
Kraut, Richard. "Comments on Julia Annas' 'Self-Love in Aristotle'." In "Aristotle's Ethics," Spindel Supplement, *Southern Journal of Philosophy* 27 (1988): 19–23.

BIBLIOGRAPHY

Kraut, Richard. "Eudaimonism and Platonic *Erōs*." In Destrée and Giannopoulou, *Plato's "Symposium,"* 235–252.

Kraut, Richard. "How to Justify Ethical Propositions: Aristotle's Method." In Kraut, *Blackwell Guide to Aristotle's "Nicomachean Ethics,"* 76–95.

Kraut, Richard. "Introduction to the Study of Plato." In *The Cambridge Companion to Plato*, edited by Richard Kraut, 1–50. Cambridge: Cambridge University Press, 1992.

Kraut, Richard. Politeia *in Greek and Roman Philosophy*. Cambridge: Cambridge University Press, 2011.

Kraut, Richard. "Return to the Cave: *Republic* 519–521." In Fine, *Plato*, 2:235–254.

Lännström, Anna. *Loving the Fine: Virtue and Happiness in Aristotle's "Ethics."* Notre Dame, IN: University of Notre Dame Press, 2006.

LaVeist, T. A., R. J. Thorpe, J. E. Galarraga, et al. "Environmental and Socio-Economic Factors as Contributors to Racial Disparities in Diabetes Prevalence." *Journal of General Internal Medicine* 24, no. 1144 (2009). https://doi.org/10.1007/s11606-009-1085-7.

Lawrence, Gavin. "Human Excellence in Character and Intellect." In Anagnostopoulos, *Companion to Aristotle*, 419–441.

Lesher, James, Debra Nails, and Frisbee Sheffield, eds. *Plato's Symposium: Issues in Interpretation and Reception*. Washington, DC: Center for Hellenic Studies, 2006.

Long, Anthony. "Aristotle on *Eudaimonia*, *Nous*, and Divinity." In Miller, *Aristotle's "Nicomachean Ethics,"* 92–113.

Lorenz, Hendrik. "Virtues of Character in Aristotle's *Nicomachean Ethics*." In *Oxford Studies in Ancient Philosophy*, vol. 37, edited by Brad Inwood, 177–212. Oxford: Oxford University Press, 2009.

Louden, Robert. "On Some Vices of Virtue Theory." *American Philosophical Quarterly* 21, no. 3 (1984): 227–235.

Lukianoff, Greg, and Jonathan Haidt. *The Coddling of the American Mind: How Good Intentions and Bad Ideas Are Setting Up a Generation for Failure*. New York: Penguin Press, 2018.

MacIntyre, Alasdair. *After Virtue*. Notre Dame, IN: Notre Dame University Press, 1984.

Mamo, Heran. "Rihanna's 2023 Super Bowl Halftime Show Is Now the Most-Watched of All Time." *Billboard*, May 22, 2023. https://www.foxsports.com/presspass/blog/2023/02/13/fox-sports-presentation-of-super-bowl-lvii-scores-six-year-high-with-113-million-viewers/.

Marrou, H. I. *A History of Education in Antiquity*. Translated by George Lamb. Madison: University of Wisconsin Press, 1956.

Martin, James. *The Jesuit Guide to (Almost) Everything: A Spirituality for Real Life*. New York: Harper One, 2010.

Matthews, Gareth. *Socratic Perplexity and the Nature of Philosophy*. Oxford: Oxford University Press, 1999.

McGrew, Susanna. "Carving Out Space for Aristotle's *Megalopsychos*." *Episteme* 31 (2021): 44–56.

McPherran, Mark. "Medicine, Magic, and Religion in Plato's *Symposium*." In Lesher, Nails, and Sheffield, *Plato's Symposium*, 71–95.

McPherran, Mark, ed. *Plato's "Republic": A Critical Guide*. Cambridge: Cambridge University Press, 2010.
Meikle, Scott. *Aristotle's Economic Thought*. Oxford: Oxford University Press, 1995.
Meyer, Susan Suavé. "Living for the Sake of an Ultimate End." In Miller, *Aristotle's "Nicomachean Ethics,"* 47-65.
Miller, Jon, ed. *Aristotle's "Nicomachean Ethics": A Critical Guide*. Cambridge: Cambridge University Press, 2011.
Miller, Mitchell. "Beginning the 'Longer Way'." In Ferrari, *Cambridge Companion to Plato's "Republic,"* 310-344.
Miller, Patrick Lee. "Finding Oneself with Friends." In Polansky, *Cambridge Companion to Aristotle's "Nicomachean Ethics,"* 319-349.
Miller, Stephen. *Ancient Greek Athletics*. New Haven: Yale University Press, 2004.
Miller, Stephen, trans. *Arete: Greek Sports from Ancient Sources*. Berkeley: University of California Press, 2012.
Miller, Stephen. *The Berkeley Plato: From Neglected Relic to Ancient Treasure*. Berkeley: University of California Press, 2009.
Moon, Warren G. *Polykleitos, the Doryphoros, and Tradition*. Madison: University of Wisconsin Press, 1995.
Moore, Christopher. *Socrates and Self-Knowledge*. Cambridge: Cambridge University Press, 2015.
Moore, Christopher, and Christopher Raymond, trans. *Plato: Charmides*. Translated, with Introduction, Notes, and Analysis. Indianapolis: Hackett, 2019.
Moss, Jessica. "Aristotle's Ethical Psychology." In Bobonich, *Cambridge Companion to Ancient Ethics*, 124-142.
Myers, David G. *The Pursuit of Happiness*. New York: Harper Collins, 1992.
Nagy, Gregory. *The Best of the Achaeans: Concepts of the Hero in Archaic Greek Poetry*. Baltimore: Johns Hopkins University Press, 1999.
Natali, Carlo. "The Book of Wisdom." In Polansky, *Cambridge Companion to Aristotle's "Nicomachean Ethics,"* 180-202.
Nehemas, Alexander. "Aristotle's *Philia*, Modern Friendship." In *Oxford Studies in Ancient Philosophy*, vol. 32, edited by Brad Inwood, 213-247. Oxford: Oxford University Press, 2010.
Neils, Jenifer. "Myth and Greek Art: Creating a Visual Language." In *The Cambridge Companion to Greek Mythology*, edited by Roger Woodard, 286-304. Cambridge: Cambridge University Press, 2007.
Newman, Mark. "1947: A Time for Change." MLB.com, April 13, 2007. Archived 2009. http://mlb.mlb.com/news/article.jsp?ymd=20070412&content_id=1895445&vkey=perspectives&fext=.jsp&c_id=mlb.
Nightingale, Andrea. "The Mortal Soul and Immortal Happiness." In Destrée and Giannopoulou, *Plato's "Symposium,"* 142-159.
Nightingale, Andrea. *Spectacles of Truth in Classical Greek Philosophy: Theoria in Its Cultural Context*. Cambridge: Cambridge University Press, 2004.
Nightingale, Andrea Wilson. "The Folly of Praise: Plato's Critique of Encomiastic Discourse in the *Lysis* and *Symposium*." *Classical Quarterly* 43, no. 1 (1993): 112-130.

Nussbaum, Martha. *The Fragility of Goodness: Luck and Ethics in Greek Tragedy and Philosophy*. Cambridge: Cambridge University Press, 1986.

Nussbaum, Martha. *The Therapy of Desire: Theory and Practice in Hellenistic Ethics*. Princeton: Princeton University Press, 1994.

Nutton, Vivian. *Ancient Medicine*. New York: Routledge, 2004.

Obdrzalek, Suzanne. "Aristophanic Tragedy." In Lesher, Nails, and Sheffield, *Plato's Symposium*, 70–87.

Oswaks, Molly. "Over 3 Million People Took This Course on Happiness: Here's What Some Learned." *New York Times*, March 13, 2021.

Owen, G. E. L. "Aristotelian Pleasures." *Proceedings of the Aristotelian Society* 72 (1971/2): 135–152.

Pakaluk, Michael. *Aristotle's "Nicomachean Ethics": An Introduction*. Oxford: Oxford University Press, 2005.

Pakaluk, Michael. "The Meaning of Aristotelian Magnanimity." In *Oxford Studies in Ancient Philosophy*, vol. 26, edited by David Sedley, 241–275. Oxford: Oxford University Press, 2004.

Pakaluk, Michael. "On an Alleged Contradiction in Aristotle's *Nicomachean Ethics*." In *Oxford Studies in Ancient Philosophy, Summer 2002*, edited by Brad Inwood, 201–219. Oxford: Oxford University Press, 2002.

Pakaluk, Michael. "On the Unity of the *Nicomachean Ethics*." In Miller, *Aristotle's "Nicomachean Ethics,"* 23–44.

Pangle, Lorraine Smith. "Friendship and Self-Love in Aristotle's *Nicomachean Ethics*." In *Action and Contemplation: Studies in the Moral and Political Thought of Aristotle*, edited by Robert Bartlett and Susan Collins, 171–201. Albany: SUNY Press, 1999.

Partenie, Catalin, ed. *Plato's Myths*. Cambridge: Cambridge University Press, 2009.

Pears, David. "Courage as a Mean." In Rorty, *Essays on Aristotle's Ethics*, 171–187.

Penner, Terry. "The Unity of Virtue." *Philosophical Review* 82, no. 1 (January 1973): 35–68.

Penner, Terry, and Christopher Rowe. *Plato's Lysis*. Cambridge: Cambridge University Press, 2005.

Perry, Richard. "The Unhappy Tyrant and the Craft of Inner Rule." In Ferrari, *Cambridge Companion to Plato's "Republic,"* 386–414.

Pew Research Center. "What Makes Life Meaningful? Views from 17 Advanced Economies." November 2021.

Polansky, Ronald, ed. *The Cambridge Companion to Aristotle's "Nicomachean Ethics."* Cambridge: Cambridge University Press, 2014.

Polansky, Ronald. "Giving Justice Its Due." In Polansky, *Cambridge Companion to Aristotle's "Nicomachean Ethics,"* 151–179.

Popper, Karl. *The Open Society and Its Enemies*. Princeton: Princeton University Press, 1963.

Portmann, Peter, ed. *The Cambridge Companion to Hippocrates*. Cambridge: Cambridge University Press, 2018.

Preston, Charles, Sammy Almashat, Samuel Peik, Meghana Desale, and Miriam Alexander. "Role of Preventive Medicine Residencies in Medical

Education: A National Survey." *American Journal of Preventive Medicine*, 41, no. 4, Supplement 3 (2011): S290–S295. https://doi.org/10.1016/j.amepre.2011.06.021.

Price, A. W. "Acrasia and Self-Control." In Kraut, *Blackwell Guide to Aristotle's "Nicomachean Ethics,"* 243–254.

Price, A. W. "Varieties of Pleasure in Plato and Aristotle." In *Oxford Studies in Ancient Philosophy*, vol. 52, edited by Victor Caston, 177–208. Oxford: Oxford University Press, 2017.

Pritchard, David. "Costing Festivals and War: Spending Priorities of the Athenian Democracy." *Historia: Zeitschrift für Alte Geschichte* 61 (2012): 18–65.

Reeve, C. D. C. "Aristotle's Philosophical Method." In Shields, *Oxford Handbook of Aristotle*, 150–170.

Reeve, C. D. C. "Blindness and Reorientation: Education and the Acquisition of Knowledge in the *Republic*." In McPherran, *Plato's "Republic,"* 209–228.

Reeve, C. D. C., trans. *Plato: Republic*. Indianapolis: Hackett, 2004.

Reeve, C. D. C., trans. *Plato on Love: Lysis, Symposium, Phaedrus, and Alcibiades with Selections from Republic and Laws*. Indianapolis: Hackett, 2006.

Reid, Heather. "Athletic Beauty as *Mimēsis* of Virtue: The Case of the Beautiful Boxer." In Reid and Leyh, *Looking at Beauty*, 77–91.

Reid, Heather. *Athletics and Philosophy in the Ancient World*. London: Routledge, 2011.

Reid, Heather. "Athletic Virtue and Aesthetic Values in Aristotle's Ethics." *Journal of the Philosophy of Sport* 47, no. 1 (2020): 63–74.

Reid, Heather. "Heroic *Parthenoi* and the Virtues of Independence: A Feminine Philosophical Perspective on the Origin of Women's Sports." *Sports, Ethics, and Philosophy* 14, no. 4 (2020): 511–524.

Reid, Heather. "Plato on Women in Sport." *Journal of the Philosophy of Sport* 47, no. 3 (2020): 344–361.

Reid, Heather. "Sport and Moral Education in Plato's *Republic*." *Journal of the Philosophy of Sport* 34 (2007): 160–175.

Reid, Heather, and Tony Leyh, eds. *Looking at Beauty: To Kalon in Western Greece*. Sioux City, IA: Parnassos Press, 2019.

Reid, Heather, and Georgios Mouratidis. "Naked Virtue: Ancient Athletic Nudity and the Olympic Ethos of *Aretē*." *Olympika* 29 (2020): 29–55.

Reid, Heather, Mark Ralkowski, and Coleen Zoller, eds. *Athletics, Gymnastics, and Agon in Plato*. Sioux City, IA: Parnassos Press, 2020.

Reid, Jeremy. "Unfamiliar Voices: Harmonizing the Non-Socratic Speeches and Plato's Psychology." In Destrée and Giannopoulou, *Plato's "Symposium,"* 28–47.

Richardson Lear, Gabriel. "Aristotle on Moral Virtue and the Fine." In Kraut, *Blackwell Guide to Aristotle's "Nicomachean Ethics,"* 116–136.

Richardson Lear, Gabriel. *Happy Lives and the Highest Good: An Essay on Aristotle's "Nicomachean Ethics."* Princeton: Princeton University Press, 2004.

Richardson Lear, Gabriel. "Permanent Beauty and Becoming Happy in Plato's *Symposium*." In Lesher, Nails, and Sheffield, *Plato's Symposium*, 96–123.

Richardson Lear, Gabriel. "Plato on Learning to Love Beauty." In Santas, *Blackwell Guide to Plato's "Republic,"* 104-124.

Rider, Benjamin. "A Socratic Seduction: Philosophical Protreptic in Plato's *Lysis*." *Aperion* 44 (2011): 40-66.

Riedweg, Christopher. *Pythagoras: His Life, Teaching, and Influence*. Ithaca, NY: Cornell University Press, 2002.

Robbins, Alexandra. *Fraternity: An Inside Look at a Year of College Boys Becoming Men*. Boston: Dutton, 2019.

Rorty, Oksenberg Amélie, ed. *Essays on Aristotle's Ethics*. Berkeley: University of California Press, 1980.

Rowe, Christopher. "The Literary and Philosophical Style of the *Republic*." In Santas, *Blackwell Guide to Plato's "Republic,"* 7-24.

Russell, Daniel. "Aristotle's Virtues of Greatness." In *Oxford Studies in Ancient Philosophy, Supplementary Volume*, edited by Rachana Kamtekar, 115-147. Oxford: Oxford University Press, 2012.

Russell, Daniel. "Phronesis and the Virtues." In Polansky, *Cambridge Companion to Aristotle's "Nicomachean Ethics,"* 203-220.

Sachs, David. "A Fallacy in Plato's *Republic*." *Philosophical Review* 72, no. 2 (April 1963): 141-158.

Salmieri, Gregory. "Aristotle's Non-'Dialectical' Methodology in the *Nicomachean Ethics*." *Ancient Philosophy* 29 (2009): 311-335.

Santas, Gerasimos, ed. *The Blackwell Guide to Plato's "Republic."* Oxford: Blackwell Publishing, 2006.

Scanlon, Thomas. *Eros and Greek Athletics*. Oxford: Oxford University Press, 2002.

Schmid, Walter. *On Manly Courage: A Study of Plato's "Laches."* Carbondale: Southern Illinois University Press, 1992.

Schneider, Carol. "Carol Geary Schneider on Educating Students for Unscripted Problems." https://youtu.be/WVQdVVFyLA4. Accessed July 19, 2022.

Schofield, Malcolm. "Music all pow'rful." In McPherran, *Plato's "Republic,"* 229-248.

Scott, Gary Alan. "Setting Free the Boys: Limits and Liberation in Plato's *Lysis*." *disClosure: A Journal of Social Theory* 4 (1995): 24-43.

Seaford, Richard. "Dionysiac Drama and the Dionysiac Mysteries." *Classical Quarterly* 31, no. 2 (1981): 252-275.

Sears, Matthew. *Understanding Greek Warfare*. New York: Routledge, 2019.

Sedley, David. "Divinization." In Destrée and Giannopoulou, *Plato's "Symposium,"* 88-107.

Seligman, Martin. *Flourish: A Visionary New Understanding of Happiness and Well-Being*. New York: Atria Paperback, 2011.

Shanzer, Danuta. "Augustine's Disciplines: *Silent diuitius Musae Varronis?*" In *Augustine and the Disciplines*, edited by Karla Pollmann and Mark Vessey, 69-112. Oxford: Oxford University Press, 2005.

Sheffield, Frisbee. "*Erōs* and the Pursuit of Form." In Destrée and Giannopoulou, *Plato's "Symposium,"* 125-141.

Sheffield, Frisbee. *Plato's Symposium: The Ethics of Desire*. Oxford: Oxford University Press, 2006.

Sheffield, Frisbee. "The Role of the Earlier Speeches in the *Symposium*: Plato's Endoxic Method." In Lesher, Nails, and Sheffield, *Plato's Symposium*, 23–46.

Sheffield, Frisbee. "The *Symposium* and Platonic Ethics: Plato, Vlastos, and a Misguided Debate." *Phronesis* 57 (2012): 117–141.

Shields, Christopher, ed. *The Oxford Handbook of Aristotle*. Oxford: Oxford University Press, 2012.

Shields, Christopher, "Perfecting Pleasures: The Metaphysics of Pleasure in *Nicomachean Ethics* x." In Miller, *Aristotle's "Nicomachean Ethics,"* 191–210.

Shields, Christopher. "Plato's Challenge: The Case against Justice in *Republic* II." In Santas, *Blackwell Guide to Plato's "Republic,"* 63–83.

Shields, Christopher. "Plato's Divided Soul." In McPherran, *Plato's "Republic,"* 147–170.

Smith, Nicholas. "Return to the Cave." In Barney, Brennan, and Brittain, *Plato and the Divided Self*, 83–102.

Sokolowski, Robert. "Phenomenology of Friendship." *Review of Metaphysics* 55 (2002): 451–470.

Spivey, Nigel. *The Ancient Olympics*. Oxford: Oxford University Press, 2012.

Sprague, Rosamond Kent, trans. *Plato: Laches and Charmides*. Indianapolis: Hackett, 1992.

Stafford, Emma. *Herakles*. New York: Routledge, 2012.

Stephenson, Bruce. *Portland's Good Life: Sustainability and Hope in an American City*. Lanham, MD: Lexington Books, 2021.

Stergiou, Gianna. "*Ponos* and *Aretē* in Pindar's Poetry." In *Ageless Aretē*, edited by Heather Reid and John Serrati, 91–108. Sioux City, IA: Parnassos Press, 2022.

Stover, James, and Ronald Polansky, "Moral Virtue and Megalopsychia." *Ancient Philosophy* 23 (2003): 351–359.

Tarrant, Harold. "Socratic Method and Socratic Truth." In *A Companion to Socrates*, edited by Sara Ahbel-Rappe and Rachana Kamtekar, 254–272. Oxford: Oxford University Press, 2006.

Totelin, Laurence. "Therapeutics." In Portmann, *Cambridge Companion to Hippocrates*, 200–216.

Tremblay, Michael. "Athletic Imagery as an Educational Tool in Epictetus." *Journal of the Philosophy of Sport* 49, no. 1 (2022): 68–82.

Tremblay, Michael. "Digestion and Moral Progress in Epictetus." *Journal of Ancient Philosophy* 13, no. 1 (2019): 100–119.

Tremblay, Michael. "MMA as a Path to Stoic Virtue." In *The Philosophy of Mixed Martial Arts*, edited by Jason Holt and Marc Ramsay, 122–133. London: Routledge, 2021.

Trilk, Jennifer, Leah Nelson, Avery Briggs, and Dennis Muscato. "Including Lifestyle Medicine in Medical Education: Rationale for American College of Preventive Medicine/American Medical Association Resolution 959." *American Journal of Preventive Medicine* 56, no. 5 (2019): e169-e175. https://doi.org/10.1016/j.amepre.2018.10.034.

Trivigno, Franco. "A Doctor's Folly: Diagnosing the Speech of Eryximachus." In Destrée and Giannopoulou, *Plato's "Symposium,"* 48–69.

Tsouna, Voula. "Epicurean Therapeutic Strategies." In Warren, *Cambridge Companion to Epicureanism*, 249–265.
United States Census Bureau. "Quick Facts." https://www.census.gov/quickfacts. Accessed March 22, 2021.
Urmson, J. O. "Aristotle's Doctrine of the Mean." In Rorty, *Essays on Aristotle's Ethics*, 157–170.
Urmson, J. O. *Aristotle's Ethics*. Oxford: Basil Blackwell, 1988.
Verity, Anthony. *Pindar: The Complete Odes*. Oxford: Oxford World Classics, 2007.
Vlastos, Gregory. "The Individual as an Object of Love in Plato." In Fine, *Plato*, 2:137–163.
Vlastos, Gregory. "The Socratic Elenchus." In Fine, *Plato*, 1:36–63.
Warren, James. "Aristotle on Speusippus on Eudoxus on Pleasure." In *Oxford Studies in Ancient Philosophy*, vol. 36, edited by Brad Inwood, 249–281. Oxford: Oxford University Press, 2009.
Warren, James. "The Bloom of Youth." *Apeiron* 48, no. 3 (2015): 327–345.
Warren, James, ed. *The Cambridge Companion to Epicureanism*. Cambridge: Cambridge University Press, 2009.
Warren, James. "Removing Fear." In Warren, *Cambridge Companion to Epicureanism*, 234–248.
Weiss, Roslyn. "Wise Guys and Smart Alecks in *Republic* 1 and 2." In Ferrari, *Cambridge Companion to Plato's "Republic,"* 90–115.
West, Martin. *East Face of Helicon*. Oxford: Oxford University Press, 1997.
White, Nicholas. "Conflicting Parts of Happiness in Aristotle's Ethics." *Ethics* 105 (January 1995): 258–283.
White, Nicholas, trans. *Handbook of Epictetus*. Indianapolis: Hackett, 1983.
Whitting, Jennifer. "Psychic Contingency in the *Republic*." In Barney, Brennan, and Brittain, *Plato and the Divided Self*, 174–208.
Wilberding, James. "Curbing One's Appetites in Plato's *Republic*." In Barney, Brennan, and Brittain, *Plato and the Divided Self*, 128–149.
Wolfsdorf, David. "Φιλία in Plato's *Lysis*." *Harvard Studies in Classical Philology* 103 (2007): 235–259.
Young, Charles. "Courage." In Anagnostopoulos, *Companion to Aristotle*, 442–456.
Zakaria, Fareed. *In Defense of a Liberal Education*. New York: W. W. Norton, 2015.
Zoller, Coleen. *Plato and the Body*. Albany: SUNY Press, 2018.
Zoller, Coleen. "Plato's Rejection of the Logic of Domination." In Reid, Ralkowski, and Zoller, *Athletics, Gymnastics, and Agon*, 223–238.
Zovko, Marie-Élise. "*Agōn* and *Erōs* in Plato's *Symposium*." In Reid, Ralkowski, and Zoller, *Athletics, Gymnastics, and Agon*, 143–156.
Zuckerberg, Donna. *Not All Dead White Men: Classics and Misogyny in the Digital Age*. Cambridge, MA: Harvard University Press, 2018.

Index

Academic skeptics, 198-199
Achilles, 60-61, 152-153, 155-156
Alcibiades, 75-77, 152
American Association of Colleges and Universities, 19
American Ninja Warrior, 216n6
appetite, 85-86, 102-106, 135, 168
aristocracy, 103-104, 156, 179
   natural vs. unnatural, 84
Aristophanes, 25, 39, 62-67, 75-76
Aristotle, xvi, 74, 111
   endoxic method, 119-120, 166-167, 188, 224n2, 226n14
   Lyceum, 111, 133, 199
   response to Plato, 122, 129, 136, 167, 178-180, 192
   response to Socrates, 126, 152, 161-162
Atalanta, 89, 107
athletic events
   chariot racing, 43, 112-117, 223n9
   footraces, 89-91
   long jump, 3-4, 47-48, 55
   wrestling, 26, 91, 135, 155, 175, 198
   See also music

beauty. *See kalos/kalon*
blessed. *See* godlike
bloom of youth, 92, 189-190

care
   about virtue, 10, 41, 44-45
   lack of, 139
Chaerephon, 11, 14, 39-40
charm bracelet, 129, 131
Charmides, 14-18
Christianity, xii, xv-xvii, 41, 68, 146, 176
competition (*agōn*)
   athletic, 113, 115-116, 133, 142
   between friends (*hamilla*), 183-184, 176
   culture of, 58

erotic, 62, 89
   as legal trial, 38
   physique, 139
   of plays, 58, 68
   verbal sparring, 30, 33, 37
   See also music; poetry
Critias, 14-18
customs (*nomoi*), 54, 62, 66, 71
   vs. lawlessness (*paranomos*), 102

definition, substantial vs. dictionary, 5
Diotima, 68-77, 94, 98
dogs, 82, 86
drinking
   alcoholism, 136, 139
   games, 58
   Socrates's tolerance for, 77
dualism, austere vs. normative, 74, 222n13

education, modern
   culture of testing, xii, xiv, 10, 45
   and return on investment, xiii
   value vacuum, xii, xiv, xvi
endy (*teleion*), 122-126, 129-130, 160-161, 178, 189-195
   translation issues, 122-123
Epicurus, 120, 197-198
erotic love (*erōs*), 58-67, 69-77
   heterosexual relationships, 63, 89
   homoerotic relationships, 21-23, 58-62, 71, 75, 189
   vs. passion/lust, 103
Euripides, 73

fine. *See kalos/kalon*
forms, 90, 92, 94-100, 105, 107-108
freedom, 5, 103-105, 139, 143
function (*ergon*) arguments, 35, 126-129, 161, 190

INDEX

Glaucon's challenge, 80–81
godlike, 106, 116, 128, 142
  becoming, 50–51, 72, 112–117, 132, 192–195, 228n29
  blessedness (*makarios*), 132–134
  bodybuilding and sculpture, 50–51, 98
  See also immortality; virtues: wisdom
gods
  Aphrodite, 61, 64, 70, 189
  Apollo, 16, 39–42, 112
  Artemis, 89
  Demeter, 59, 69
  Dionysus, 58–59, 73
  Eros, 57, 58 (*see* erotic love)
  Hera, 89, 113, 223–224n9
  Herakles, 112–117, 132–134, 142, 172, 182, 195
  Zeus, 112–113, 115–116, 133, 189, 195
good(s)
  division of, 71–75, 80–81, 85–85, 102–106
  form of, 94–100
gymnasium (*gymnasion*) layout, ix, 11–13

happiness (*eudaimonia*)
  defining, 120–134
  narrow vs. expansive, 122–126, 130, 191–195, 219n18
  nonphilosophical contexts, 111, 113, 116–117
  translation issues, xvii, 120
health
  bodily, 50–55, 80–81, 143, 160–161
  civic, 82, 84–86, 101–106
  social/environmental determinants of, 51–55, 65, 108 (*see* customs)
  spiritual/mental, 8, 51–55, 83–86, 101–106, 136–138
  valuable in itself, 72, 79–81, 122
Heraian Games, 89
Hippocrates, 51–55, 108
  See also health; medicine
Hippothales, 23, 25, 94
Homer
  and athletic contests, 23, 155
  heroic ethos, 60–61, 83, 152–153, 172
  Hymn to Demeter, 69
honor/reputation (*timē*)
  and greatness of spirit, 146, 148–154
  role in happy life, 120–121, 132–133, 142
  and shame, 60, 66–67, 76–77
  and spirit, 86, 103–105

immortality
  of human soul, 50
  striving for, 69–72, 76–78, 108–109, 112–113, 117, 192–195

Jefferson, Thomas, 84, 156

Kaepernick, Colin, 29, 87
kalos/kalon, 181
  beautiful goodness (*kalokagathia*), 150, 230n19, 234n17
  competing for, 176, 182–183
  goal of virtuous activity, 141–145, 147–150, 162–164, 187
  and immortality, 142
  in nonphilosophical contexts, 23, 112–117
  translation issues, 112, 141–142, 164–165, 172, 230n19
knowledge vs. belief, 96–97, 169–170
Kyniska, 218n3, 223–224n9

Laches, 4–7, 9, 37
Landy, John, 159
liberal arts curriculum
  ancient, 5, 82–84, 93–99, 215n25
  censorship of, xv, 83
  modern, xiv, 19
love. *See* erotic love; *philia/philos*
Lysis, 23–26, 37, 45, 94

mathematics
  in education, 93–95, 94–99, 219n18
  as eternal, 72, 76
  in justice, 156–158
  in sensible beauty, 48–51
medicine, 161, 198
  holistic, 14, 51–55, 65
  as a science, 17–18, 24–25, 52–53, 62–63, 76
  valuable for consequences, 80–81
Milo of Kroton, 135–137, 143
money, xii–xv, 33–34, 43
  moneymaking class, 85, 101–103
  valuable only for consequences, 80–81, 120–121, 123, 129–130
  virtuous use of, 147–148, 162, 183
music
  and character development, x–xi, 3–5, 55, 79–80, 82–84
  experience of, 73, 78
  flute (*aulos*), 4, 47
  kithara, 119, 127–128, 130, 171, 194

INDEX

musical art (*musikē technē*), 48, 62–63, 76, 208n4
musical contest (*musikon agōn*), 40, 47, 128
tuning, 34–35
mystery cult/Eleusis, 59, 68–69, 70–75

nude athletics (*gymnastikē*), 11
  applied to soul, 14
  and character development, 3–4, 55
  co-ed, 87, 89–91, 93
  dog leash, 13
  historical development, 13
  ideals of, ix–x, 13, 33, 114

Olympic Games
  ancient, 28, 89, 111–117, 120, 133, 197
  celebration of victors, 23, 43, 91
  modern, 28, 87, 89, 147, 159
  site, 11–12
  victors as role models, 8, 127–131, 135, 142, 150–152, 172, 194
ornament (*kosmos*), 112–115, 117, 131–133, 142, 147–154, 164–165, 189–190, 193
outdoing (*pleonexia*), 34–37, 135, 150
Owens, Jesse, 28

perplexity (*aporia*)
  in Platonic dialogues, 70, 79, 97, 107
  in Socratic dialogues, 2, 6–10, 23–25, 30, 43–44, 50
  vs. puzzles (*aporiai*) in Aristotle, 119, 167, 180
philia/philos
  love of gym training (*philogymnastia*), 62
  love of listening (*philēkoos*), 92
  love of winning (*philonikia*), 9
  love of wisdom (*philosophia*), 9, 24, 26, 33–34, 62, 92–93
  See also virtues: friendship
Pindar, 113–117, 132, 142, 150–151, 189
Plato
  gym manager (*gymnasiarchos*), 48–49
  method of hypothesis, 50, 66–67, 70, 76–77, 99–100, 107–109
  response to Socrates, 93, 96–100, 107–109
pleasure (*hēdonē*), 120–121, 123, 126, 129–130, 132, 150
  and pain in education, 137–138, 171–174

of touch, 143–145, 153, 168–171
pluralism, xv–xviii, 44
poetry
  competitions, 58
  love poetry, 21, 23
  and moral development, 3, 40, 83
  victory odes, 113–117
practice (*askēsis*), 176, 184–187, 189, 195
psychology, modern
  adaptive level phenomenon, 36
  cognitive behavioral therapy, xvi, 8–9, 36, 45
  flow, xv–xvi, 72, 78, 150, 171–174, 188–191, 195
  grit, 124–125, 164–165, 187, 194
  interest, xv, 41, 44–45, 94, 105, 109, 174–175, 187
  mindset: growth vs. fixed, 8–10, 45
  purpose exploration, xv, 41–42, 45, 94, 108–109, 122, 153, 163, 177, 187
  purposeful role models, 42
Pythagoras, 48, 135
Pythian Games, 39–40, 48, 128, 135
  oracle, 39–41
  site, 16, 39
  See also gods: Apollo

Rapinoe, Megan, 87–88, 153
Rihanna, 57
Robinson, Jackie, 146–147, 153

Sappho, 21
self-sufficient (*autarkēs*), 123–126, 129–130, 176–180, 184, 191–192
slavery, 5, 22–24, 29, 90–91, 103, 155, 178
social media, 78, 96, 121, 169
Socrates
  cross-examination (*elenchos*), 6–7, 67, 198
  critique of, 36, 50, 64, 107
  of an oracle, 40
  and tough love, 45, 76
  and followers, 197–199
  historic individual, 1–2, 151–153, 197
  praised by Alcibiades, 75–77
sophists, 33–37
Sparta, 9
  See also Kyniska
spirit (*thymos*), 82–83, 86, 97, 102–106
Stoicism, xvi, 197–198, 203n8, 208n8, 228n28, 229n13, 234n15

INDEX

study (*theōria*), 120–121, 123–125, 136, 160–161, 171, 178, 192–195

Thrasymachus, 28, 30, 33–37, 94, 100, 106
training (*ethos*), 136–140, 162–163, 167–168, 170–172, 185–187, 190, 228n6
tyranny, 62, 103–104, 107, 114, 180

virtue (*aretē*)
  of character vs. of thought, 136, 159–165
  having vs. using, 127–128
  and the mean, 137
  translation issues, 8, 111, 116, 128
virtues
  big spending (*megaloprepeia*), 148–149, 151, 181, 189, 194
  bravery (*andreia*), 4–7, 10, 54, 64, 82–83, 85, 140–141
  discipline/moderation/temperance (*sōphrosunē*), 14–20, 82–86, 102–104, 143–145
    vs. weakness of will (*akrasia*), 166–171

friendship, 23–25, 31–32, 121–122, 126, 175–187 (see *philia/philos*)
  toxic friendship, 24, 42, 176
generosity (*eleutheriotēs*), 147–148
greatness of spirit (*megalopsychia*), 146–154, 160, 163–165, 185–187
hope (*euelpis*), 231n23
justice (*dikaiosunē*), 31–37, 51, 84–86, 156–159
  and decency/equity (*epieikeia*), 158–159
  retributive vs. rehabilitative, 32
  social justice, 53–54, 74, 108
  valuable in itself, 80–81, 99–106
wisdom, 6, 8, 97–100
  human vs. divine, 17, 40–41, 44, 107
  practical (*phronēsis*) vs. theoretical (*sophia*), 136, 160–164, 192
  as the whole of virtue, 5–7

women
  athletes in antiquity, 89
  ancient feminism, 90–91, 218n8
  marriage/family norms, 91, 112, 179
  modern feminism, 22, 87–88

Xenophon, 90–91

www.ingramcontent.com/pod-product-compliance
Lightning Source LLC
Chambersburg PA
CBHW022002220426
43663CB00007B/923